Learning from Latino Teachers

JB JOSSEY-BASS

Learning from Latino Teachers

Gilda L. Ochoa

John Wiley & Sons, Inc.

Published by Jossey-Bass
A Wiley Imprint
989 Market Street, San Francisco, CA 94103-1741 www.josseybass.com

Wiley Bicentennial logo: Richard J. Pacifico

Jossey-Bass books and products are available through most bookstores. To contact Jossey-Bass
directly call our Customer Care Department within the U.S. at 800-956-7739, outside the
U.S. at 317-572-3986, or fax 317-572-4002.

Jossey-Bass also publishes its books in a variety of electronic formats. Some content that
appears in print may not be available in electronic books.

Library of Congress Cataloging-in-Publication Data

Ochoa, Gilda L., date.
  Learning from Latino teachers / by Gilda L. Ochoa.
    p. cm.
  Includes bibliographical references and index.
  ISBN 978-0-7879-8777-0 (cloth)
  1. Hispanic Americans—Education. 2.   Discrimination in education—United States.
  3.   Educational equalization—United States. I.   Title.
  LC2670.O28 2007
  371.1008968—dc22

                                                                    2007017894

Printed in the United States of America
FIRST EDITION
HB Printing   10 9 8 7 6 5 4 3 2 1

The Jossey-Bass
Education Series

Contents

To my parents,
Francesca Palazzolo Ochoa and Henry José Ochoa,
my most influential teachers

Preface

There is a crisis in education, and the most immediate victims are children. The culprits, however, are not those we think they are. They are not teachers, students, or parents. The faults run much deeper, and the damages reverberate throughout time. This book details how the scars are felt in the lives of Latinas/os.

Part of understanding Latinas/os and education involves a critical reflection on racial/ethnic labels. Although I acknowledge the politics surrounding labeling and the ways that panethnic terms may mask within-group heterogeneity, I use the terms most commonly used by the teachers in this book. Thus, *Latina/o* is used when referring to anyone of Latin American descent currently residing in the United States. To distinguish between the genders, *Latina* and *Latino* are used. *Mexican American* is used when describing Mexicans born in the United States. *Mexican* is used when referring to both Mexican Americans and Mexican immigrants.

Segregation, vocational training, English-only policies, and inferior facilities mar the history of Latinas/os in schools. Even after decades of struggle and landmark desegregation cases such as *Mendez* v. *Westminster* (1947) and *Brown* v. *Board of Education of Topeka, Kansas* (1954), inequalities in schools and opportunities persist. Latina/o students attend some of the most segregated schools, and these schools tend to be "high poverty schools" (Orfield, 1996). Furthermore, Latinas/os are vastly underrepresented in honors and advanced placement courses, and over 40 percent do not complete high school. Along with these old patterns, new injustices have taken shape in federal policies such as No Child Left Behind, where inflexible curriculum, standards-based teaching, and high-stakes testing drive education.

With this weight of history on us, is another system of education possible? Can we imagine a time when no child is truly left behind, when teachers have a voice in structuring schools, and when all communities and families are valued? Fortunately, the teachers profiled in this book are not pessimistic about the possibilities. They may be frustrated with the persistence of inequality and top-down policies, but they remain committed to change.

This book, based on observations in schools, conversations with students, recent literature on education, and in-depth interviews with Latina/o elementary, middle, and high school teachers, offers insightful stories and powerful visions in the movement for just schools. The teachers' narratives form the bulk of this book, and they are filled with complex accounts from their days as students to their current positions as teachers. They juxtapose disturbing memories of humiliation and ridicule in schools with the strength and wisdom infused in them by their family, teachers, and friends. In their reflections as students and in their roles as teachers, school practices are paramount. In particular, they are critical of the devastating impacts of curriculum tracking and high-stakes testing on the very students they are teaching: students just like themselves—working class, immigrant, and Latina/o.

Teachers' are not the only voices in this book. The ideas of students, family members, and other school officials are also integrated in the concluding chapters. As the immigrant rights movement and the school walkouts from spring 2006 demonstrated, Latina/o students have much to say. Just as they found ways to make their voices heard in the immigration debates, they have strong views on schooling. Their ideas, when combined with those of others, must be part of any movement for changing schools.

The narratives and strategies for change offered throughout this book provoke introspection, reflection, and action and will appeal to all those who have ever questioned the U.S. educational system. Teachers and teachers in training will encounter critical information from their colleagues on Latinas/os and education. Families and students will be inspired by the stories of resilience and resistance, and policymakers will find concrete recommendations for achieving more just schools.

Too few politicians, educational bureaucrats, and researchers have taken the time to listen to individuals who have intimate knowledge about the schooling experiences and lives of Latinas/os: Latina/o teachers. Thus, by focusing on the voices and experiences of Latinas/os, a group underrepresented as K–12 teachers, this book offers an insider's perspective on the challenges and strategies that many Latina/o students still face in schools.

This book is not offered as a step-by-step guide for improving the educational system. The changes needed are too complicated to be neatly laid out in a quick-fix manual. Instead, it is my hope that the teachers' narratives will cause the terms of the debate about education to start to shift. Rather than simplistically blaming teachers, students, or parents for not caring about schools and then imposing more standards, tests, and paperwork, we must envision and work toward a radical restructuring of schools and society. When it comes to public education, the stakes are too high—not just for Latinas/os but for everyone in the United States—to do anything less.

In the following chapters, Latina/o teachers describe their families, schooling experiences, decisions to become teachers, and experiences in the profession. Their narratives are filled with accounts of coping, challenging, and resisting multiple barriers on the paths to becoming teachers. One teacher remembers that her immigrant mother feared school and tried to keep her from attending, yet other teachers share stories of how racial discrimination fueled their parents' determination to get their children into college.

All speak fondly of key individuals who shaped the direction of their lives. Many are equally as passionate about the exclusion they faced in schools because of their identities as Mexican, poor, or undocumented students. It is the combination of these experiences that has influenced their teaching and the high aspirations they maintain for the students who fill their classrooms. Nevertheless, they are torn, and some are growing weary of school policies such as No Child Left Behind, where more testing and paperwork are chipping away at students' spirits and teachers' energies.

These narratives capture each teacher's unique voice, life history, and philosophy. When they are read as a whole, several prevailing and overarching themes emerge that emphasize the elements of education that make a difference. Along with listening to Latina/o teachers, these elements and chapters emphasize understanding the diverse experiences of Latinas/os, learning from Latina/o families, recognizing what is lost for a formal education, supporting students, challenging unequal school practices, and envisioning inclusive and loving schools and society. Much is to be learned from these teachers' compelling stories, and after the background chapters in Part One, I end each chapter by connecting, comparing, and reflecting on the teachers' narratives. These conclusions consider the lessons learned from Latina/o teachers and include recommendations that are relevant for us all.

Each chapter may be read alone, of course, but when they are read in order, this book reveals the exclusionary ideologies used to explain unequal Latina/o educational outcomes, the elements of an education that make a difference, and the life trajectories of the Latina/o teachers. Underlying each chapter is a critical analysis of our educational system and the larger policies and belief systems that shape our schools and society. This book concludes by integrating the teachers' narratives with recommendations from today's high school and college students about improving educational opportunities and schools.

We must connect the experiences of Latina/o teachers with today's youth and with our pasts. Each generation influences the other and has something to teach. However, these lessons are lost when voices, histories, and perspectives are excluded in the classroom, the curriculum, and academia. By listening to the stories of those Latina/o teachers who have navigated through sixteen years of formal education, we are better positioned to work together for schools and communities that are premised on love and justice over inequality and marginalization.

Acknowledgments

Many people deserve credit for helping me envision and complete this book. First and foremost, I thank my parents—middle school teachers who dedicated their lives to public school education. As first-generation college students, they made my path through schooling easier. They also provided me with unconditional love and support, instilled a sense of justice, and introduced me to the power of teaching.

The politics of education, classroom dynamics, and school bureaucracy have permeated many of our family conversations. I have been influenced by my mother's forty years of classroom experiences and her conversations with my sister-in-law, Julie Kaup, also a public school teacher, on the joys and difficulties of teaching. My brother, Enrique Ochoa, paved the path for me through graduate school and life as an academic committed to social justice. He and my mother introduced me to teachers to interview, read and commented on each chapter, and assured me of the importance of writing an accessible book. Watching my niece and nephew, Elisa and Ricky, find their own ways to resist oppressive school practices through hairstyles, T-shirts, and school walkouts keeps me optimistic about the future. The stories that my aunt, Luce Palazzolo, reminds me of about my own childhood help me remember my youth. Finally, mi esposo Eduardo Ruiz's unyielding support and messages to "write the book that *you* want to write" sustain me.

I am indebted to the teachers, principals, instructional aides, families, and K–12 students who opened their schools, classrooms, and homes to me. They generously shared their stories, experiences, and classes. I hope that I have done their work justice.

I appreciate the continued support and encouragement from colleagues, friends, and students, particularly through the Claremont Colleges Intercollegiate Department of Chicana/o Studies and Pomona College Sociology Department. Thanks also to Estela Ballon, Jeanett Castellanos, Edith Chen, Daniel Malpica, Kimberly Nettles, Vilma Ortiz, Daniela Pineda, María Tucker, and Alicia Velazquez. Their work and everyday examples have furthered my thinking about Latinas/os and education.

Several wonderful research assistants, funded through Pomona College, helped me at various stages of this book. They are Ana Cisneros, Elizabeth Cobacho, Laura Enriquez, Laura Kaneko, Diana Khuu, Dianna Moreno, Vivian Pacheco, Christopher Ramos, and Tojuana Riley. My thinking has also been enhanced by students enrolled in my courses, especially in Chicanas/Chicanos in Contemporary Society and Chicanos/Latinas and Education. Students Brenda Beas, Rosalba Chamu, Andrés Gallegos, Silvano Gonzalez, David Henderson, Monica Hernandez, Marleene Martín, Bonnie McGinnis, Maria Rojas, Corrina Wood, and Yim Fan Yan affirmed the importance of this work and pushed me to think more deeply when they selected this topic as the subject of their course research papers. Finally, through the Pomona College Summer Scholars Program, Stephanie Roman (West Covina High School in Southern California) and Jennifer Victoria (Montclair High School in Southern California) worked with Laura Enriquez to read various chapters and provide helpful comments.

My work has benefited from the financial support of institutions, including the American Sociological Association's Minority Fellowship Program, Pomona College, and the John Randolph Haynes and Dora Haynes Faculty Fellowship.

Special thanks go to the staff of Jossey-Bass Publishers, especially Lesley Iura, for helping to see this book to completion.

The Author

Gilda L. Ochoa is associate professor of sociology and Chicana/o studies at Pomona College. She received her B.A. from the University of California, Irvine, and her Ph.D. in sociology from the University of California, Los Angeles. She is the author of *Becoming Neighbors in a Mexican American Community: Power, Conflict and Solidarity* (2004), coeditor of *Latino Los Angeles: Transformations, Communities, and Activism* (2005), and coeditor of *Chicano/a and Latino/a Studies in Sociology: Syllabi and Instructional Materials*, Fifth Edition (2003). She has written articles on college-community connections, parent organizing, and Mexican American women's activism, and she teaches courses on Chicanas/os and Latinas/os, education, Los Angeles communities, and race/ethnicity. Through student-centered classrooms, she aims to foster dialogical and collaborative spaces that are social justice oriented. She is the recipient of two teaching awards: one as a UCLA teaching assistant and another as a Pomona College professor. She speaks annually at school career days and teaches in college programs that aim to increase the number of underrepresented students in higher education. She also works with middle and high school students as part of the Henry J. Ochoa Community Scholars Program, which she cofounded with her family.

Part I

Background

Listening to Latina/o Teachers

*For much of US history, Chicanas have not existed outside
of our communities. Our stories have not been included
in literary anthologies, our books have not been found in
mainstream bookstores, and our perspectives have not been
included in college classrooms.*

L. A. Flores (2000)

Despite important struggles and movements to include multiple histories, experiences, and perspectives, the voices of Latinas/os remain marginalized in education. In the curriculum, the structure of the classroom, and the expectations of traditional social science research, this subjugation is multileveled and has significant ramifications.

Within the course curriculum, if scholarship on and by Latinas/os is not outright excluded, it is often tokenized: added on at the end of the semester, not fully analyzed, or only included in ways that do not disrupt traditional theories or frameworks. As a result, students are often provided with incomplete histories, experiences, and perspectives of the United States. This incomplete and even inaccurate knowledge may perpetuate stereotyped assumptions and reduce the possibilities for becoming informed citizens who can implement effective policy changes. In addition, students' relationships to schools may be hindered when they do not see themselves or their families reflected in the course curriculum. They may perceive school or certain academic subjects as irrelevant to their lives.

Although Latinas/os may be absent in the curriculum, Latina/o students may stick out within the classroom, especially when they are underrepresented in four-year colleges and universities (Madrid, 1995). Within classrooms lacking adequate curriculum, teachers and students may call on Latina/o students to become "native informants" because they are assumed to be experts on their presumed racial/ethnic groups and asked to share the history, experience, and perspective of Latinas/os (see hooks, 1994). Since Latina/o students may have been schooled in the same narrow curriculum as their peers, there is no guarantee that they are familiar with the heterogeneous histories and backgrounds of the millions of Latinas/os in the United States. In these situations, such pressure to represent Latinas/os and to educate their classmates and teachers can be daunting, leading some students to withdraw.

Being invisible or tokenized in the course curriculum often combines with the structure of traditional classrooms to reinforce another form of marginalization—one that privileges individualism, competition, and speaking standard English over collaboration, community building, and multiple ways of communicating. For students who enter school speaking a language other than English and who come from collectivist households where working together is the norm, traditional classrooms, which emphasize individualism and competition, may be antithetical to what they have learned in their family. Such classrooms may be uncomfortable environments at best. When teachers do not permit or support diverse ways of communicating, the classroom can be a hostile place. Too many Latina/o college students have shared with me that in school, they were punished for speaking Spanish, ridiculed for their supposed accents, reprimanded for assisting their peers, or ignored by their instructors. Over time, some stopped participating in class; they withheld their voices.

The traditional pedagogy in many U.S. classrooms is referred to as the banking model: students are treated as empty receptacles in which knowledge is deposited (Freire, 1970). When this happens, what students' know and experience are typically devalued and disregarded. Personal experiences may be trivialized as irrelevant to the course material, while theory and "facts" are perceived as more rigorous and important (Torres, 2003). The focus on other people's theories and histories as disconnected from students' lives may also limit student engagement in the classroom.

Finally, just as individual Latinas/os may be excluded and silenced because of course curriculum and classroom pedagogy, the structures of academia have fostered a system that favors the perspectives of the dominant classes at the expense of subjugated groups. Since women, members of the working class, and groups of color have a history of exclusion from institutions of higher education, their voices, theories, and perspectives are largely absent from the disciplinary canons that frame contemporary scholarship and academic debates. And university positions where new ideas and theories are constructed and review boards that determine which research is funded and published remain skewed in favor of whites, the upper-middle class, and men (Baca Zinn, Weber Cannon, Higginbotham, and Thornton Dill, 1990; Kennelly, Misra, and Karides, 1999).

The exclusionary practices within academia are far reaching and include publication hierarchies that shape whose voices and perspectives are heard. When the normative expectation for tenure is publishing in what are regarded as top academic journals and academic presses, individuals who are committed to community involvement, action-oriented research, and accessible writing may find that their work and contributions are undervalued.

Furthermore, the domination of positivist research methodologies over feminist, Marxist, and other critical approaches has limited new perspectives, voices, and theories. Positivist research methodologies tend to position researchers as "experts," assert that scholars maintain distance from the people being studied, advocate that researchers adopt a value-free stance from their topics, and employ large sample sizes because they are believed to enhance the reliability and generalizability of studies (Guba and Lincoln, 2004). Acceptance of these approaches—over collaboration, reciprocity, dialogical, social justice, and life history research that are common among critical theorists—fosters a hierarchy of importance and validity within the academy, where large-scale surveys are perceived to present unbiased facts while community-oriented research and individual stories are devalued. There are many examples of positivist researchers who have entered working class neighborhoods and communities of color with their own unnamed biases and have completed research that misrepresents these communities and reproduces power hierarchies by race/ethnicity, class, and college community. Although such researchers may have advanced their careers, it has often been at the price of faulty representations of communities.

Fortunately, there are models of scholarship in sociology, women's studies, ethnic studies, and education that critique patterns of marginalization that ignore, silence, and subjugate multiple voices. This burgeoning body of scholarship (1) centers personal experiences as forms of knowledge, (2) believes in the importance of dialogue and storytelling where participants have the opportunity to frame the issues that concern them, (3) encourages the use of emotions as a way to validate what we know, (4) emphasizes writing in accessible ways for a wide audience, and (5) advocates for research that is social justice oriented (Collins, 1991; Delgado Bernal, 1998; Flores, 2000). These models of research, along with my identity as a Latina feminist, daughter of public school teachers, and qualitative researcher, have influenced my approach to writing this book. By centering the voices and perspectives of Latina/o teachers, this book offers a unique and overlooked view into the educational system and provides recommendations for educational improvements applicable to all students and teachers.

Expanding What We Know About Latina/o Teachers

There are nearly three million K–12 public school teachers in the United States; most love teaching and are committed to contributing to society by helping others (Nieto, 2005).

They give of themselves in spite of their fifty-hour workweeks, thirty-two-minute lunches, and less profitable salaries than professionals with similar credentials (Nieto, 2005). Although an extensive literature documents the commitments, passions, and experiences of white teachers (see Paley, 1978; McIntyre, 1997; Howard, 1999; Michie, 1999) and there is a burgeoning amount of scholarship on black teachers (see Ladson-Billings, 1994; Foster, 1997), there is much less material written on Latina/o teachers.

What we do know is that although Latinas/os constitute a growing percentage of the K–12 student population, they are significantly underrepresented as teachers. This underrepresentation is a national phenomenon that stems from historical and institutional factors that continue to skew who has access to critical thinking courses, higher-level learning, college attendance, and careers in teaching. Today, 40 percent of public school students are of color, but 90 percent of teachers are white. According to the National Center for Education Statistics, there is not a single teacher of color in nearly 40 percent of U.S. public schools (National Collaborative on Diversity in the Teaching Force, 2004). Within California's K–12 public schools, Latinas/os account for only 14 percent of teachers, although nearly half of all students are Latina/o. In Los Angeles County public schools, Latinas/os make up 60 percent of the student body but less than a quarter of the teachers (Education Data Partnership, 2004c). As the number of students of color increases at rates faster than those of teachers of color, these gaps are expected to grow (National Collaborative on Diversity in the Teaching Force, 2004; Grant and Murray, 1999).

Current research highlights the importance of increasing teacher diversity. The National Collaborative on Diversity in the Teaching Force suggests that teachers of color often have high expectations for students of their same racial/ethnic background. They may be role models for all students who enhance educational experiences, raise student self-esteem, and decrease absenteeism and disciplinary referrals for students of color (National Collaborative on Diversity in the Teaching Force, 2004). These benefits help to explain some research indicating that Latina/o and African American students prefer teachers of their race/ethnicity and that regardless of their own bilinguality, students have positive attitudes toward bilingual teachers (Galguera, 1998).

Expanding what we know about Latina/o teachers is an important step in increasing the diversity of our teaching force, recognizing the contributions of Latina/o educators, and allowing others to learn from their approaches to schooling, students, learning, and education. Listening to these teachers sharpens our understanding of how some Latinas/os have navigated through a K–12 system where as many as 40 percent of Latinas/os are not completing high school. At a time when work is needed to improve the educational opportunities of Latinas/os, yet public discourse on education often ignores or blames Latinas/os, the Latina/o teachers featured in this book offer their perspectives to teachers, students, families, communities, and politicians.

Centering the Narratives of Latinas/os

I hope that you don't take this the wrong way, but I wanted to talk to you because I felt like you were blaming teachers. The teachers at this school are so dedicated. We are here way before and after school. We give our all to these students. To be honest, I was not happy with your talk; I felt like you were blaming us, but I didn't say anything then because you're Latina and I didn't think it was right to question you in front of the group. Most of the people that lead in-services are White. We never hear from Latinas [Field notes, December 2004].

Hours after I wrote these comments in my notebook, I still thought that elementary school teacher Angelica Vasquez had misunderstood me. That day in 2004, while speaking to a group of fifty school officials about Latinas/os and education, I never meant to blame teachers. On the contrary, having been raised by two public school teachers myself, I consciously tried to avoid casting judgment or sounding as if I was the expert on Latina/o students. However, I had been invited by a school principal to talk about diversity and how teachers could work with students better. But this microscopic focus on teachers' attitudes and interactions left the many larger factors that teachers are encountering in schools—standardized testing, bureaucracy, and limited resources—under-explored. Despite my intentions, Angelica Vasquez saw me as an outsider who, like so many others in our society, was ready to blame teachers for all of the problems in schools. However, she was reluctant to critique me in front of her colleagues because she identified with me as a Latina, and as she stated, "We never hear from Latinas." Within today's climate where everyone supposedly knows how to improve schools and is quick to blame teachers, no wonder Angelica thought that I was reproducing this pattern.

Angelica was right: we never hear from Latinas/os, especially when it comes to education. Yet although Angelica was pleased to hear from someone she identified with as a Latina, she was not satisfied with my approach or perspective. Her critical response to my talk captures the complexities posed in centering the narratives of Latinas/os. Diverse perspectives on education are needed, and we must hear from Latinas/os, especially given their marginalization in education. However, no one perspective or narrative speaks for or to all Latinas/os.

Bearing in mind Angelica Vasquez's response to me, this book aims not to homogenize or essentialize the experiences of Latinas/os or present only my perspective. Instead, I have relied extensively on Latina/o teachers' stories and comments to create a collaborative project that captures a diversity of experiences and perspectives and fosters reflection, dialogue, and learning for the betterment of teachers, students, and communities.

Teachers and Other School Officials

Over the past fifteen years, Latina/o school personnel, families, and students have graciously invited me into their classrooms, offices, and homes. I have attended classes and school events as both a guest speaker and an observer, participated in the organizing activities of Latina/o parent groups, and worked with students in seventh through twelfth grades in various educational programs. These experiences have shaped my perspectives and helped me to better understand Latinas/os in education and the narratives of the public school teachers who are centered in this book.

This book draws primarily from eighteen interviews that I completed with Latina/o teachers (Table 1.1). In meetings ranging from one to six hours and spanning one to several days, these teachers generously shared their stories and thoughts on their schooling experiences, family expectations, decisions to teach, school practices, and the state of education. Although most encouraged me to use their names in this book, not all were comfortable with administrators at their school knowing their perspectives. Some new teachers did not have tenure and worried about the ramifications of their comments. Thus, to respect these teachers' confidentiality, I have changed the names of all individuals, schools, and districts. Though actual names are excluded, their stories are not easily forgotten.

At the time of our initial meetings, these teachers had been in the classroom from one to forty-one years. Two were retired, and eight were in their first five years of teaching. On average they had been teaching for ten years and were thirty-seven years old. Most are women, the children of Mexican immigrants, first-generation college students, and Spanish-English bilingual.

All live in Los Angeles County, and most have taught in the same school district—one whose size, location, and racial/ethnic demographics make it a microcosm of school districts throughout the county. Its campuses have twelve hundred teachers and more than twenty-five thousand kindergarten through twelfth-grade students

Table 1.

Name				
Angel...				
Ana C...				
Crist...				
Davi...				
Diar...				
Em...				
Eric...				
Ga...				
Ge...				
Ile...				
J...				
Lisa ...				...ol
Manuel Cadena	26	Second		
Margarita Villa	29	Second	Ten	Middle school
Marie Marquez	32	Second	Five	Middle school
Marta Escobar	77	Second	Forty-one	Elementary (retired)
Miguel Elias	34	First	Seven	Elementary
Vivian Sosa	25	Fourth	Four	Middle school

(Education Data Partnership, 2004a, 2004c). It serves neighborhoods that have established Mexican Americans and a growing percentage of Mexicans, Central Americans, and Asian Americans. Similar to the larger Los Angeles County, Latina/o students predominate in this district at 71 percent, but Latinas/os are less than a quarter of the teachers (Education Data Partnership, 2004b).

I combined what I learned from these teachers with the information that Latina/o parents, over twenty additional Latina/o, white, and Asian American school officials, and many K–16 students have shared with me over the years. Table 1.2 lists some of these individuals whose experiences, perspectives, and activities are explicitly included in this book.

I sent most of these teachers, principals, counselors, and instructional aides written transcripts of our taped meetings, and I maintained e-mail and telephone contact with the eight teachers whose stories form the bulk of this book. In 2006, six of these teachers came to my home for an informal discussion on Latinas/os and

Table 1.2. Description of Additional Selected School Officials and Latina/o Parents

Name	Age	Generation in the United States	Occupation
Denise Villarreal	46	Third	Elementary school principal
Erica Handel	62	Third	Elementary instructional aide
Gloria Dominguez	65	Second	Retired elementary instructional aide
Jane Hanson	55	Third	Elementary instructional aide
Lourdes Fernandez	41	Third	Elementary school principal
Raquel Heinrich	40	First	Union representative
Roberta Zavala	47	Third	Elementary school principal

education. This additional meeting provided a space for the teachers to meet one another and discuss shared concerns that form the crux of this book; the meeting also allowed me to reflect on what I had learned from the teachers.

After arranging the sofa and dining room chairs in a circle, I take a step back to survey the room and breathe deeply. The recorders, tapes, and interview guide are neatly arranged on the coffee table. As I scan the room one last time, the doorbell rings at 3:50. I rush to open it to see Diana Cortez smiling. Just seven months earlier she had been to my home for a one-on-one interview, and today she returned for a discussion on Latinas/os and education with five other teachers.

Of all of the teachers I interviewed, Diana is one of the most experienced. Born in 1940, she attended school in Pasadena, California, during a period of de jure segregation when Mexican Americans and Asian Americans in her community attended separate schools from whites. Although she has fond memories of her early school years, such blatant discrimination significantly limited the educational pursuits of many of her Mexican American classmates. As the first member of her family to graduate from college (Pasadena City College and La Sierra College), Diana attributes her desire to teach and her love of learning to her mother, an avid reader. She also credits her Seventh Day Adventist Church for encouraging education.

Diana began teaching in 1963, and she enjoyed the thirty-four years that she spent teaching language arts to seventh graders in a predominantly working-class Mexican American community. For her, teaching was rewarding and kept her young, and her colleagues, she said, were "some of the greatest people in the world." Now she is trying to understand why the current generation of students seems more lackadaisical about learning, and with the tremendous amount of paperwork now required of teachers, she is glad that she has retired.

Before Diana and I make our way to the family room, there is a knock at the door. This time, it is Marie Marquez at the doorstep, and Miguel Elias is coming up the walk. It has been a year since I interviewed each of them in their middle and elementary school classrooms.

During our initial meeting, thirty-two-year-old Marie Marquez shared with me her schooling experiences in Orange County, California. She was a quiet student who completed her homework, received good grades, and stayed out of trouble. However, with the exception of one high school counselor who took a special interest in her because she knew her four older siblings, Marie went through school unrecognized. She was not encouraged to enroll in honors classes until tenth grade, and as the child of Mexican immigrants, she was unfamiliar with college grants and scholarships. However, with support from her parents and inspiration from a high school English teacher, Marie completed college at California State University, Fullerton, and became a language arts teacher at a middle school that serves primarily working-class Latina/o students. Having taught for the past five years, Marie believes that education is a business where there is little value placed on teachers and the needs of students. Instead, she believes, policies are passed and implemented by politicians, superintendents, and principals who are detached from schools. Despite her criticisms of the educational system, Marie sees herself as a leader pulling students through the educational pipeline. She hopes that people thinking about becoming teachers will enter the profession only if "they really want to be there for kids."

In a profession where women predominate, thirty-four-year-old Miguel Elias is one of only four Latino teachers whom I interviewed, and he is the only male teaching elementary school. During our first interview, we sat talking in his first-grade classroom, squeezed into the students' small chairs and desks. Miguel's stories transported me to his childhood, marked by several trips across the U.S.-Mexico border. With each move, he adjusted to a new school and community. Born in Mexico, he first came to the United States at the age of three. Just two years later, his father died, and his family returned to Mexico. When Miguel was eight, his family moved permanently to the Los Angeles area. As an undocumented Mexican immigrant, he faced constant ridicule by his classmates and several teachers. But he fought back against his peers' attacks, and several influential teachers and friends introduced him to the possibilities of teaching. Now, as a teacher for the past seven years, Miguel aims to be a role model in a profession where there are few Latinos, and he hopes to inspire students who also come from single-parent families.

The next teacher to arrive at my home is twenty-five-year-old Vivian Sosa. A math and science teacher, Vivian first invited me to her middle school classroom in December 2004, where after the school day had ended, students returned to her room seeking advice on their science projects. A fourth-generation Mexican American woman, Vivian teaches not just at her alma mater in the Los Angeles area but also in the same school district where her mother, a pregnant teenager, was ridiculed, humiliated, and finally excluded. Despite her mother's hostile school experiences, she loved learning and was determined that Vivian and her other four children attend college. She raised strong children and inspired them by sharing stories of her life. As a teacher for the past four years, Vivian exhibits her mother's strength and has adopted her method of telling stories to build students' self-esteem.

With two teachers scheduled to arrive late because of meetings and coaching responsibilities, we begin our group conversation. We are just starting to talk about plans for this book when Erica Burg and Gabriela Muñoz arrive.

I had known Erica when she was a college student, and she was one of the first teachers to agree to share her experiences. She met me for our one-on-one interview in my office at Pomona College. Born in El Paso, Texas, to a Mexican mother and a German father, twenty-four-year-old Erica Burg has been teaching for two years at a middle school that serves over one thousand mostly working-class Latina/o students. During our meeting, she contrasted her experiences teaching at this large school with her fond memories as a student in a small family-like Catholic school. Erica is drawing on her own schooling experiences, trying to recreate a similar loving and caring atmosphere in her classroom. Although the impermanent administrators, budget cuts, large class sizes, malfunctioning equipment, and poor school grounds intensify her workload and push her patience, Erica is flexible; she is asking others for help and trying everything she can to help her students.

I first met thirty-year-old Gabriela Muñoz while I was interviewing another teacher. After listening to the nearly two-hour interview, Gabriela graciously volunteered to share her experiences. Born and raised in East Los Angeles to Mexican immigrant parents, she has been teaching elementary school students for eight years. She describes her first few years of teaching as a "battlefield." Administrators yelled at and fought with teachers; teachers disrespected students, and students did not seem to care about school. Gabriela endured administrators who threatened her own child, but she loved teaching too much to allow such abuse to persuade her to leave the profession. Instead, she looked for a different district and has found a school with a loving environment for the working-class Latina/o community.

I was sorry that Cristina Martinez and Angelica Vasquez, two of the other teachers whose contributions are critical to this book, were unable to attend this gathering. During our individual meeting, twenty-five-year-old Cristina Martinez invited me into her classroom. It was the end of a busy week of teaching middle schoolers and meeting with their parents in individual conferences. However, Cristina spoke passionately about her family and schooling. Her parents sacrificed to help her become one of the few members of her New Mexican extended family to graduate from college and the only one to earn a master's degree. Her path to becoming a teacher was not easy. She explained that she has forsaken traditional aspects of her background and laments living away from her family. Hoping that her middle school students will also challenge themselves, Cristina pushes them and shares her own stories of struggle. Nevertheless, as a third-year

teacher, the emphasis on testing in schoo
students, and the learning process. The c
high that shortly after our initial interview,

It was at our first meeting that thirty-six
expressed her reservations about my pers
the talk I had given to school officials. Chall
a harsh critique of teachers, she explaine
and education by focusing on the role of fa
on families stems from her own experiences, and during our meeting, she recounted how her immigrant mother turned off her alarm clock to keep her home from school, her older brothers worried that an educated Latina would have difficulty finding a husband, and school officials rattled off statistics about the small percentage of Latinas/os who graduate from college. Rather than heed these negative messages, Angelica transformed them into motivating factors to earn a master's degree, and today they influence her teaching philosophy. For the past nine years, Angelica has been introducing the primarily working-class Latina/o students in her classrooms to the opportunities outside their community so that they do not feel limited by others' expectations.

By the time that the six teachers and I finally sit down together, we only have ninety minutes for discussion. Luckily, they need little prompting to share their experiences and thoughts. I ask a few questions, and they expand on the issues that they had raised during our individual interviews. Their stories include experiences of navigating through the educational pipeline from kindergarten through college. They share their enlarged views of education that involve helping students to feel loved and cared for, and they reflect on ways that the educational system could be improved with multicultural curriculum, less bureaucracy, and a reduced emphasis on standardized testing. Laughter fills the family room, and the teachers affirm each other's many thoughts and experiences by sharing similar stories and suggestions. I am pleased with the way our conversation is unfolding. The camaraderie is transparent.

e conversation comes to an end, the following dialogue
es about the revealing lack of opportunities to have open
scussions about education even within a school environment:

Miguel Elias: I have learned a lot today.

Gilda Ochoa: Just out of curiosity, do you have chances as teachers to
sit down and talk about what it is that you do and how you feel
about education?

Marie Marquez: The only time that we ever say anything is when we're
at lunch. . . . We don't get a chance at our staff meetings because we
need to do data analysis. We need to get into groups and discuss
what we did wrong. Why are the students not doing well on the
tests? . . . It's just work, work, work, work. Fill out the sheet. Make sure
that everyone's name is on it.

Erica Burg: That's why I miss graduate school. Getting my master's
in education, I was in small classrooms where I could actually talk
about stuff.

Vivian Sosa: I want to go back. I miss school. . . . We had fifteen people in
our classes in graduate school. So we were able to talk to the teachers.
We were able to communicate by e-mail what ideas we had. These
were current ideas. There's research that we could access. . . . I miss
being around an environment of positive people that really want to do
something.

Long after the teachers left my home that night, I replayed their
conversation on this apparent contradiction. How can a nation
allow its students and teachers to spend so many hours in spaces
that are not positive, learning environments? What is happening
in schools and classrooms that is leading these teachers to crave
a return to graduate school? Shouldn't K–12 public education

also be characterized by learning, dialogue, and support? While it is no surprise that teachers are negatively affected by the speed-up of our fast-paced society, what may be less obvious are the detrimental impacts that teachers encounter in our system of schooling where standardized testing drives education and top-down policies often limit teacher autonomy. The results of this shift in schooling are felt by teachers such as Vivian Sosa and Erica Burg who long for a positive, supportive space. Since they do not see such places in their schools, they yearn to return to graduate school. It is disconcerting to think of schools as places filled with teachers such as these who have so much energy, desire, and creativity but because they are constantly working and kept focused on testing, they have little time for dialogue and reflection.

Dynamic exchanges such as these shaped this book and my decision to focus on Latina/o K–12 teachers. As these teachers offered their stories, I realized that I must be willing to tell my own story—not to decenter or counter their narratives but to make more personal how our stories are interconnected and the ways that school practices continue to result in unequal opportunities.

Telling Stories: Weaving Together Educational Biographies to Understand Self and Society

> When I theorize, I tell a story, and by this I try to understand, try to make sense of, my universe. This is my theorizing, my storytelling. This is the place and the movement where I was born, and where I grew. It is also my place and my movement in relation to my family, my community, and my society [Martínez 1996, p. 117].

By sharing how they navigated through at least sixteen years of formal education, Latina/o teachers' stories of their families and schooling provide important strategies on how students might better resist the barriers they encounter throughout the educational pipeline from kindergarten through graduate school. Also, their reflections on contending with current school policies as teachers provide insiders' recommendations on improving schools and the roles that policymakers, school officials, and families can play in this endeavor. They provide a vision of how we can all work together for schools and communities that are premised on love and justice over competition and inequality. But too few are listening to the individuals intimately involved in Latina/o education: Latina/o teachers. In listening to their stories, we can learn much about our selves, schools, and societies.

As a Latina, a professor, and the daughter of two middle school teachers, the topic of Latinas/os and education is both intimately personal and political. When I think about education, I recall the stories of my parents, remember my schooling, and hear today's students' experiences. Most salient in these stories and my memories are the struggles of coming to voice by acquiring the English language, speaking in the classroom, and challenging exclusionary comments and practices. It is this process of coming to one's voice that makes telling stories so critical to the structure of this book.

As first-generation college students and English-language learners, my parents faced various struggles. My mother entered kindergarten in the New York City public school system speaking Italian. She is the oldest child of Sicilian immigrants and remembers crying her first week of school while her mother sat outside her classroom door trying to console her. My mother made her way through school and was the only member of her nuclear family to complete college. My father was fifteen years old when he and his parents left Nicaragua for Los Angeles. For his first seventeen years in the United States, he struggled to learn English and earn a college degree. Like my mother, he attended community college and then transferred to California State University, Los Angeles. With their passion for social justice, my parents used their education for the good of society: they became middle school teachers.

My parents' struggles and their knowledge of the educational system assisted me in my schooling. Although I spoke English, I rarely spoke in the classroom. My quietness in the classroom intensified as I progressed through school, and by the end of my first year of college, one of my professor's comments on a final paper exemplified this silence: "honors work from an almost invisible student." Among my memories of school was how my classroom personality contrasted with my interactions outside the classroom—ones characterized by laughter and loudness. Thus, I understand the difficulties of coming to voice within an academic setting.

Finally, I hear the voices of today's Latina/o students. There are the college students who describe their own difficulties within school: being silenced in undemocratic classrooms, experiencing a chilly or even hostile climate on campus, and feeling that schooling has separated them from their families and communities. Despite these difficulties, many students remain optimistic about their futures and aspire to become agents of change. They want justice for their communities and are concerned about their younger brothers and sisters. Then there are the high school and middle school students. Some worry about their futures and are looking for an education that empowers them, but others express defeat. They say that they do not care about school, but their actions or emotions convey other messages. They do care, and they wonder why their teachers have repudiated them. These stories of rejection and neglect are haunting.

Such stories, experiences, and memories influenced how I heard the narratives told to me by Latina/o teachers. Our own lives are brought to bear when we listen and learn from the lives of others. Thus, although the lives of the eighteen Latina/o K–12 teachers are centered in this book, I have not suppressed my own voice, experiences, and emotions. I hope that the stories that unfold throughout this book will inspire others to reflect on the opportunities, struggles, and forms of resistance that characterize their educational biographies. As we think about our own stories and learn from others, it is harder to rationalize or individualize the persisting gaps in opportunities. Certainly each story is unique and cannot be generalized, yet patterns emerge that are part of larger systems of power and inequality. I hope that readers combine the stories of these teachers with other stories to construct creative approaches in the struggle for social justice for past, present, and future generations of students.

2

Explaining the Achievement Gap

. . . [E]fforts to understand why so many students from
subordinate populations drop out of high school without
engaging a theoretical analysis of the impact of racism and
class inequality (as so often happens) produces fragmented
and decontectualized "truths."

Darder (2002)

As my brother and I slowly make our way from the high school administration building to the school parking lot, it is not the stream of students, the security guard, or the cumbersome pizza boxes that slow our movement. Instead, we are weighed down with what we have just learned over lunch from a group of ninth-grade Latina/o students. Having worked with these six students the previous year as part of an after-school program on Latina/o Studies, we were eager to see them and to know how they were adjusting to high school. On the surface, the students seemed to be enjoying their school and were happy to be meeting new people. However, as our lunch meeting progressed, they gradually scaled back their initial upbeat reports. First, there was Marco. Raised in a Mexican immigrant household, he is Spanish-English bilingual and was hoping to take Chinese in high school. However, his school counselor thought that it would be too difficult for him and assigned him to a Spanish-language class instead. Then there were Ana and Mariela. With their heads bowed and their voices lowered, each revealed that she was failing a class— English and Spanish, respectively. As we listened to students describe their classes and course schedules, the school bell interrupted us. There was just enough time to say our good-byes before the students headed off to their classes. With the students gone, we begin walking away from the administration building, sharing notes, and asking each other a barrage of questions: "Why was Marco steered away from Chinese? That's not right! What about Ana and Mariela? Why aren't they passing their classes?"

While we stand in the parking lot searching for answers to how the school can better serve these first-generation working-class students, a military recruiter walks toward the administration building. We glance in his direction and angrily think out loud which students he will be targeting. We know that military recruiters have greater access to high school students under section 9528 of the No Child Left Behind Act, and on campuses that serve working class communities and communities of color, military recruiters are common (Inouye, 2006). At some schools, military recruiters outnumber college counselors. In the context of the war on Iraq and U.S. involvement in Afghanistan, there is an urgent need to address the unequal opportunities that result in a path to the military for some students and college for others.

Next, we see Mr. O'Brien, an experienced teacher whom my brother and I both had when we were students. We have fond memories of him and greet him warmly. He is on his way to class and has only a few minutes to spare, but he stops long enough to give us his theory on what is happening at the school. He boldly states that the students who come to Grant High School from the predominantly working-class Latina/o middle school that Marco and his classmates attended "get the dirty end of the stick." He is referring to the elimination of vocational classes such as auto mechanics and wood shop as evidence of this inequality when his words begin to fade and my mind drifts away. Although I have mixed views on vocational courses because of the ways that working-class students have been funneled into them, I understand Mr. O'Brien's example as an illustration of the

unequal allocation of resources at Grant High School that are linked
to race/ethnicity and socioeconomic class.

One thing is clear: the experiences of Marco, Ana, and Mariela
are not unique, and Mr. O'Brien's theory for understanding such
experiences by exploring larger phenomena is an important step
in changing unequal school practices and outcomes. Latina/o students are pushed out of school or leave school at disturbing rates.
According to a Harvard University report released in 2005 on
California youth, only 60 percent of Latina/o and 57 percent of
African American students graduated with their high school class
in 2002. These percentages compare with 78 percent of white
and 84 percent of Asian American students. In the Los Angeles
Unified School District, the percentages are even more staggering:
39 percent of Latina/o, 47 percent of African American, 67 percent
of white, and 77 percent of Asian American students graduating on
time (Helfand, 2005; "Confronting the Graduation Rate Crisis in
California," 2005). These percentages suggest that too many students across race/ethnicity are not on track to graduate from high
school, but overall, Latina/o and African American students are
disproportionately being derailed.

This relatively low level of educational attainment is alarming
when we consider the limited employment opportunities in our
economy. The opportunities for social and economic advancement
at the beginning of the twentieth century for people without a college or high school diploma do not exist in our post-industrial and
globalized economy. Deindustrialization within the United States
has dramatically reduced the number of traditional high-wage,
medium-skill manufacturing jobs that provided benefits and stable
salaries for previous generations of workers. The decline in the production of automobiles, steel, and rubber in the United States has
been accompanied by a growth in the service economy and in jobs

in retail sales, health care, legal services, restaurants, and hotels. These jobs are often part time and subcontracted, without benefits and possibilities for unionization. Although there has also been an increase in high-skill, technologically advanced sectors, such as electronics, aerospace, and defense, these jobs are typically unavailable to people who have not completed high school. As a result, there is a growing polarization of jobs, incomes, benefits, and life chances, and this polarization has racial and gender dimensions. With the feminization of the labor market, women high school graduates may find limited work opportunities as secretaries and nurses, but men of color without college degrees often struggle to find employment, and if they do, they often then face marginalization in low-paying jobs (Amott, 1995; Eitzen and Baca Zinn, 1995; Lopez, 2003). Thus, receiving the "dirty end of the stick" in school continues into the workforce and beyond.

The persisting educational inequalities, especially with today's economic structure, have major implications for individuals, families, and communities. The U.S. Census Bureau reports that people twenty-one to sixty-four years of age who do not have a high school diploma have median incomes of about $21,000 per year. In comparison, college graduates of the same age group earn over twice as much: about $43,000 each year (Vasquez, 2006). Over a lifetime of working for forty years, this wage gap translates into a $880,000 difference, shaping life chances, opportunities for home ownership, and funding for children's college education.

Not only are the potentials of students untapped by unequal access to education, but the differences in educational outcomes have important ramifications for all in the United States. According to Russel Rumberger, a professor of education, "The 66,657 dropouts reported by California in 2002–03 could cost the state $14 billion in lost wages over the students' lifetimes, and add 1,225 inmates to state prisons" (Helfand, 2005, p. A26). As a society, we all lose when adults and schools give up on students by providing them with less than they provide others.

There must be a national debate about the inequalities in our educational system and how these inequalities are a manifestation of systemic injustices. Creative social justice strategies must be devised and implemented to address the root causes of these injustices. Unfortunately, many explanations for differing educational experiences and high school completion rates blame students, families, communities of color, and the working classes. The dominant discourse is that we live in a meritocratic society where students and families can pull themselves up by their bootstraps by working hard. Thus, the assumption is that students who do not perform well in school are to blame: they are lazy, they lack the intellectual ability, or their parents do not value education. Unfortunately, these facile explanations ignore the root causes of disparities, camouflage structural injustices, and actually perpetuate various discriminatory school practices.

Typically, individuals who are disconnected from the classrooms and the communities that they blame have perpetuated these explanations and school practices. Such top-down, one-size-fits-all approaches to education objectify teachers and students as they are acted on and their funds of knowledge are ignored and minimized. For example, few have focused on what Latina/o students and teachers may know from having experienced years of schooling in the United States. In particular, few politicians, policymakers, or researchers have considered the lessons that may be learned from the approximately 6 percent of college graduates each year who are Latina/o and the factors that enabled them to navigate through the educational pipeline to acquire their college degrees. Rather than being dismissed or unexplored, this insider knowledge should be mined because of the unique perspective that it can offer to our understanding of Latinas/os and education.

Since traditional explanations of Latinas/os and education have been largely ineffective, I take a countervailing approach to understanding Latinas/os and education that does not blame students or their families. Instead, my approach, like that of

Mr. O'Brien, considers how as a group, Latina/o students are shortchanged in schools and society. In particular, I use a framework that focuses on the historical and contemporary theories, practices, and ideologies that have perpetuated a pattern of inequality within schools. As part of this approach and detailed in Chapter Three, I emphasize the salience of generation, language, socioeconomic status, skin color, and gender on educational experiences. Furthermore, I center the perspectives, experiences, and lessons of Latina/o teachers who have a unique vantage point from which to understand Latina/os and education. Taken together, this integrated power-conflict approach combines broader factors with the everyday experiences, perspectives, and actions of Latina/o teachers to argue for restructuring schools from hierarchically organized, competitively driven, and exclusionary entities to collaborative, affirming, and loving spaces. As part of delineating the theoretical approach undertaken in this book, the remainder of this chapter presents a critical discussion of the dominant theories—especially biological and cultural deficiency theories—used to explain Latinas/os and education. It also highlights how these past theories and practices have reemerged under neoconservativism and neoliberalism, and how they are negatively shaping today's schools.

Explaining the Educational Outcomes of Latina/o Students: From the 1900s to the Present

For decades, academics and politicians have offered various explanations for differences in educational attainment. These explanations range from arguments that blame individuals and groups for their supposed deficiencies, to ones that critique biased school officials, unequal schooling facilities, or narrowly defined academic standards in schools. The popularity of these theories has changed over time and varied in scope. However, biological and cultural deficiency perspectives have been the most influential in shaping schools and the overall racial, economic, political, and social order.

In the following review of theories, the focus is on the histories and experiences of Mexican Americans in California. Of all of the Latinas/os in the state, Mexicans have predominated historically and numerically. Thus, many of the educational theories and school practices specifically targeted this group. Although Latinas/os from various countries have lived in California for decades, it is mainly over the past thirty to forty years that significant percentages have moved to the area. In particular, during the 1970s and 1980s, many Central Americans fled oppressive conditions imposed by U.S.-supported dictatorships. Since this period, Central Americans and other Latinas/os have often attended schools with Mexican Americans, where they have been subjected to similar exclusionary school practices and ideologies.

Biological Deficiency Theories

> Authorities on the Mexican mind agree that after the age of 12–14 educational and higher ambitions turn to inclinations of sex impulse. . . . The average [Mexican] boy and girl revert to the native instinct [quoted in Gonzalez, 1990, p. 37].

For much of history, biological deficiency perspectives, such as these comments by the Los Angeles assistant supervisor of the Compulsory Education Department in 1928, dominated academic and public discourse on education (Gonzalez, 1990). The underlying premise of biological deficiency theories was that non–Anglo Americans, including Mexicans and Puerto Ricans, were biologically different and inherently inferior to Anglos (Barrera, 1979). This official actually believed that Mexican teenagers were naturally inclined toward sex rather than education and that they did not have the capacity to control their sexual urges. Such beliefs shaped and reinforced school practices.

Some researchers and superintendents used biological deficiency arguments to argue that school segregation best enabled educators to address Mexican students' needs. Therefore, in California during the 1920s and 1930s, Mexican American and Mexican immigrant students were segregated into Mexican classrooms or Mexican schools. These schools, inferior in structure and resources, followed a program of Americanization that emphasized the English language, gender-specific vocational training, hygiene, and U.S. patriotism. By not challenging students academically, these schools perpetuated the ideology of biological determinism. It was believed that Mexican students were intellectually inferior; as a result, they were excluded from academically rigorous classes, and they then became less academically prepared. These practices also reproduced the existing social and economic order by preparing Mexicans to fulfill the role of low-wage laborers (Gonzalez, 1990).

Theorists and school officials who believed that biological or innate differences were to blame for educational outcomes found support for their perspective in intelligence tests. Since the tests included vocabulary and content typically familiar to middle-class, English-speaking Anglo students, these students consistently outperformed their working-class, Spanish-speaking, Mexican counterparts, and a disproportionately high number of Mexican youth were labeled "educationally mentally retarded" and placed into slower-learner classes (Gonzalez, 1990).

Theorists seemed to overlook the fact that IQ tests were designed and administered by middle- and upper-class whites, and that middle-class, English-speaking Anglo students were the group by which all others were compared. Thus, these biased tests appeared to confirm the theories that Mexican students were inherently inferior to whites (Gonzalez, 1990). Had middle-class white students been given tests constructed and administered by working-class Mexican adults, they probably would have been the ones deemed intellectually deficient. However, by the twentieth century, the social structures privileging white upper-class males and granting them the power to determine intelligence and educational policies had already been well established in U.S. society.

In the Southwest, biological deficiency theories and unequal school practices were buttressed by the history of Anglo colonization, where through the Mexican-American War (or the War of the North American Invasion, as it is referred to in Mexico), the United States acquired nearly half of Mexico's territory in 1848, including the current states of Arizona, California, western Colorado, Nevada, New Mexico, Texas, and Utah. This conquest of northern Mexico and the events following it reduced many Mexicans in the Southwest to a landless people who became politically and economically powerless and had a foreign language and culture imposed on them (Weber, 1973; Barrera, 1979; Almaguer, 1994).

The ideologies of manifest destiny and white supremacy rationalized the conquest and subsequent subordination of Mexicans. These ideologies also justified a racial/ethnic hierarchy that placed Anglo practices and values such as the English language above Mexican cultural practices, including the Spanish language (Weber, 1973). The effects of these exclusionary practices and ideologies were experienced in all facets of life for Mexicans in the Southwest, and their negative impacts persisted during the period of education characterized by cultural deficiency theories.

Cultural Deficiency Theories

> The Mexican's basic community organization of life is not of the efficient Japanese type; neither is it of the industrial-individualistic American form. On the other hand, it differs widely from the family clan-village Chinese form of community organization. It is unorganized . . . resting on daily needs, and taking little thought of the morrow [Bogardus, 1934, p. 23].

By the 1920s, cultural deficiency or assimilationist theories became more common, and by the early post–World War II era, they had replaced biological determinist perspectives in popularity

(Gonzalez, 1990; Frankenberg, 1993; Omi and Winant, 1994). As a result, rather than define Mexican Americans as biologically different from Anglos, more theorists began equating the experiences of Mexicans with those of southern, central, and eastern European immigrants. Furthermore, as the 1934 quotation opening this section shows, supposed cultural factors such as disorganization, collectivism, and delayed gratification were blamed for hindering the progress of Mexicans.

Such theorists assumed that immigrants from Mexico would follow the path of Irish, Italians, and Jewish immigrants who were believed to have adopted the culture of the dominant society and were integrating into mainstream organizations, institutional activities, and general life (Park, 1950; Gordon, 1964). Some assimilationists, ignoring the significance of exclusionary practices, have argued that groups that have not acquired socioeconomic parity are to blame because they possess cultural characteristics that are at odds with the values and practices that are perceived to be superior—those associated with middle-class white America (Lewis, 1966; Glazer and Moynihan, 1975; Sowell, 1981; Harrison, 1999).

To explain the educational outcomes of Latinas/os, social scientists working within this model have focused on presumed cultural deficiencies (Barrera, 1979). They have claimed that Latinas/os are "too clannish," "present time oriented," "do not care about education," or have a "language handicap" (Madsen, 1964; Heller, 1966; Chavez, 1991). Thus, many of the same school policies implemented early in the twentieth century, such as segregated schooling, vocational training, and the emphasis on the English language, persisted between 1950 and 1965, but the ideologies justifying them shifted from biological to cultural explanations (Gonzalez, 1990). Overall, deethnicization and acculturation were goals, and a key role of schools was to integrate immigrants into society by transmitting the dominant values, norms, and expectations as quickly as possible (Parsons, 1951). Although cultural integration was emphasized and the California Supreme

Court ruled against segregation in the 1947 decision of *Mendez* v. *Westminster*, the segregation of Mexican students into vocational courses and schools with inferior facilities ensured that most Mexicans continued to receive unequal schooling and were segregated from middle- and upper-class whites. Thus, regardless of how well Mexican Americans of this generation spoke English, knew Anglo customs, and identified with the United States, institutional integration was prohibited for most.

Such cultural deficiency theories and unequal schooling dramatically shaped educational outcomes, opportunities for work, and life chances. Through the 1960s, Mexican American students faced blatant exclusion and racism by school officials. They were punished for speaking Spanish, provided with little opportunities for economic advancement, and steered toward labor-intensive, dangerous, and poorly paid jobs (Gonzalez, 1990). For example, at the Central Avenue Americanization School in La Puente, California, very few Mexican students completed eighth grade between 1920 and 1935. Life history interviews with La Puente residents Carlos and Leticia Mendoza who attended Central Avenue School revealed that of the couple of hundred students who attended this segregated school in the 1930s, only four other Mexican students advanced to high school with them. The Mendozas remember their high school principal "throw[ing]" Mexican youth out of school if they got in any trouble (Ochoa, 2004a). Although the Mendozas were among a small group of Mexicans to receive a high school diploma during this period, they encountered overt racial discrimination when looking for jobs and trying to purchase a home in an Anglo neighborhood. Their leisure-time activities were also constrained by segregated beauty salons and movie theaters (Ochoa, 2004a). During this period, Mexican Americans were prohibited from using public swimming pools, or were allowed to swim only just before the pools were to be cleaned (Camarillo, 1979). It was not until the victories achieved during the civil rights movement and the growing use of power-conflict perspectives to understand societal dynamics and educational practices that this overt racism in the treatment and in the ideology of cultural deficiency slowly began to change.

Power-Conflict Theories

The civil rights movement of the 1960s and 1970s ushered in new ways of understanding society, education, and the experiences of Latinas/os. As part of the Chicana/o movement, students during this decade pushed for improving the high school completion rates of Mexican students, opening the doors of universities, and establishing Chicano studies classes and departments. Such popular movements critiqued cultural deficiency perspectives and introduced new theories. Some espoused a cultural nationalist ideology that promoted a race-based identity; others linked the struggle for Chicana/o rights to a critique of capitalism, internal colonialism, and/or sexism and heterosexism (Barrera, 1979; Moraga, 1983).

In general, power-conflict approaches critique deficiency theories for blaming students, their families, or their cultures for educational outcomes. As power-conflict theorists have described, these deficiency theories tend to ignore or minimize the different conditions under which groups entered the United States, from individual and voluntary migration for southern and eastern Europeans to conquest and colonization for Mexicans (see Barrera, 1979). These differences have influenced groups' receptions in the United States. Although each group has been expected to acculturate, not all have been equally accepted into U.S. institutions and social groups. For example, although various groups of European immigrants faced exclusionary treatment, they were not subjected to the same institutional practices of de jure segregation as Mexicans were. Finally, the enduring patterns of economic, political, and military U.S. domination over Latin America perpetuate asymmetrical power relations that persist between whites and Latinas/os in Latin American and the United States. Thus, power-conflict theories emphasize the macroscopic factors that perpetuate and reproduce power and inequality by race/ethnicity, class, and gender (see Barrera, 1979; Collins, 1991; Almaguer, 1994). Such theories seek to understand U.S. society by highlighting historical patterns, and they also consider how structural factors and dominant ideologies like capitalism and a system of white supremacy result in unequal institutional practices within schools, at work sites, and in other arenas.

Since the 1960s, those adopting power-conflict approaches to education have analyzed how the structure of schools and their practices mirror and reproduce U.S. capitalism (Bowles and Gintis, 1976; Gonzalez, 1990). Coupled with these arguments has been a growth in research exploring how specific institutional policies and practices have negative impacts on Latina/o students. In particular, researchers have focused on race/ethnicity, class, gender, and curriculum tracking, that is the unequal placement of students into vocational, college-preparatory, and honors courses (Oakes, 1985); the rise in segregated schools (Orfield, 1996); the growing emphasis on biased and high-stakes testing (Valenzuela, 2005); the limited use of culturally relevant curricula (Segura, 1993); the elimination of bilingual education (Soto, 1997); and unequal school facilities and resources (Kozol, 1991). Most recently, scholars have been analyzing the intersecting aspects of domination by considering how racism, classism, *and* sexism are intimately connected and cannot be separated (Bettie, 2003; Lopez, 2003). Compared to previous theories, these approaches to understanding education offer a fuller and more complex analysis of Latinas/os and education, and they parallel the perspectives offered by the Latina/o teachers throughout this book.

Neoconservatism and Neoliberalism

The civil rights movements and power-conflict theorists effectively critiqued cultural deficiency perspectives and their accompanying school practices such that they declined in popularity during the 1960s and

1970s. However, in the past twenty-five to thirty years, there has been a revival of cultural deficiency arguments and Americanization school practices in the form of neoconservatism. Simultaneously, neoliberal policies have resulted in the elimination and disinvestment in important social programs such as affirmative action and bilingual education that emerged during the civil rights struggles. Together, neoconservative and neoliberal approaches have camouflaged and exacerbated inequality, and these frameworks have become the defining economic and political paradigms shaping U.S. schools and other public services (Omi and Winant, 1994; Apple, 2001).

Starting in the late 1970s and under Ronald Reagan's presidency, a backlash against civil rights gains and power-conflict frameworks resulted in the reemergence of cultural deficiency perspectives in the form of neoconservatism (Omi and Winant, 1994). A neoconservative perspective assumes that we live in a meritocratic and color-blind society where racism, sexism, and other forms of discrimination are something of the past. In popular discourse, some who accept this perspective argue that "we are all the same," that there is "a level playing field," and that programs stemming from civil rights victories are examples of "reverse racism." Within this framework, people may say that they do not see race, or they may equate being color conscious with being racist. By failing to consider the larger societal factors that result in a stratified society, this approach blames groups of color for their positions in society and reinforces the prevailing notions of rugged individualism and meritocracy (Frankenberg, 1993). Individual and cultural factors, as opposed to historical, political, economic, and social ones, are then used to explain group position. These sentiments led California voters to approve the 1996 ballot initiative to eliminate affirmative action, Proposition 209. This proposition, named the California Civil Rights Initiative, equated affirmative action with racial preferences for people of color and discrimination with white men. Lost within this proposition was the continuing significance of historical and contemporary racism.

Most recently, neoconservatism has fueled anti-immigrant and anti-Latina/o sentiment. Conservative academics and leaders of nativist movements have depicted immigration as "the most serious challenge to America's traditional identity" (Huntington, 2004, p. 32), and they believe that immigrants have negative impacts on all aspects of the United States. This sentiment has fueled English-only movements and anti-immigrant campaigns to militarize the U.S.-Mexico border and charge undocumented immigrants with felonies.

Just as past cultural deficiency theorists advocated for acculturation through Americanization programs, neoconservatives support acculturation and a core Western-based curriculum. They oppose multicultural and bilingual education because they perceive them as threats to a U.S. national identity—narrowly defined as white, Protestant, middle class, English speaking, and heterosexual. There is concern that multicultural and bilingual education will result in the disuniting or the fragmenting of the United States (see Schlesinger, 1991). However, as will become apparent in the following chapters, multicultural and bilingual education are important precisely because they foster critical awareness, a sense of empowerment, and knowledge bases and frameworks critical for living in a multiracial and multiethnic society.

While neoconservatives focus on "cultural restoration" and maintaining a core national identity (see Apple, 2004), their perspectives on the economy merge with neoliberal ideologies that emphasize consumer choice and free market approaches such as privatization and deregulation of social services. Such neoliberal approaches have resulted in massive defunding of social programs like education, health care, transportation, social security, and public housing. There has also been a concurrent move to privatize public services (Hursh, 2005) and an emphasis on individualism over a concern for community and the public good (Garcia and Martínez, 2006). Such practices have intensified the economic chasm between the poor and the wealthy in the United States.

Today's educational system has been dramatically shaped by reports and practices stemming from neoliberal policies during the Reagan-Bush era of the 1980s and continuing under George W. Bush's No Child Left Behind Act. In 1983, a commission appointed under Ronald Reagan's secretary of education released *A Nation at Risk*, a report critiquing the "rising tide of mediocrity" among U.S. schools in science, industry, and innovation in comparison with Japanese and Western European educational systems (National Commission on Excellence in Education, 1983, p. 1). The report blamed teacher education programs and teachers for the nation's economic problems (Berliner and Biddle, 1995).

Although the report has been challenged as lacking evidence, "manufactur[ing] a crisis," and an attack on America's public schools (see Berliner and Biddle, 1995), *A Nation at Risk* became a rallying call for conservatives and ushered in a wave of criticism about the educational system. It opened the doors to the neoliberal school policies that are ubiquitous today: inflexible curriculum, standards-based teaching, high-stakes testing, increased teacher requirements, reduced teacher autonomy, and opportunities for greater privatization through school vouchers and charter schools (Pearl, 2002). According to professor of education David Hursh (2005), corporate and political leaders advocate that these reforms are necessary "to increase educational and economic productivity in an increasingly globalized economy, to decrease educational inequality, and to improve assessment objectivity" (p. 609). However, as will become apparent from the teachers' narratives in this book, these reforms are damaging schools, teachers, students, and communities by reproducing inequality. Thus, any movement for progressive educational change must involve an interrogation of these school policies and their linkages to larger economic, political, and social policies that undermine love and justice for the common good.

The Reproduction of Inequality

> For the most part, the social scientists who discussed and
> studied the importance of nature versus nurture were
> white males, all middle class by profession, some upper
> class by aspiration. They did not represent the inter-
> ests—political, educational, or social—of the groups
> considered intellectually inferior, whether by nature or
> nurture [Gonzalez, 1990, p. 66].

Analyzing these various social science theories and policies reveals
the relationships between knowledge production and unequal
access to power. What we know from the academic literature about
Latinas/os has been influenced by a long history of discriminatory
ideologies and practices. Contending with organizational barriers or
outright exclusion from educational institutions, publishing boards,
and grant review panels, few working class, women, and people of
color have been in positions to research, publish, and share new
ways of knowing (Baca Zinn, Weber Cannon, Higginbotham, and
Thorton Dill, 1990; Collins, 1991). Thus, until the 1960s, while
biological and cultural deficiency perspectives dominated in the
United States, those researching, writing, and acting on Latinas/os
did so primarily from privileged raced, classed, and gendered positions. Removed from Latina/o communities, they often researched
and wrote about Latinas/os from vantage points that perpetuated
stereotypes about Latinas/os and normalized dominant society.

It is only within the past thirty to forty years, with the policies achieved through the civil rights struggles, that we are seeing
theories and approaches within academia that focus on systems of
power and inequality rather than blaming individuals. Nevertheless, as will unfold in the following chapters, the roots of biological and cultural deficiency theories and the school practices that
they shaped remain. These deficiency theories and their concurrent

school practices form the foundation of today's unequal structures in the United States, and they are maintained and reproduced by current practices and ideologies. Thus, just as the history recounted in this chapter should not be forgotten in contemporary educational debates, neither should the detrimental impacts of current neoconservative and neoliberal approaches. Most of today's school policies and practices are premised on these exclusionary historical and contemporary frameworks, and they have devastating costs. The political elite continue to possess stereotyped assumptions and to devise educational plans that reflect, justify, and maintain the dominant classes and unequal school practices that Mr. O'Brien sees daily in the lives of Grant High School students such as Mario, Ana, and Mariela.

3

Understanding the Experiences of Latinas/os in the United States

*The mass media and politicians exploit data about the
youth, higher fertility rate, and growth rate of the
"Hispanic" population in ways that, ultimately, intensify
racist fears . . . and strengthen stereotypes about "Hispanic"
cultural traits and the perception that their presence will
contribute to increased social problems and tax payers'
burdens. . . .*

Gimenez (1997)

To the extent that the patterns of discrimination and inequality
detailed in Chapter Two are ignored and Hispanics or Latinas/
os are presented as a homogenous group of people who all share
supposedly negative cultural characteristics, Gimenez is correct.
Individual stereotypes, racist ideologies, and incorrect policies will
persist.

Latinas/os are not monolithic. As of the 2000 U.S. Census,
there were over 35 million Latinas/os in the United States with
diverse backgrounds that influence their schooling experiences,
life chances, and others' perceptions. Most (59 percent) of the
nearly 13 percent of U.S. residents who identified as Hispanic or
Latino were of Mexican descent. Ten percent were Puerto Rican,
4 percent Cuban, 2 percent Dominican, 5 percent Central
American, 4 percent South American, and the remaining
16 percent wrote in a pan-Latina/o label such as *Hispanic* or
Latino. During this period, 33 percent of California residents and
45 percent of Los Angeles County residents identified as Latina/o.

Mexicans predominated at over 70 percent of all Latinas/os in the state and county, and Central Americans represented nearly 10 percent of all Latinas/os (Suárez-Orozco and Páez, 2002).

Within and across these varying national origin groups, Latina/o students may share cultural characteristics, working-class experiences, and encounters with discrimination in the United States. Nevertheless, there may also be as much variation among Latinas/os as between Latinas/os and other racial/ethnic group. Thus, an awareness of Latina/o heterogeneity is important to delineate the distinct manifestations of various forms of discrimination and prejudice, prevent stereotyped assumptions about Latinas/os, assist school officials in better understanding the diverse backgrounds of students, and ensure a clearer perspective for enacting school policies.

The following sections detail the ways in which generation, language, socioeconomic position, skin color, and gender are made significant for Latinas/os in education, and each of these factors is interrelated and compounded. Nevertheless, for purposes of elaboration, I discuss each of them separately.

U.S. Involvement, Latina/o Immigration, and Generational Diversity

Each Latina/o ethnic group has a distinct history in the United States that has been shaped by U.S. power and domination in Latin America (for further discussion, see Gonzalez, 2000). These histories, combined with generation in the United States and immigration status, influence life chances, including educational experiences.

Though often left out of popular discourse about immigration and education, the history of Mexicans in the Southwest predates the United States and must be understood in the context of U.S. conquest and persisting discrimination. Waves of labor recruitment and migration are salient aspects of this history. Throughout the

1900s, the U.S. government and capitalists engaged in an unequal and exploitative pattern of recruitment and deportation of Mexican workers that changed depending on fluctuations in the U.S. economy. U.S. businesses recruited Mexicans to work in agricultural fields, meat-packing industries, brickyards, and canneries and to build up the railroads during World Wars I and II. From 1942 to 1964, this labor recruitment was instituted as part the bracero program, a U.S. contract worker program with Mexico that brought five million Mexicans with temporary labor contracts, termed *braceros*, to work in U.S. agribusiness (Calavita, 1992), along with about five million more undocumented Mexican workers (Hondagneu-Sotelo, 1994). During the 1980s and 1990s, migration from Mexico was fueled by global economic restructuring that disrupted subsistence living, employment networks established while working in transnational corporations within Mexico, and family networks from earlier immigration waves.

Depending on the U.S. economy and labor market, these recruitment campaigns and migration waves have fluctuated with rampant anti-Mexican practices. During the Great Depression of the 1930s, nearly one million people of Mexican descent, including U.S.-born children, were deported and repatriated to Mexico (Balderrama and Rodríguez, 1995). During the post–Korean War recession, there were similar deportation campaigns under what was called Operation Wetback, where the Immigration and Naturalization Service (INS) deported about two million Mexican immigrants and their Mexican American children (Acuña, 1988). Most recently, the 1990s California recession and the post-9/11 so-called antiterrorism campaigns have resulted in increased militarization and surveillance at the U.S.-Mexico border, anti-immigrant policies, summary raids in neighborhoods and workplaces, and nativism.

These patterns of recruitment, exploitation, and deportation of Mexican immigrants have had enduring impacts. Not only have they fostered stereotypical images of Mexicans as cheap labor and forever foreigners, but the labor of Mexican workers has been critical in supporting the U.S. economy and enhancing the lives of U.S. residents. Nonetheless, as a group, Mexican workers have been poorly compensated for their labor, and their many contributions to the building of the United States have gone largely unacknowledged. Over time, some of these same experiences have befallen other groups of Latinas/os in the United States. Non-Latinas/os do not always distinguish between Mexicans and other Latin Americans. Thus, as new groups of Latinas/os, such as Central Americans, have entered the United States, they too have encountered some of the same anti-immigrant and anti-Latina/o sentiment that Mexicans have experienced.

Compared to Mexicans, most Central Americans have a relatively recent history in California. Nonetheless, U.S. economic, political, and military power and domination in Central America reach back to the middle of the nineteenth century. This history ranges from invasions to investments by U.S. citizens to the efforts of the U.S. government to control waterways, and to the use of U.S. Marines to squelch popular uprisings and impose U.S.-supported governments (for examples, see Ochoa and Ochoa, 2005). As U.S. involvement in Central America increased with the sponsoring of wars that resulted in abduction, torture, and death, violence, destruction, and poverty intensified, and hundreds of thousands of Central Americans began moving to the United States in the late 1970s and early 1980s (Hamilton and Chinchilla, 2001).

Fleeing oppressive conditions imposed by U.S. government-supported dictatorships, many Central Americans, especially Salvadorans and Guatemalans, were largely denied political asylum and forced to live without documents and the rights that they bestow. Within a context of anti-immigrant policies, declines in high-wage manufacturing jobs, and a weakening labor movement, Central Americans have encountered many economic and political difficulties in the United States. Older immigrants also encounter the psychological trauma of war from their lives in Central America.

These larger patterns of U.S. power and domination are critical to understanding Latinas/os and education, especially in California. For example, these asymmetrical power relations between the United States and Latin America, the exploitative treatment of immigrant workers, and the denial of documents to immigrants have fueled negative perceptions of Mexicans and Central Americans. Looking at public opinion polls on immigrants, sociologists Espenshade and Belanger concluded in 1998 that "Latin American and Caribbean immigrants in general, and Mexican immigrants in particular, rank somewhere near the bottom in terms of how Americans view immigrants. . . . European immigrants are most favored, and Asians fall in the middle. In comparison with Latin American immigrants, Asian immigrants are perceived as less likely to use welfare or to commit crimes, and more likely to work hard, to have strong family values, and to do well in school" (quoted in Suárez-Orozco and Páez, 2002, p. 22). These inaccurate and stereotyped perceptions not only ignore historical phenomena and institutional inequalities, but maintain a racial/ethnic hierarchy that influences how school officials and others may perceive students. One of the results may be that school officials accept the biological or cultural deficiency ideas of the past and view white and European students more favorably than Asian students, and they may view Latina/o students poorly. Students are aware of others' perceptions of them, and the rampant anti-immigrant sentiment that continues to plague the United States can damage a child's sense of self and belonging.

The devastation caused by U.S. involvement in Latin America and the establishment of family ties throughout the Americas spur immigration. So the majority of Latinas/os in the United States are either immigrants or children of immigrants. However, there is a wide range of generations that experience schools differently. Studies suggest that Latina/o immigrants, in comparison to their

U.S.-born Latina/o peers, tend to describe schooling as a more positive experience, and they perceive their teachers as more approachable and caring (Olsen, 1997; Valenzuela, 1999). For example, in a Texas high school study, Angela Valenzuela (1999) found that teachers typically interpreted Mexican immigrants' more conservative styles of dress and interactions as indications that they were more concerned about school than their Mexican American peers were. Given this research, it is not surprising that immigrant and often second-generation Mexican Americans and Central Americans in non-college-bound courses have higher grades, test scores, and high school completion rates than their third- and fourth-generation counterparts. However, access to college-bound courses tends to eliminate these generational differences (Valenzuela, 1999) because these courses are typically more rigorous, and teachers often have higher expectations for the students enrolled in them.

There are also important variations among Latina/o immigrant students by age and skill level that influence educational outcomes. In particular, recent work suggests that at rates of 84 to 85 percent, Latina/o youth who arrive in the United States at younger ages are more likely to earn high school diplomas than older immigrants, whose high school completion rate is about 56 percent (Quijada and Alvarez, 2006). In particular, Mexican immigrants who migrate before the age of five graduate from high school at rates comparable to those of U.S.-born Latinas/os (Fuentes, 2006).

Immigrants who start school at older ages in the United States do well if they are able to establish strong skills in reading, writing, and mathematics in Spanish. These skills are significant in helping students transfer their knowledge to English. So older immigrant students who are able to establish a strong foundation in their home language tend to do better in U.S. schools than older immigrant youth who did not have access to formal schooling in their home countries (Valenzuela, 1999). These difference in students' educational foundations are heavily influenced by class position and whether or not children come from homes where their families were able to provide them with formal schooling in their countries of origin.

Latina/o Linguistic Diversity and the Struggle for Bilingual Education

As a result of the history of immigration and the generational differences among Latinas/os, there is also great linguistic diversity: Latin Americans in the United States speak English, Spanglish, Spanish, Portuguese, an indigenous language such as Zapoteco, Mixteco, and Mayan, or a combination of any of these languages.

Over 75 percent of Latina/o children over the age of five enter U.S. schools speaking Spanish (Quijada and Alvarez, 2006). This is an important resource that schools can build on through additive bilingual education programs where students improve both their English-language abilities and their Spanish-language verbal and literacy skills. In fact, bilingual children demonstrate superiority in concept formation, mental flexibility, and verbal problem-solving abilities (Lindholm, 1995). However, as part of the neoconservative agenda to make English the official language and to push a national identity, bilingual education programs are under attack throughout much of the United States; some have already been eliminated. In California, the passage of Proposition 227, English for the Children, in 1998 dramatically reduced bilingual education programs in the state. Such attacks on bilingual education are detrimental to the psychological development of young children, who may internalize the belief that speaking English is better than speaking their home language. Moreover, as a society, we limit the possibilities of raising bilingual, biliterate youth who reap not only educational and occupational advantages but also the social advantages of interacting in a diverse and interconnected world. In many schools throughout the United States, opportunities for bilingualism and biliteracy are stunted.

It is not until high school that most students are able to study a language other than English, and the effectiveness of these language classes at fostering bilingualism is questionable. Pedagogically, these courses may be taught in English with an emphasis on grammar and vocabulary over immersion. Furthermore, it is believed to be more difficult to learn a language after childhood, and it takes five to seven years to acquire average levels of proficiency (Cummins, 1996).

Latina/o Socioeconomic Backgrounds

As a result of patterns of immigration, U.S. restrictions on documentation status, racial/ethnic discrimination, and economic restructuring, Latinas/os are likely to be poor or working class. In 1999, the median family income for all Latinas/os in the United States was about thirty-four thousand dollars in comparison to about fifty thousand dollars for all families in the country. During this same period, more than one in every four Latinas/os under age eighteen (28 percent) was living in poverty compared with one in six of the general population (17 percent) (Ramirez, 2004).

Despite the relatively low median family income, there is income variation among Latinas/os, including a growing middle class. In particular, there are differences by subgroup: South Americans and Cubans have median family incomes ten thousand to fourteen thousand dollars higher than median family incomes of Mexican, Puerto Rican, Central American, and Dominican families (Ramirez, 2004). These income differentials are linked to immigrants' educational and class disparities in their countries of origin, skin color differences, and the context of reception when these groups entered the United States. For example, in comparison to most other Latina/o immigrants, the first wave of Cuban immigrants in the 1960s came primarily from middle- and upper-class backgrounds, tended to be lighter skinned, and were granted documentation status and governmental assistance as political refugees. These advantages markedly enhanced the social, political, and economic opportunities for Cubans as a whole, but there are also variations among Cuban Americans depending on the same criteria of premigration class position, skin color, and documentation status in the United State.

Perhaps most staggering of all is the dramatic wealth gap that exists in the United States. In 2002, the average Latina/o household had a net worth of $7,932. This includes all of the assets owned by the household minus the liabilities. In comparison, the average for white households was $88,651. One in four Latina/o households had zero or negative net worth during this period, meaning that they owed more than they owned. The wealthiest 25 percent of Latina/o households possessed over 90 percent of the wealth among Latina/o households. Thus, not only is there a large wealth gap between white and Latinas/os, but there are important gaps among Latinas/os. For example, among Latina/o immigrants, Cubans had a combined net worth of nearly $40,000 compared with $7,602 for Mexicans (Kochhar, 2004).

Home ownership is a critical factor shaping the wealth gap between households. Since nearly two thirds of white households own homes compared to less than 50 percent of Latina/o households (Kochhar, 2004), the overall amount of wealth for white households will appreciate more than for Latina/o households. Not only do home owners benefit from this home appreciation, but they also receive tax deductions, and if they also own a rental property, they receive additional income from individuals and families who cannot afford to buy their own homes. All of these home owner benefits reproduce this wealth gap, which has significant implications for life chances, including having the ability to finance children's college education through home mortgages. As home prices continue to soar, home ownership becomes increasingly prohibitive for working-class and lower-middle-class families, especially in areas where many Latinas/os, live such as Los Angeles and Orange counties in California.

The poor and working-class position of many Latina/o families should not be taken lightly when considering the type of education that students are receiving. Not only may students have to contend with economic hardships, but many must also negotiate the competing demands of school and work. In addition, living in working-class urban communities, Latina/o students are likely to attend schools that are segregated by race/ethnicity and class. In fact, Latinas/os are attending more segregated schools than they did in the 1970s, and in California, the situation is approaching "hypersegregation" (Orfield and Yun, 1999). As with the past, typically these schools are poorly funded and characterized by inferior facilities, limited curricula, insufficient resources, and overcrowded classrooms (Orfield, 1996).

Latina/o Racial Identities and Colorism

For Latinas/os with a history of conquest, colonization, and migration, there is a wide range of racial identities, skin colors, hair types, and facial features. In the 2000 U.S. Census, Latinas/os identified in various ways, with over a third selecting more than one racial category. Eight percent identified as white, 2 percent as black or African American, 15 percent as American Indian and Alaskan Native, 11 percent as Asian, Native Hawaiian, and Pacific Islander, and 97 percent as Other (Ramirez, 2004).

In a racially stratified society, physical features influence life chances, and research shows that Latinas/os with lighter skin and more European features earn more money, complete more years of schooling, and have higher-status jobs than Latinas/os with darker skin and more indigenous features (Telles and Murguia, 1990; Gándara, 1995). Students experience these inequalities at an early age. For example, a study on bilingual teachers and teachers in training, many of whom were Mexican American, found that these teachers rated lighter-skinned students more favorably than darker-skinned students (Bloom, 1990). Thus, not only may whites accept a color hierarchy that privileges light skin, but Latinas/os and other groups may also internalize these pervasive messages (Moraga, 1983). The early messages and unequal treatment that students receive because of their appearance often continue through adult-hood, to the extent that Mexican American women "described as very dark brown-skinned will have completed one less year of education than very light brown [women] with similar background characteristics" (Hunter, 2005, p. 43).

Gender Differences Among Latinas/os and Education

Finally, by gender, Latinas and Latinos are experiencing schools differently. Girls and women across race/ethnicity and generation tend to outperform their male counterparts (Valenzuela, 1999; Lopez, 2003). In 1996, 8.4 million women were enrolled in U.S. colleges in comparison to 6.7 million men; women are also more likely to be in honors courses, and they earn higher grades (Lopez, 2003). A 2005 report on California graduation rates reveals that a gender gap exists for all races/ethnicities. In 2002, 87 percent of Asian American, 80 percent of white, 65 percent of Latinas, and 60 percent of black women completed high school compared to 80 percent, 75 percent, 55 percent, and 50 percent, respectively, of their male counterparts ("Confronting the Graduation Rate Crisis in California," 2005). Despite these gender differences, because overall Latinas/os have such a low high school comple-tion rate, we need to be especially aware of what is happening with Latino students and the reasons that they are not advancing educationally.

Why, since the mid-1970s, have Latinos not been able to make more educational progress (Contreras and Gándara, 2006)? In one of the few studies to explore this question, Lopez (2003) finds that among Afro-Latinas/os in a New York City high school, various school factors, teachers' interactions, and family dynamics have resulted in different race-gender experiences and outlooks.

The criminalization of men of color, combined with poor school facilities, intensive policing at school, low-curriculum tracks, and limited job opportunities, have fostered a situation of "institutional expulsion" for the young men in her study. In contrast, young women, who are less likely to be punished for breaking certain school rules and tend to find support and encouragement from female teachers and mothers, seem to exhibit "institutional engagement" and optimism for the future amid oppression (Lopez, 2003).

Latinas' higher level of school engagement in comparison to Latinos should not be misinterpreted as success or an end to sexism. Gendered expectations and pressures for heterosexual romance may lead some Latina high schoolers to scale back their educational aspirations (Valenzuela, 1999), and in comparison with all other girls, Latinas are underrepresented in advanced placement courses and less likely to graduate from high school and college (Ginorio and Huston, 2000). Although there are various explanations for these patterns, power-conflict theories that focus on unequal school practices and structural factors best explain these differing educational outcomes.

The Effects of Exclusionary Beliefs

When considering schooling experiences and strategies for change, we must remember this diversity among Latinas/os and the larger phenomena that shape educational outcomes. All too often, these differences are forgotten and the macroscopic factors are overlooked. When such factors are ignored, students such as Marco, Ana, and Mariela at Grant High School, who were introduced in Chapter Two, are shortchanged. Not only are they provided with unequal schooling, but some students may even come to blame themselves for their difficulties in school.

We cannot subject another generation of youth to the damaging school practices and inequalities that characterize the U.S. educational system, and we should not allow top-down policies and individuals far removed from education to dictate school practices that are also testing the spirit, energy, and creativity of too many teachers. With these larger goals in mind, we turn to teachers' reflections on the significant elements of education that have made a positive difference in their schooling, lives, and teaching.

The following chapter focuses on the education that happens within families, a topic that too often is dismissed. Latina/o teachers' narratives remind us of the wisdom that comes from our families and how more of this knowledge should be integrated into classrooms and the structure of schools. From their voices, we hear how through resilience, resistance, and family support, they have navigated many exclusionary beliefs and practices. Their stories and perspectives offer hope for the future and concrete strategies for change.

Part II

Family and School

4

Learning from Latina/o Families

*I am constantly told, usually by non-Latinos, that Latino
parents just don't care about the education of their children.
And I've always, of course, rejected that because my mom
was never able to attend any parent conferences, and I
know a lot of teachers see that as not caring. But my mom
had two jobs and she was a widow. There are a lot of
obstacles for parents . . . economics, problems at home with
divorce . . . that maybe make parents not want to take on
something else.*

(Ana Camacho, high school teacher)

The daughter of Mexican immigrants, Ana Camacho is the first
member of her family to graduate from college. She saw how
her mother struggled and sacrificed to get her through school. So
when she is "constantly told," especially by non-Latinas/os, how
Latina/o parents feel about education, she cannot help but get
angry. Maybe that is why when Ana was asked how Latina/o parents feel about education, she smiled and replied, "Hmm. *I* get to
answer that question."

By drawing on the example of her hard-working mother, Ana critiques dominant conceptions of Latina/o families and definitions of
parent participation that assume parents who do not attend school
events are not involved in their children's education. Parents believe
that all forms of raising children are critical, including providing
food, clothing, and verbal encouragement (Williams and Stallworth, 1983; Gándara, 1995). However, studies confirm what Ana
knows: some teachers possess stereotyped perceptions of Latina/o
families and narrow notions of parent participation in education.

Such teachers may mistakenly equate parents' absences at school events with not caring (Lareau, 1989; Quijada and Alvarez, 2006).

Continuing with a more complex response than the one that is usually told to her, Ana juxtaposes schools' expectations for parental involvement with the significance of parents' economic responsibilities. Working-class parents may not be able to attend school functions because of their work schedules or because they may lack transportation or child care (Lareau, 1987). School officials with more privileged class backgrounds may not always understand the financial and time constraints of working-class families. So schools may schedule open houses, parent-teacher conferences, and other events at times that are not conducive for working families, and school officials may then accuse parents of not caring about education when they are simply unable to attend these functions.

Ana highlights other often overlooked factors that may fuel some teachers' negative perceptions of Latina/o parent participation: "Latino parents assume, especially if they are new immigrants, that the teacher and the school know what to do and that they don't have the education to be able to tell the school what to do." Studies find that working-class white parents also believe that schools and teachers are responsible for teaching students to learn (Lareau, 1987). Working-class, immigrant, or Latina/o parents who place much of the responsibility of education on teachers do not devalue education. Instead, they may just believe that teachers have the proper training to educate students (Lareau, 1987). Furthermore, some Spanish-speaking parents may fear that that they will appear ignorant or unaware to teachers (see Valdés, 1996) or that there will be no school personnel who speak Spanish. Thus, lack of familiarity with the U.S. educational system may prevent some parents from visiting their children's schools (Moreno, 2004), especially if the environment is unwelcoming to them.

Unfortunately, what Ana is constantly told about Latina/o parents is not an anomaly. There are many misperceptions that blame Latina/o families and assume that if Latina/o families only cared about education, then educational inequalities would be addressed.

There is a long history of programs aimed at Latina/o families, especially mothers, under the pretense that families need to be improved: they need to learn how to speak English, prepare nutritious meals, and raise their children (for examples, see Gonzalez, 1990; Valdés, 1996; Villenas, 2001). These cultural deficiency perspectives and the programs that they justify misrepresent Latinas/os and perpetuate school practices such as English-only classrooms that may divest Latina/o students of family and cultural resources, including the Spanish language and family values (Valenzuela, 1999). In the end, programs based on a cultural deficiency framework may do nothing but exacerbate the structural and institutional inequalities that persist by segregating students and providing them with inferior schooling. When families are blamed, larger processes such as educational practices and the growing disinvestment in public education can be ignored.

Other Latina/o teachers share Ana Camacho's perspectives. From the teachers' narratives in this chapter, we learn the multiple ways that their families have been involved in education and their recommendations for how community members might work collectively for love and justice in our schools and society. Most of the teachers recounted the wisdom that they acquired from their family members, especially their mothers, and how this wisdom sustained them through school and now informs their teaching philosophy and classroom pedagogy. Overall, these narratives remind us that education comes in many forms and extends beyond the classroom doors and the school gates.

Woven throughout many of the teachers' memories are reflections on how they navigated between the multiple and intersecting worldviews of society and family. They are cognizant of how mainstream conceptions of education that emphasize individualism, competition, and acculturation—acquiring the dominant language, values, and traditions—are privileged over approaches to education that emphasize familial connections (*familismo*), respect (*respeto*), and/or the Spanish language. The dominant emphasis permeated the so-called Americanization movements of the past and persists today under neoconservative frameworks.

Despite the pervasive impacts of mainstream approaches to education and the teachers' various family expectations, the teachers and their parents have not simply resigned themselves to others' requirements of them. Just as their families are challenging assimilationist imperatives and discriminatory actions, teachers' narratives are filled with examples of resilience, resistance, and redefinition. Like high school teacher Ana Camacho, they are countering dominant stereotypes, constructing their own perspectives on Latinas/os and education, and carving out their own lives that are characterized neither by complete assimilation nor by passively accepting the demands of their families. Their stories reveal how many of the teachers have developed "a tolerance for contradictions, a tolerance for ambiguity" and the skill to juggle multiple cultures and competing demands (Anzaldúa, 1987, p. 79).

Though the family and cultural resources of Latina/o and working-class students may be minimized in schools, the following stories of family support, inspiration, and sacrifice reveal how much can be gained by listening to them. In this case, teachers' retellings inspire a rethinking of the role of Latina/o families in education, the encouragement of diverse forms of knowledge, and an awareness of the multiple paths toward being educated.

Latina/o Family Involvement and Education: An Introduction

Countless studies link parental involvement in school with student academic success (for discussions, see Gándara, 1995; Lopez, Scribner, and Mahititvanichcha, 2001). These studies highlight how middle-class white parents are more likely than working-class and Spanish-speaking Latina/o parents to visit their children's schools, and how working-class, immigrant, and Latina/o families lack the cultural capital necessary for academic success in middle-class Anglo institutions. This cultural capital includes access to U.S. middle- and upper-class knowledge, cultural competencies, and worldviews (see Bourdieu and Passerson, 1977). More recently, some of this work has been critiqued for maintaining the narrow notions of parental participation that teacher Ana Camacho previously debunked, ignoring the range of ways that Latina/o and working-class parents are committed to education, and minimizing the cultural capital of working-class and Latina/o families (Gándara, 1995; Moreno, 2004).

Contemporary studies also suggest that working-class and Latina/o parents may face a double bind when it comes to parents' involvement in schools. First, they are often accused of not participating. However, when they do attend the events advocated by schools such as the Parent Teacher Association meetings and question school officials about their practices or activities, they may be ignored, intimidated, or excluded. During an informal meeting, one Los Angeles–area Mexican American high school principal clearly gave me this perspective: "I don't know what parent participation means. Parent participation is not always a good thing. For example, when I was the principal at [another] school, we had to check with the different parent groups before we could get anything done. I don't want to have a bitch session" (quoted in Ochoa, 2004a, p. 193). Studies suggest that teachers often want parents to defer to them and "assume the role of audience" in their relationship to schools (Lareau, 1987; Shannon, 1996), so when working-class parents challenge school officials, they may be dismissed or labeled "irrational" (Shannon, 1996, p. 83). The school principal quoted viewed some parents as "bitching," a gender-specific term that may be a direct attack on Latinas who at this school are the family members who attend most school activities.

Just as school officials may structure and limit parental involvement, they may overlook the important everyday activities occurring in homes, families, and communities that are critical components of education. After all, parental physical involvement in schools may not be as important to student academic success as parents' expectations for higher education, the extent of parents' conversations with their children, and the learning opportunities provided to children (Gándara, 1995). According to the teachers featured in this book, their parents, especially their mothers, transmitted their high educational values by pushing them to go to college and teaching them family and community histories and cultures. Parents' teachings were often conveyed though inspiring and instructional personal stories of challenging discrimination and humiliation. These teachings, typically overlooked as important forms of education and cultural capital, "can serve as a vehicle of social mobility" by modeling and engendering a sense of hope, a commitment to justice, and a desire for advancement (Gándara, 1995, p. 51). Overall, the narratives from Latina/o school officials suggest how their families supplemented unequal schooling and incomplete curriculum by sharing experiences, histories, and cultures and by demonstrating their commitment to a broad understanding of education.

Parental Educational Expectations

Contrary to the beliefs of some school officials, studies suggest that Latina/o families place a high value on education (Moreno and Valencia, 2002). The verbal support that middle school teachers Margarita Villa and Vivian Sosa received from their families was common among the teachers:

> Our parents were behind us [saying], "You are going to go to college." I was going to be the first one in my family, so college was pushed upon us. . . . We had to go on and become higher than what our parents were because that was told to us from the beginning . . . it was put in our heads. I was told since I was five years old, even before that, my parents were saying "You're going to Cal

State LA; you're going to Cal State LA." I went to Cal State LA. They never gave us a choice that we were not going to go to college [Margarita Villa].

Education was extremely important. We could not bring home any C's, D's, or F's. That was not acceptable. It was A's and B's. Period. Education was valued very highly. No matter what my parents struggled with personally, my mom working two jobs to make sure we had enough—and my dad working, it didn't matter. It was, "You are going to school" [Vivian Sosa].

Such encouragement for first-generation college students is an important way that families demonstrate their strong commitment to schooling (Gándara, 1995).

Another way that parents of first-generation college students convey their value for education is by modeling hard work. In particular, twenty-five-year-old Cristina Martinez felt empowered by knowing her father's struggles and always seeing him learn:

My dad talks about having to teach himself how to read, having to push himself to be able to write. He got his trade in mechanics. Then he went back to school to work on diesel trucks. I remember my father going to school when I was in elementary school, and he would always get A's and B's. He would be at the top of his trade. Seeing him do that was very empowering, seeing no matter what kind of learning it was, Dad was always right up there. It was also important seeing my mom as an avid reader.

Although college was a new experience for this family, the actions of her parents were powerful influences on Cristina's determination to excel in school.

Parents as Teachers

Listening to the teachers' narratives and thinking about my own life, it is hard not to notice the crucial role that our parents have played as our first, and perhaps most important, teachers. However, typically, parents' experiences and knowledge basis are left out of textbooks and class discussions. By sharing what they know, these parents helped their children succeed, filled an important void in knowledge, and instilled pride and a strong sense of self-esteem that seemed to inspire their children's curiosity and enabled them to contend with the anti-Latina/o messages that they received from others. Although the following examples are presented in separate sections, they emerged throughout the teachers' narratives in complex, multiple, overlapping, and intersecting ways.

Teaching Our Histories, Cultures, and Languages and Helping to Make Us Kind and Grateful

Middle school teacher Margarita Villa's family members taught her the most about Mexican Americans, a topic excluded from the primarily Mexican American K–12 schools that she attended:

> I learned a lot about Chicano studies through my parents. . . . We weren't taught much of the history [in school]. My mom and dad told us about Rubén Salazar; they told me about the high school walkouts. They knew who Rodolfo Acuña was, and I read his biography later on. They told me who Cesar Chavez was. Cesar Chavez was not taught to me in school. I got that a lot from my parents, and when I got curious, I would look them up. But I remember my parents telling me about when Rubén Salazar was killed at the Silver Dollar. They would always talk about those things. . . . My uncles also taught me a lot. They would always remind us that people used to be embarrassed to speak Spanish.

Margarita Villa's immigrant parents moved to the United States during the start of the 1960s Chicana/o movement. Thus, they remember critical events in recent Chicana/o history: the 1968 Chicana/o school walkouts for educational justice, the struggles of Cesar Chavez and the United Farm Workers, and the 1970 National Chicano Moratorium against the Vietnam War and where Chicano news reporter Rubén Salazar was killed by members of the Los Angeles Police Department. They also taught her about renowned Chicana/o studies scholar Rodolfo Acuña. He has authored several books, including *Occupied America*, an extensively read and referenced history of Chicanas/os that is in its sixth edition. Since the history and the experiences of Mexican Americans remain largely invisible in the K–12 curriculum, Margarita's parents had to compensate for the school's deficiencies by teaching her about these important individuals and history. In college, Margarita learned more by enrolling in a Chicana/o Studies course. Learning this history from her family and in college was key for instilling a sense of pride and affirming Margarita's family message: "Don't ever be embarrassed by who you are."

Seventy-seven-year-old Marta Escobar, who taught K–8 students for over forty years, echoes the important role of parents' teachings:

> My mother was very much devoted to México because our relatives were there, and she enriched us about the Mexican part of our heritage. . . . Thanks to my mom, she took us to see where she had lived as a young person, and that really made me very proud of México. . . . That's what kept us having pride about the Mexican part just like we had the American part because we were growing up here and knew everything. So she kept all of that with us, and it enriched us.

As it did with Margarita, this enrichment motivated Marta to seek classes in college to add to the knowledge she received from her mother. Whereas Margarita took Chicana/o Studies courses, these courses did not yet exist when Marta was a student. Inspired by her mother, she completed four years of Spanish literature where she learned more "wonderful things about México."

In the United States, where Chicana/o and Mexican history and culture are absent in most K–12 schools, families who convey such knowledge to their children through relating counterhistories disrupt dominant constructions of history. Sometimes this resistance involves not only challenging what schools teach but also what other family members accept as important knowledge and skills. This was the case for fifty-five-year-old Jane Hanson, a third-generation Mexican American woman who married a European American. As an elementary instructional aide who assists Spanish-speaking students, Jane confronted her husband and defended her right to teach her daughter Spanish: "That day that she was born, my husband said, 'This baby's going to speak English.' I said, 'This baby's going to speak what I teach her because you're going to be at work, and I'm the mother, and she's learning what I want her to learn'" (quoted in Ochoa, 2004a, p. 150).

Raised during the 1940s and 1950s, Jane vividly remembers the Spanish-language repression that permeated her schooling. She recalls the pain of not being allowed to speak Spanish in El Monte, California, schools because of the intense prejudice toward Mexicans. These memories fueled her strong desire to speak Spanish to her daughter. However, when Jane was raising her daughter in the 1970s and 1980s, the value of Spanish was still minimized; assimilation was the goal, even if it meant being limited to speaking English. Jane had to battle her husband, but she successfully raised a bilingual daughter who is now a Spanish-English medical interpreter.

The teachers' families conveyed more than history and language to their children. After all, education is not just about learning history and culture; it also encompasses the acquisition of values and morals that make one a good person. In Spanish, *bien educado* means knowing "how to live in the world as caring, responsible, well-mannered, and respectful, human beings" (Valenzuela, 1999, p. 23). An emphasis on being *bien educado* is similar to conceptions of *educación*, where level of education, occupation, or socioeconomic class position are not necessarily related to having *una buena educación*. How one behaves and interacts with other people is crucial, as is learning social and personal responsibilities (Valenzuela, 1999; Villenas, 2001).

Researchers have described how this broader conception of education is important for many Latina/o families (see Delgado-Gaitan, 1992; Valdés, 1996; Valenzuela, 1999; Villenas, 2001), and Marta Escobar captures its significance in her family when she recounts, "The training that we get from our family. You know, my mom always taught me to be kind and grateful and things like that."

Gabriela Muñoz's account coincides with Marta's that her mother has been responsible for shaping the person she has become. Her mother's teachings have provided her with much "rich[ness]": "I know where I came from, and my mom has really instilled that; you have to be proud of your values, of your ethical moral values, your traditions and keep those alive. . . . If my mom had spoken just English to me I would have never been so rich in that sense . . . language-wise."

From their mothers, teachers such as Marta Escobar and Gabriela Muñoz see the benefits of educating the whole person and being bilingual. Yet it is precisely this richness of language and the focus on respect and educating the whole person that is depleted and overlooked in our school system. Students who enter school speaking a language other than English may be perceived as lacking English-language skills rather than as possessing resources that can be strengthened (see Valenzuela, 1999). Moreover, the competitive structure of schools and the emphasis on quantitative evaluations of a person's worth, such as how students perform on standardized tests, minimize the significance of being caring and respectful people. Thus, the resources that these teachers and other students possess as they begin school may be diminished in favor of speaking English and qualities that favor individualism and competition.

Sharing Family Stories of Struggle and Inspiration

During our meetings, teachers generously shared their family stories, which trace family histories and often transmit important lessons about inequalities, struggles, and forms of resistance. In some cases, the stories helped teachers develop a greater awareness of power and inequality, a desire to persist against hardships, and a commitment to effect positive change. As such, the telling and retelling of these stories have consequences that extend beyond the narrator and the recipient of the story: they have the power to inspire multiple generations. This is the case with the family stories that thirty-two-year-old Marie Marquez and twenty-five-year-old Vivian Sosa grew up hearing. These stories capture the critical role their parents had in shaping their educational aspirations and their approaches to teaching. Their impact can be seen in the ways both carry these stories and their parents' determination into their classrooms, where they are influencing another generation of students.

Marie Marquez's immigrant parents instilled the importance of education into their six children by modeling their love of politics, telling their stories, and attending school meetings. Marie's mother died while she was in high school, but Marie's father continued to motivate her with his own life philosophy of doing "whatever you want." The result was her "dad's crowning achievement": all six of his children graduated from high school. Two graduated from college, including Marie, who received a bachelor's degree in English literature and a master's degree in education.

Marie Marquez describes her father's love of learning: "School was really important to my parents, mostly to my dad because he's self-taught. He only has a third-grade education. He's seventy-one, and he reads the newspaper every day from front to back, and that's his education. He loves to carry on conversations about politics."

Just as watching her father read and listening to him discuss current events encouraged Marie to advance in school, knowing his experiences of struggle and resistance also inspired her. Marie Marquez's father left Mexico in the 1950s at the age of nineteen. Although his mother warned him that he would "starve to death," he took some money from her purse, crossed the desert in the middle of the night, hopped on a train, and ended up in southern California. Born over ten years after her father's migration, Marie remembers her family's financial struggles—eating "frijoles and tortillas for dinner just to make ends meet." She also knows her father's history because "he talks all kinds of stories about how he actually ran away from home." These stories make her laugh because she believes that if she had done "something like that at nineteen, it would have been a totally different story." However, when we listen to Marie's narrative, we find many parallels with her father's life.

While Marie's father struggled with the decision to follow his mother's admonition and stay in Mexico or migrate to the United States, Marie encountered her own competing pressures as a working-class Mexican American female living in a middle-class and predominantly European American neighborhood. She remembers the gender differences that existed between Marie and her three sisters and their brothers: "The girls stayed at home; we didn't really go out. We weren't allowed to have boyfriends until we got out of high school. We were pretty sheltered. The guys had a little more leeway. . . . The girls had to beg and plead just to go play at a neighbor's house because my mom was very strict with the girls. We had to stay close by."

Although Marie sometimes resented the gender restrictions that her mother placed on the girls in her family, an ironic twist to such restrictions is that of the six children, the two who received college degrees were the girls. Thus, as other studies on the children of immigrants have suggested, while being kept closer to home may limit young girls' movements, greater contact with adults and time for studying and reading may have a positive influence on their educational aspirations (see Lopez, 2003). Thus, although Marie's mother initially limited Marie's movement, in the end, Marie's education enhanced her career and life opportunities.

At times, Marie's awareness of these differing gender restrictions in her family combined with the varied messages that she received from her parents about her participation in school: "There was a tug of war. My dad wanted us really involved in school, as much as possible, whereas my mom would question everything. If I was going to stay after school, 'Why are you going to stay after school?'"

Marie also had different experiences and family commitments than did her middle-class white friends in her southern California neighborhood:

> Going through school with girls and guys who were able to go to coed parties in elementary school, we couldn't do that. . . . It was difficult because I wanted to be like some of the white kids I went to school with, but I couldn't because I had these restrictions. . . . I knew that they didn't understand where I was coming from—having to go to the store and translate for my mom and having to go with relatives to translate for them at the doctor's office. It's a whole different life you're leading, and your friends don't get it.

Studies on children of immigrants like Marie who become "cultural brokers" (Buriel and De Ment, 1997) suggest that there are many benefits of interpreting between family members and mainstream institutions. One of them is learning how to navigate new places (Lopez, 2003). Marie's childhood experiences translating for institutional representatives may have facilitated her ability to negotiate the two forms of tug of war that she recounted earlier: the one with her parents—between her mother's desire to have her home and her father's desire that she get involved with school—and the one between her family's expectations and her friends' experiences. And although Marie may have wanted fewer restrictions from her family, she had a strong sense of pride that she "could speak another language while some people couldn't." Thus, in comparison to her white middle-class peers, Marie's language skills and understanding of U.S. institutions may have allowed her to develop broader perspectives and an expanded ability to interact with people from varied backgrounds. What may have felt like restrictions to her as a child have become critical assets in a diverse society.

Despite learning how to navigate between various expectations and experiences, Marie was still "thrown for a loop" when her father had a talk with her about his desire that she "make something" with her life: "My dad was, 'You can do whatever you want.' We were talking about a cousin of mine who was in a bad situation; she was in a relationship and had kids. My dad told me, 'You have the opportunity to make something with your life. I don't want you to ever have to depend on anyone else except for yourself. I want you to be able to support yourself, if anything bad happens.'"

Marie knew that her parents had high educational expectations for her and her siblings. However, she had not anticipated that her father would advocate that she should do whatever she wanted, especially considering her uncles' expectations: "Seeing my uncles who were even more traditional than my dad—they valued education, but I think in their minds, once a daughter finished school, she's to get married and have a family. My dad was like, 'No, you can do whatever you want.'"

Perhaps the "totally different story" that Marie believes would have happened had she been the one to leave home at the age of nineteen, as her father had, was not that different from her father's life after all. Both Marie and her father navigated between different expectations, followed their dreams, and ushered their family into new places—the United States and college, respectively. Maybe Mr. Marquez shared his stories about leaving home against his mother's wishes precisely to inspire Marie to do the same.

In the classroom, just as her father inspired her with "all kinds of stories," Marie is trying to motivate students by sharing her stories. For the past five years, she has been teaching middle school students at a predominantly Latina/o and working-class school. Because she grew up in a household similar to that of most of the students in her classes, Marie believes that she "understands what the kids are going through because [she] went through the same exact thing—not having anyone at home sometimes and not having anyone to help with homework. . . . Parents can't always help because they don't speak the language." With these equivalent experiences, Marie tries to encourage students by telling them, "I've been there. I've done that. Trust me." By the end of each school year, the students know Marie's stories. Students reply to Marie, "We know, Ms. Marquez, we know. We heard the story."

Like Marie Marquez's father, Vivian Sosa's mother is also teaching more than her daughter with the stories of her life. Vivian is the fourth generation of her family to be born in the United States and the first to receive a master's degree, which Vivian describes as "big for me, because this is what I've wanted to do since I was in high school."

Vivian teaches middle school at her alma mater, a practice that is not uncommon for this generation of teachers who are returning to their alma maters. One poignant example of returning to teach in one's community is Garfield High School in East Los Angeles, where one-third of the teachers are alumni (Landsberg, 2005). However what might surprise some is that Vivian teaches in the same school district where her mother was also a student. In this district, Vivian's mother, a pregnant Mexican American teenager, was ridiculed, humiliated, and excluded. Despite this hostile environment, her mother loved learning and was determined that her five children attend college. So she raised strong children and inspired them by sharing stories of her life. Vivian has internalized her mother's stories and her will to challenge injustices against working-class Latinas/os and is relaying her mother's messages to today's students:

> My parents' story is amazing. Both of my parents were in Texas when they were young. My mom remembers my dad walking down the street with his baseball cap, pulling a wagon. They didn't know each other, but at the age of five, they both moved to Los Angeles. They grew up in the same neighborhood in East LA. Then both sets of my grandparents moved separately to the same city when my parents were in junior high. So my mom and dad both came to this school, and they met here.
>
> They married when my mom was a senior in high school, and she got pregnant two weeks after they married. It was really rough for her because she was pregnant, and she had bad experiences with some of the teachers. She was kicked out of high school to go to a continuation high school [students believed to have behavioral problems or to be academically at risk are referred to these alternative high schools]. They told her she couldn't go to her school, but she kept going because my mom was a fighter. She's a very strong woman. She went to the principal and said, "What are you doing? This isn't fair. I'm married. This isn't out of wedlock. This is totally legal." He said, "Sorry, no." She and her best friend were both married, both pregnant. Because she fought it, they said, "You have to go to the continuation school, but you can still participate in prom and everything else." Now, she says, "If I would have realized what that was back then, I could have hired a lawyer. That was wrong. Me and my friend were both Mexican girls who had to be shipped away because it was seen as really bad that we were pregnant, but there was one female, who was white, who was pregnant, and she was

allowed to stay in school." That was really rough for my mom. But that made her stronger, and it made her raise us in a certain way.

My mom has told me of several other incidents where she was discriminated against at school. Teachers insinuated that she was a prostitute. A teacher threw a quarter on the floor and told her to pick it up, and he made a comment about her being not necessarily a whore, but . . . . Once my mother told me those stories, it made me question people: "How could they be so cruel, so mean?" Having to go to another school and being an outcast because she was Hispanic and pregnant was wrong. Instead of hindering her, these experiences pushed my mother further. She's tough; she would make sure that if we fell or something occurred, we were strong and got over it. That was the mentality that she raised us with. So since we were born, it was, "You are going to do this. You're going to college." The way my parents raised us was based on how they grew up and what stereotypes existed for them and for my grandparents.

Now, as a math and science teacher for the past four years, Vivian has adopted her mother's method of being "tough" and telling her own stories in the classroom to build students' self-esteems. She does this by drawing on her own experiences and conveying unconditional love and support:

I love teaching here, especially because this is where I went to school, and I just wanted to come back and tell students, "There's no excuse." It's probably my mom talking, but no matter what you're getting yourself into, wherever you're coming from, you can still do something positive. It just comes down to personal determination. What do you want to do? If you want to do it, you're going to do it. That's something that I hope I bring to these kids. I tell them, "Look, I didn't have the struggles that some of you have. I wasn't involved in gangs. I was a very quiet girl, but I was persistent and knew what I wanted." These kids can do so much. I have such a big heart for my students, and I tell them all the time, "I care so much about you guys." I truly love these kids. On the first day of school, I have no idea who the students are, if I'm going to like them or not. But I know what I want to do with them. And I know that they all could be successful. I think that every kid is in deficit of something: love, confidence, or parents. I'm hoping that when they come to my class that it's a positive place where they can get that need filled and feel, "Wow, she really cared about me."

Some readers may interpret Vivian's philosophy as one that reinforces a cultural deficiency perspective, where students and families are blamed for school performance. However, Vivian's narrative illustrates that she is aware of the inequalities and stereotyped perceptions working against Latinas/os. Since these injustices and stereotypes are so pervasive, Vivian tries to offset them by instilling in students a sense of personal agency.

Vivian's holistic approach to teaching is apparent not only in her desire to create a positive classroom space where students are cared for by her, but she also aims to teach students to be good people who care about each other. She instills this ethos by focusing on

skills that students need to learn for life. Out of all the jobs that I could do, this is definitely something that I wanted to be a part of because you don't just mold students academically; you mold them with who they are and who they will become. They might not remember me, and if they don't, oh, well. But I want to make sure

that I'm instilling values in them—respect, being kind
to each other. This is how you have to act in the world.
You can't be mean to people.

With such a powerful commitment to instilling determination,
love, and respect, it is easy to see how Vivian's classroom philosophy has been nurtured by her mother's stories of the tremendous
hostility that she encountered in the same school district two
generations earlier.

For Vivian, part of building a classroom environment of respect
and kindness involves encouraging students to see each other not
simply as individuals who compete against each other but as part of
a family:

> Right now, I have the progress graphs for period 1 on my
> wall. I told the kids, "You guys have got to look at these
> graphs because there are a lot of people failing, a lot of
> people getting D's. You need to help each other. We're a
> family in here. You need to support each other. If some-
> one doesn't know what they're doing, you help them.
> I'm one person, and I'm trying to get through to every-
> body, and it's just impossible." I'm trying. I get through
> to as many kids as I can in a day, but I hope that the
> kids are helping each other and they're seeing that for
> all of us to be successful, we need to help each other. My
> vision is that we prove some people wrong.

In her classroom, Vivian is teaching much larger lessons than
algebra and science. Often in classrooms, posted progress graphs
are used to reward students who receive high grades. However,
these graphs often have the double effect of publicly ridiculing,
humiliating, and punishing students who have not completed their
homework or performed well on tests. From her mother's experiences, Vivian knows the damaging impacts of public humiliation.

Thus, she does not use posted progress graphs in traditional ways that foster competition and create hierarchies among students. Rather than simply praise the top-scoring students in class and ridicule the other students, Vivian inverts the tradition: she encourages the students who are receiving high grades to assist their classmates and adopt a collaborative orientation in the classroom.

Overall, the significance of family is one of the many themes that emerge from Marie and Vivian's reflections. The stories that their parents shared have had far-reaching impacts, influencing their teaching philosophies and classroom pedagogies. Like her father, Marie tells her stories to the many working-class and Latina/o students in her classes. And Vivian uses what she learned from her mother: she maintains high expectations of students and aims to create a family environment where all of the students work together for the good of the class and the larger community. Mrs. Sosa's lessons of struggling against injustice persist in Vivian's challenge to traditional approaches to education, where individualism and competition are valued in the United States over her more collaborative ethos. Overall, such family stories of resistance and resilience can be seen as forms of cultural capital that parents transmit to their children to motivate them and instill strength as they too enter new situations and struggles (see Gándara, 1995).

Although teachers such as Marie Marquez describe the important role that their fathers have in their lives, in conversation after conversation, most of the teachers were like Vivian Sosa. Regardless of their gender, they touted their mothers as being the major influence in shaping their educational aspirations.

Mothers as Supporters

"For me," said Vivan Sosa, "my mom was the stronghold of the family. Ever since we were five years old, she sat us down and said: 'You are going to college, no ifs, ands, and buts about it. You're going.'" She and the other teachers were in my family room, gathered in a circle and sharing our thoughts on Latinas/os and education. Vivian accurately gauged the role our mothers have in our lives. Most of us were nodding as she spoke. During our earlier one-on-one meeting, Vivian had already shared this:

> My mom loved school; she loved learning. She tried to continue to go to college, but it was just extra classes; she didn't really pursue it. But she really wanted to. She worked as a bookkeeper in her earlier years, and then she did clerical work. She worked until I was a sophomore in high school, and at that time, she got injured. So, she had to go on workman's comp and disability. . . . Even though my mom worked, she was able to come to school functions. So we heard from my mom that education was a priority.

The love of learning that Vivian's mother conveyed has been contagious to her daughter. Now, during a difficult time in her family, Vivian is the one encouraging her mother to pursue her education: "My mom has talked about wanting to go back to college. I keep telling her to do it, even to take a computer class. But my dad has prostate cancer, so she's trying to enjoy life with him while the time is here."

Sixty-five-year-old Diana Cortez also described her mother as a role model who instilled in her a love of learning. Diana was a student in the 1950s, when women were often steered toward marriage. Within this context, Diana's mother's encouragement was especially notable:

> My sisters and my parents didn't have the attitude of, "Why do you want to go to school if you're just going to get married and have kids?" I didn't get that signal from home.
>
> My mother was an avid reader. She would read all the time, and I always liked to learn. I didn't care if it was astronomy, or how the blood system works, I always

loved to learn different things. And my mom had a curiosity about learning too. I think the modeling was there, and her being bilingual was important. It seemed to broaden her horizons and give us the idea that it was good to know not just one thing, but more things. The fact that my mom could read and write in both languages was impressive.

De jure segregation and Americanization programs structured Diana Cortez's early years in school. Schooling during this period focused on the English language, vocational training, and American patriotism (see Gonzalez, 1990). Nevertheless, Diana's mother resisted such a narrow focus in schools. By modeling the strengths of bilingualism and biliteracy, she inspired her daughter to pursue an advanced education and speak both Spanish and English.

Not only were mothers seen as role models, but as was the case with Margarita Villa, mothers were usually described as the parent who checked homework, went to school if there were problems, and attended school events: "I remember my mom: 'Did you do your homework? Did you do this class? Did you do this class?' The minute that something went wrong with my three sisters or me, she would go to school and find out what was wrong."

Knowing that their mothers had high educational aspirations for them also enabled these Latina teachers to turn whatever sexist comments that they encountered into educational motivators. Thirty-year-old Gabriela Muñoz recalls an uncle who received a college degree in Mexico and assumed that she was not interested in education. Fortunately, Gabriela had already internalized her mother's messages, so she was able to offset her uncle's negativity with her mother's determination and her own strong sense of self:

I grew up with very demeaning people, and that gives you more power somehow. . . . My uncle said to my mom, "You know, Gabriela's just using college as an excuse

to get out of this house. She just wants to get out; she
wants to be free and have independence." I did want
independence in a sense because I wanted to have fun;
don't get me wrong, but give me some slack here. He just
told me I was going to get pregnant, and I was going to
mess up. He never knew anything about me—never even
cared to ask. So I kept hearing my uncle's voice behind
me. Every time I wanted to give up or was too tired to
go to class, I kept thinking [whispers], "I have to go to
class." So that kind of pushed me to go into higher education because my mom was always saying, *"Tienes que ir
al colegio, tienes que ir a la Universidad"* [You have to go to
college, you have to go to university.]. You couldn't say
no to this woman. . . . My mom was so overprotective of
us. She used to drop us off at the high school; she used
to pick us up. She was so involved; she used to go to the
meetings; she used to go to the college fairs. She knew
the college counselor like the back of her hand.

Gabriela was determined to challenge her uncle's pejorative image
of her, and fortunately her mother's resolve to get her into college
helped Gabriela to fulfill her dreams.

Not all mothers have the time, transportation, or energy
to visit their children's schools. Although Gabriela's mother's ability to attend school functions was helpful, her verbal messages to
Gabriela were just as powerful in inspiring her to excel in school
and challenge people's low expectations.

Mexican mothers have been described as the "guiding force in
the home behind the children's powerful educational ambitions"
(Gándara, 1995, p. 37). This involvement includes a range of
women's work, both visible and less visible, that emanates from their
reproductive labor in families. This reproductive labor involves, but
is not limited to, buying and preparing food; providing emotional

support, care and nurturance, and socialization for family members; maintaining and transmitting culture; and establishing family and community connections (Dill, 1994; Baca Zinn, 1994; Glenn, 1992). In the public space, Latina parent participation may coincide with what the school expects—attending school functions and communicating with teachers. It can also involve parents' organizing around school issues such as bilingual education and school closures (for examples, see Delgado-Gaitan, 1991; Ochoa, 2004a). However, in many cases, school officials may not always see Latina parent participation because this participation may occur in private spaces such as in the home. These private, home-based activities involve encouraging, inspiring, and conveying the importance of education through storytelling and role modeling, as well as engaging in learning activities (see also Gándara, 1995; Moreno, 2004). For example, as Lopez's work (2003) on Caribbean youth documents, young women's awareness of their immigrant mothers' struggles inspired them to pursue education and achieve independence. All of these forms of participation by Latina mothers in public and private spaces are important for students, families, and communities. They can motivate students and also lead to "activist mothering"—political activism as a central component of mothering and community caretaking" (Naples, 1998, p. 11)—where the goals are broader than just focusing on individual students and extend to community survival and social justice within schools (see Ochoa, 2004a).

Sharing Their Lessons for All

These teachers' narratives allow us to consider what Latina/o families are doing to encourage education. We see how family members—mothers in particular—often are the ones who must supplement the deficient curriculum of our schools that tends to leave out Latina/o history, the Spanish language, and the valuing of diverse ways of experiencing and interacting within society.

When schools and policymakers focus more on the technical aspects of schools, such as parental attendance at events, student performance on standardized tests, or schools' rankings, they devalue and overlook the personal ways that individuals, families, and communities are experiencing schools. In the race to achieve higher test scores, more years of education, and attend more prestigious colleges, too many students, families, and communities are being left behind, and we are perpetuating a society based more on individualism, competition, and inequality than on collectivism, love, and justice. Fortunately, the teachers' narratives offer important ideas for change.

Denise Villarreal, a forty-six-year-old Mexican American school principal, exhorts us to remember that "it takes a village to raise a child, and we're that village." Families, schools, and other community members must work together to improve the opportunities and well-being of children. However, they must do so in ways that respect the values and wealth of families and communities. This involves understanding that parents' involvement includes multiple forms of participation among all family members—verbal encouragement, modeling, and engagement in school-related events and educational activities. Second, school officials should aim to create democratic, inclusive campuses, offices, classrooms, and meetings. This entails redefining schools as community spaces where families and students feel welcome and where they and their perspectives are respected.

Schools and policymakers have much to learn, and they should not impose their approaches to education in ways that minimize or change family structures. Doing so can divest families and communities of important resources and systems of social support and can hinder students' sense of selves. Instead, a model of "power sharing" (Shor, 1996, p. 200) that brings together school officials, family members, and community residents as partners, as opposed to audience members, consumers, or clients, in school activities should be enacted. Rather than simply encouraging families to participate in the activities that are determined by school officials or assuming that families need the school's help, spaces of real dialogue and exchange should be created where families and school officials can speak as equals about education. Together, they can contribute what they know. All community members, including businesses, civic leaders, and residents, have an interest in educating youth and have resources and knowledge basis that can be drawn on.

Studies confirm what high school teacher Ana Camacho clearly stated at the beginning of this chapter: many Latina/o families value education precisely because of its possibilities for economic mobility (Delgado-Gaitan, 1992). Retired middle school teacher Diana Cortez knows this too:

> Latinos value education. When you're at the bottom of the heap in your own country and you're just trying to survive and put food on the table, you want better for your kids. Many parents say, "I want my kids to get an education because I don't want them to work"; especially the fathers say, "*Como un burro, como yo,* like a donkey." They don't want hard physical labor for their children. They want them to have more white-collar jobs.

The good news is that Latina/o students are internalizing these high expectations (Kao, 2000). However, these high aspirations are not always translating into equally high educational outcomes, indicating that we need to consider how schools and other U.S. institutions are failing students. The following chapters take us through the sacrifices, hurdles, and barriers that Latina/o students often encounter during their school years and provide examples to students about ways to navigate through the educational pipeline. Recommendations are also offered on changing dominant beliefs and institutions.

5

What Do We Give Up for an Education?

When I would return home for the holidays . . . I was reju-
venated with the love, foods, laughter, tears, and all things
shared among families. But I was saddened because I always
had to leave them, and there was a growing disparity in our
education levels, views of the world, and goals for life.

(Herrera, 2003)

Seconds after the school bell rings, students pour out of their classrooms. The air is punctuated with laughter, shouts to friends, and private conversations. "Excuse me. Oops," I hear myself say as I dodge a stream of middle schoolers. Eager mothers and toddlers wait in parked cars and outside classrooms. It's teacher-parent conference week, and I too have scheduled a meeting with a teacher, Cristina Martinez.

As I make my way to her classroom, I see that a mother and her sixth-grade son have arrived before me, and they are in the middle of their conference. Once their conference comes to end, Cristina carries her teachers' stool over to where I am seated. It has been a long week. Grades are due, and it's Friday afternoon. Undaunted by the setting of the sun and the emptying of the school, Cristina Martinez settles in to share her experiences. Like many of the other Latina/o teachers I have met, she is one of the first members of her extended family to graduate from college, travel internationally, and leave home. Her story of becoming a teacher is one of sacrifice—for her parents and for herself:

> Everybody in my life has always loved me so much.
> For whatever reason, I've always been the golden child

in my family. I got that love that so many other people in my family didn't. For whatever reason, so many other kids in my family got these negative comments: "What's wrong with you? You're worthless." Either they screwed around, they had babies way too young, or they weren't good in school. Maybe they had different families, whatever it was, but it was always in my family, a shower of, "We love you, you're awesome. You're going to do something. You're going to be somebody." It was always a lot to carry, but my parents were really great. They said, "You don't have to do any of this stuff. You choose. But you have had the opportunities that, for some reason, nobody else has had, and you have to be thankful for those."

Formal education has been a new thing for my family. My mother's parents had twelve children, six boys and six girls. My dad's parents had eleven children, nine of whom survived. I have just one uncle on my dad's side and another one on my mom's side who have bachelor's degrees. Because of that, it has kept my family in a state of poverty where it's paycheck-to-paycheck. There is no education fund.

My parents never spoke to me about going to college. They never said, "You have to go to college," or "You are going to go to college." My parents speak a lot about how being my parent was difficult because I would come home with, "I want to be in this program. I want to go to this trip." I always wanted to go to college, and I think a lot of it was my frustration with being poor, seeing other kids at my school have the name-brand shoes or go on trips with their families for summer vacation. I never got any of that stuff. My desire to go to college and to travel was hard for my parents because they didn't have the resources all the time to write out a check. It was, "We're going to have to hustle. We're going to have to do a lot of things for her to be able to do that." My parents had to let go of me at a very young age, knowing that I was going to need those things on my résumé so I could get the scholarships. My mom speaks of how hard it was for her to let me go across the country by myself on trips, and she just put that in God's hands. "Please take care of her, because these are things that she wants, and I can't give them to her. So I have to help her to get them somehow." So it wasn't ever them saying, "You have to go to school." It was very much just a part of me.

Cristina's parents showered her with love and did whatever they could to enable her to achieve her dreams of attending college. This love and support was crucial, but Cristina also credits her own determination, which emerged from her "dual frame of reference," which allowed her to contrast her family background to wealthier parents in her school who were able to purchase new clothing and take their families on summer vacations (see Ogbu, 1991; Valenzuela, 1999; Lopez, 2003). Seeing these difference in material items and opportunities, Cristina strove harder for an education to move away from poverty.

Although this dual frame of reference shaped Cristina's aspiration to attend college, motivation and hard work are not enough for achievement in a stratified society such as the United States, where unequal opportunities by class and race/ethnicity also manifest themselves in unequal experiences in colleges and universities. Cristina did well in high school and earned her entrance into the University of New Mexico, but the transition from high school to college was still very difficult as a first-generation college student:

When I was going to college, I would call home crying, "I can't do this. I don't know how to do it." The University of New Mexico is a tough school. It's a big school. When I got to college, I suffered. I didn't know how to

talk to my professors or how to write. There was nobody
to help me. There were no examples, and my parents
would tell me, "We love you. You can do it. Go ask for
help." That was the only advice that they could give
me, and with that support I pushed through.

With support from her family, Cristina eventually completed
college and applied to graduate school, which introduced her to yet
new obstacles:

While in graduate school, it was nice to be so intensely
challenged. My last semester was extremely hard for me
because I was facing my fears of, "I'm here. I am in a
private school that I can't afford, that I'm getting loans
up the wazoo for. But this campus is somewhere no one
in my family has ever been." I'm talking a huge family
of over four hundred people. It was a battle for me not
to hate myself for having that opportunity, of me saying, "It's okay to not understand where you're at, to be
scared, and to not get it all right." I'm so hard on myself.
I expect so much of myself. In that last semester, it was,
"I'm not doing too hot in my classroom because I'm
just stretched at all ends. I'm not academically where
I would like to be because I didn't have the best education." I went to graduate school with kids who had so
much background in academics, and it was hard to be in
the same room with these kids and always be the poor
kid. I didn't always want that stigma, or that quality, of
being the kid who understands the poverty side.
    At the same time, I found myself giving up a lot of
traditional things. My family—you don't leave. You stay
near home. I'm away from my family, not because I got
married and moved with my husband, not because of a
job, but because I chose my education. In that last semester of graduate school, my grandmother died. Everybody

told me my grandmother was sick, in the hospital, and that she had to have this surgery. My grandmother was equivalent to my mother. That's how close I was to her. She was my best friend. I grew up with her. There was a whole period of time where I couldn't go back home until my brother's graduation, when I had to take a day off from graduate school, which is an absolute no-no. And that was the first time I got to see her. I saw this woman who was so thin, and I knew she was dying. It was hard. I spent my brother's graduation weekend just crying, and I couldn't stop. I couldn't stay with her. I had to come back because I had two more weeks to teach my kids. 'Cause if I stop, I don't get my teaching credential on time. I don't get the master's that I need to keep this job. So I came back, and I said, "Well, when I finish school I'm going back home." I came back to school for two weeks. Sunday morning, they told me that my grandmother had a stroke, and I got on a plane, and I went home and I missed her by twenty minutes. I had to bury her and come back in four days, because I had to take the RICA [Reading Instruction Competence Assessment], and I had to pass. I walked into that test on Saturday, and for the first time in my life of taking tests, I wanted to close the book, walk up to the proctor, and say, "Here you go. I'm not doing this." I had to go to the bathroom and say, "You have to pull it together." I went back, and I took the test, and thank God I passed it. It was definitely the hardest experience, finishing my master's paper where I talked about what being a teacher meant—the sacrifice. So I spent the last two weeks in class crying because I gave up a lot. It's definitely been a wild ride to come up without other people having done it before me.

Cristina describes the love, praise, and encouragement that she has always received. However, "formal education has been a new thing" for her family, and her parents sacrificed to help her become one of the few members in her extended family to graduate from college and the only one to earn a master's degree. These family sacrifices were financial as well as emotional, as her "parents had to let go" of her at a very young age.

Just as her family struggled, Cristina's path to becoming a teacher has not been easy. She had to contend with the stigma of being "the poor kid" and has forsaken traditional aspects of her background, including not living near her family. When graduate school and teaching forced her to stay in California while her grandmother was dying in New Mexico, the sacrifices Cristina had made were simply overwhelming.

To the extent that the road to success in the United States continues to be equated with acquiring values of individualism, independence, and leaving one's family over collectivism, interdependence, and *familismo*, feelings similar to the ones Cristina Martinez expressed persist. However, individuals and families respond differently to these expectations. While Cristina believes that her family "let her go" so that she could achieve a college degree and a career, the following two examples, of Vivian Sosa and Angelica Vasquez, reveal other ways that families and individuals respond to formal schooling and socioeconomic advancement in the United States.

Forgoing the Spanish Language for Educational Advancement?

Just as Cristina Martinez has given up significant aspects of her family life, a defining component of identity for many Latinas/os was kept from Vivian Sosa—Spanish: her grandmother counseled withholding it from her granddaughter because of her own stinging memories of discrimination:

> My grandma raised us during the day, and she didn't want us to speak Spanish because she felt it was a

disadvantage. She grew up speaking Spanish during a time when Spanish was bad, so she didn't want that to be a hindrance to us. She told us, "You guys will not speak Spanish. I want you to get a good education, to go to college. So you learn English only." My mom would say, "No, I want them to learn Spanish," and my grandma said, "No, it's going to be a problem," not knowing that it would be a great asset for me.

There are very real reasons that Vivian's grandmother felt the way she did about the Spanish language. My own father felt the same way. A Nicaraguan immigrant, my father faced tremendous amounts of accent and color discrimination. After struggling to learn English, earn a college degree in history and Spanish literature, and receive his teaching credential at the age of thirty-three, he still could not get a teaching position in the late 1960s. When he went to a school in an upper-middle-class white community to apply for a job, he was told that the job for janitor had already been filled. His educational background did not shield him from stereotyped assumptions and workplace discrimination. So he wanted to shield us from the discrimination that he faced, and given the dominant discourse about assimilation, he thought that speaking to us only in English would help. Nevertheless, he yearned for us to be able to communicate fully with our Spanish-speaking grandmother, whom we saw weekly.

The beliefs expressed by Vivian's grandmother and my father are not unique. Older Latinas/os who lived in the United States before the 1960s had similarly painful experiences with language and assimilation. Individuals of this generation came of age when most Latinas/os in California were at least third generation, in comparison to today's demographics, where about two-thirds of Latinas/os in the state are the children of immigrants (see Lopez and Stanton-Salazar, 2001). These demographic patterns combined with the dominant expectation of assimilation of the period, and many

Latina/o residents encountered blatant discrimination for speaking Spanish. Some members of this generation followed a pattern common among other upwardly mobile groups of color: they attempted to assimilate. Not realizing Spanish would become as pervasive as it has today, they felt that they should forgo teaching their children Spanish in hopes that they could more easily advance economically, socially, and politically (Ochoa, 2004a).

Within the United States, the belief in Anglo superiority and the corresponding acceptance of the inferiority of the Spanish language and other Latina/o cultural practices often underpin this emphasis on acquiring the English language and the dominant norms and values. For example, although the Treaty of Guadalupe Hidalgo in 1848 that ended the war between Mexico and the United States guaranteed the right to maintain the Spanish language, the ideology of manifest destiny supported a racial/ethnic hierarchy that fostered the belief in Anglo superiority. The notion of manifest destiny "implied the domination of civilization over nature, Christianity over heathenism, progress over backwardness and whites over Mexicans and Native Americans" (Almaguer, 1994, p. 33). The oppression of the Spanish language that has existed since the colonization of the United States has powerfully influenced language patterns and Spanish-language use within Latina/o families.

The beliefs about the Spanish language have been used to justify school policies that have reinforced dominant sentiment. Historically, school practices took the form of Americanization programs, segregated Mexican schools, and the disproportional labeling of Mexican students as "mentally retarded." Children were punished for speaking Spanish at school. School officials washed their mouths out with soap, swatted them with rulers, confined them to the corner of the classroom, forced them to wear dunce caps, and ridiculed them in front of their peers (Vigil, 1997; Valenzuela, 1999; Ochoa, 2004a).

Through the 1960s, most of the research literature on bilingualism was premised on the belief that English-language learners were deficient (Soto, 1997). Summarizing a 1962 review of over two hundred studies on the supposed negative impacts of bilingualism among children, Soto (1997) writes, "Such disadvantages cited in the literature included handicaps in speech development, emotional and intellectual difficulties, impaired originality of thought, handicapped on intelligence tests, loss of self confidence, schizophrenia, and contempt and hatred toward one's parents, to name but a few" (p. 3).

Ilene Gómez, a fifty-five-year-old Mexican American educator who has taught students of all ages, explains that these early beliefs about bilingualism persist today among some in her teacher education classes. She recounts the misperceptions she has encountered by teachers in training who are opposed to bilingual education: "Well, give them more English." "You're interrupting them by giving them their classes in Spanish." "You're actually presenting barriers." "There's only so much room in that brain to acquire languages. If they're doing it in Spanish, they're not going to have enough brain." Thus, though the attacks against the Spanish language and Spanish-speaking students are not as overt as they were in the past, the ideologies are slow to change, and some Spanish-speaking students still face ridicule and the assumption that they are not intelligent. Given such studies and public sentiment, it is easy to see why some Latinas/os have made a conscious decision not to raise bilingual children or grandchildren.

Having not been taught the Spanish language because her grandmother believed that she was doing what was best for her granddaughter, Vivian Sosa has been made to feel disconnected from Spanish-speaking individuals and communities. This is especially the case when she is with people who assume that all Latinas/os speak Spanish:

> One time at the mall, a woman was speaking to me in Spanish, and I told her, "I really don't know Spanish." She was like, "You're such a disgrace to the Hispanic

culture." It was hurtful. She didn't know my background. I still have flashes of that woman saying, "You're such a disgrace," and I think, "Am I? Am I really? Or is it just I didn't learn Spanish?" I wish I'd learned, and I wish I knew. I took Spanish classes, but it just didn't stick because I didn't use it.

As Vivian's example suggests, the emphasis on assimilating can have a negative influence on self-esteem and a sense of connection with a community, especially when one is accused of being "a disgrace" by people who may be unaware of the long history of Spanish-language repression in the United States. Also, ironically, those of us who were spoken to only in English but possess college degrees may feel as though we lack important Spanish-language skills for communicating with other Latinas/os, sometimes even with members of our own families. As we turn next to Angelica Vasquez's story, we see her reflecting on these apparent losses and the ways that she sought to mitigate them as she acquired more schooling.

Straining Family Relationships for Schooling

Not all Latina/o family members, or mothers, respond to formal education in the same ways. Some may do all that they can to hold on to their children for fear of how U.S. schooling may change them and their relationship to their families and communities. This was the case for Angelica Vasquez's mother and older brothers who sought to keep her close to home. As a result, Angelica also experienced Marie Marquez's "tug of war" between her family and schooling expectation. Like Marie, Angelica responded by drawing on her family's rules and will to survive to achieve her educational goals. Like Cristina Martinez, Angelica also adopted a dual frame of reference. However, her dual frame of reference was her mother—a person Angelica did not want to emulate. Given these varied experiences and perspectives, the path toward schooling and a career in education for thirty-six-old Angelica Vasquez has been much more strained than the paths recounted by the other teachers:

> I was a gift baby. When I was born, my father was fifty-five, and my mother was forty-two. So they were significantly older, and my brothers are twenty years older than I am. Originally my father came to the United States as a bracero to work on the railroads. He stayed to work because he has so many children. But my mother didn't like that he was here alone. She was a very jealous person, so she followed him. It was not so much for economic purposes or a better life for her children. It was probably because she was afraid he would find a new wife.

Like her parents and siblings, Angelica was born in Mexico. Her parents had been living in East Los Angeles, but her mother wanted her daughter to be the same as all of the members of her family—an immigrant—so she went to Mexico to give birth to Angelica.

As the child of immigrants, Angelica grew up speaking Spanish:

> I started school not knowing how to speak English. My language, the way I communicate, is part of my personality. Once in a while I still throw in a Spanish word because it gets to the point. Your culture seeps into everything, every decision you make. It goes into religion, the way you see the world and what you think is the social norm. I have lots of girlfriends who are Anglo-Saxon, and they may see the world differently than I do, and it's because of my culture. There are things that

are so embedded in my person, because of my culture, because of what my parents taught me.

At home, Angelica's mother emphasized speaking Spanish and caring for the family:

My mother didn't have a high value for education. The way my mother would punish us was to not let us go to school. I'd see that with my brothers and sister. My sister got into a fight with my mom, and she pulled her out of high school. So she never went to high school; I knew at a very young age, you keep your mouth shut, do your job, and just get it done. You learned that you need to do whatever you need to do for yourself, and the school better not call home.

I think school frightened my mother. She wanted me to be that homey little person, to get pregnant and get married young or to be a spinster so I could stay with her forever. So she would unplug my alarm clock to go to high school or college. "Ay, mija, te ves muy cansada" [My daughter, you look very tired].

My parents laid down the law, and you knew that there were very specific and strict consequences. My mother didn't play around. If the laws were the way they are, she probably would have been sent up for child abuse for my brothers and sisters. But she needed to do what she needed to do to survive, and I understand that, because we lived in East LA with six teenage boys in the heart of the gang-infested neighborhood. My brothers were more afraid of her than they ever were of any gang. So you don't have one of them with a tattoo, not one of them with a pierced ear. That would not be acceptable because my mother would go and get them from wherever they were, and she would take care of it.

Although Angelica admires her mother's strength and will to survive, she also sought to distance herself from her:

> One of the reasons I wanted to go to college was that I did not want to be my mother. I didn't want to not have choices. My mother and father were married for fifty years; my father loved my mother, and my mother absolutely hated my father, and she mistreated him. She was miserable, and she made us miserable. But she didn't leave because she had nowhere to go. I didn't ever want to be that person. That's why I wanted to put myself in a position where I could always decide what happens to me because when I was young, everything happened to me. So, I wanted to make sure that didn't happen to me when I was an adult.
>
> I don't like anyone saying what I can and cannot do; I will do what I want. Once I was in junior high school, I told my oldest brother, "I want to go to college and to university." I didn't know that they're kind of the same. And he was not trying to hurt my feelings, but he said, "You really need to let go of that dream 'cause it's not going to happen, and you're just going to be disappointed."
>
> When I graduated from high school, I told my brothers I was going to go to Cal Poly Pomona. They told me that I should go to Cal State LA. They were saying this because they wanted to protect me. They said Cal Poly would be too hard for me. "I should go to Cal State LA because there would be more of my own kind, and it would be easier because Cal Poly was a technical school and there were too many white people there."
>
> I mustered up the courage to tell them that they had not helped me my entire life, so this was not their choice to make; it was mine. They probably didn't

talk to me for a good month, and to this day, they tell me that I was the rudest thing in the world for telling them that.

When I was in my third year of college, my older brother said, "Are you sure you want to keep going to college?" And I said, "Yeah, I want to get a good job." He said, "You know, nobody's going to marry you." And again, he's trying to help me out, according to his world, because he has never left the Latino community, and he doesn't speak English very well. He remains in his comfort zone even though he's a very bright man. He was telling me, "You need to understand that because you're a woman, you cannot marry below you; you can only marry above you. Nobody that hasn't gone to college will even look at you because you will intimidate them." He explained this to me, and he was right, "The farther you get in college and the older you get, the less choices you have of who you can marry. So your pool of eligible men to marry dwindles. Because if you graduate, you're only going to want somebody who's gone to college, and how many men have gone to college? And then you're just going to end up *una mujer soltera* [a spinster]." I was smarter then. I didn't make a scene like I did when I was eighteen. I said, "Well thank you for the advice, but I think I'm going to stay here." And I remember him telling my mother, "*Que loca* [She's crazy]."

Angelica criticizes her family's approach to schooling. She remembers that her mother tried to keep her home from school and that her brothers thought an educated Mexican American woman would never meet a husband. Although Angelica admired her mother's strength and understood her brothers' worldviews, she disagreed with them and used their messages to motivate herself. Likewise, when school officials spouted off statistics about the small percentage of Latinas/os who graduate from college, Angelica turned these negative messages into educational incentives.

As she came up through high school and college, Angelica faced "a very big struggle" that is related to her brothers' words of advice. Her family's "cultural roots" focused on "us" where "the family is important and you are second." In comparison, she found the U.S. educational system to be based on the individual. It was not easy navigating between individual notions of success in the United States and her upbringing in a Mexican immigrant household where family was emphasized. At times, it felt as though she had to choose between her family and her education. This difficulty was exacerbated because Angelica's schooling did little to help her understand the intergenerational tensions she was experiencing at home and in relationship to dominant U.S. expectations of success. However, with time, Angelica realized that she could "accommodate without assimilating" (Gibson, 1988). For Angelica, this meant reconciling the competing demands of focusing on her family or focusing on her education by believing that a college degree would better enable her to assist her family:

> When I graduated high school, I had to make a conscious decision: "I'm going to be selfish." I know that it would be best for me to work to help out my mother and father because they're old. But I had to tell myself, "You are smart enough to understand that if you get a better job, you will be able to help them more in five years than you can help them now. You just need to go to school." And I remember making that conscious choice.

Being raised to believe that "the family comes first," Angelica never wanted to withdraw from her family. However, at times her family thinks that she is different from them:

> You're in the battle within yourself sometimes. Your head
> tells you one thing, but your heart tells you another. My
> heart tells me I want to be like my family; I don't want
> to be different from my family; I don't want to alien-
> ate my family. But my head is telling me, "There's a big-
> ger, better world out there. You're destined for different
> things." And even now, my family sometimes thinks that
> I'm—"*Me quiero mucho*"—a little bit of a snob.

Thinking about her experiences, Angelica is concerned for
today's generation of students who may encounter a more difficult
struggle than she had. She sees how this struggle revolves around
some of the same generational and cultural dilemmas that she has
encountered: *familismo* (feelings of loyalty and reciprocity with
family) versus individualism, *respeto* (respect) and interactions
with elders, and the maintenance of the Spanish language.
Angelica believes that the push to assimilate is exacerbating this
clash for today's generation:

> The struggle that I suffered between my culture, family,
> and individualistic needs is nothing compared to what kids
> have now. There's a huge language divide that I see emerg-
> ing, and I knew it was going to come as soon as bilingual
> education was done away with. So many kids want to
> become individuals, and their parents are letting them
> because they want their kids to melt in, but the kids can't
> speak Spanish anymore. They can't communicate with
> their parents. And it's sad because the parents are their
> guides, and these kids are lost. So the parents will speak
> to them in Spanish, and the kids will answer in English.
> And the parents are letting it happen. My mother would
> never have let it happen. My brothers and sisters would

never let me speak to them in half a sentence in English, half a sentence in Spanish. I spoke to them in Spanish, or I spoke to them in English, none of this half-and-half stuff. I thank God for that because I grew up bilingual.

Angelica believes that the elimination of bilingual education in schools is exacerbating these intergenerational divides and is having a negative impact on educational outcomes:

> Kids are having subtractive bilingualism because they're not proficient in one language or the other. . . . They have these huge gaps, so it's making education really hard. They don't have the vocabulary in Spanish or in English. They don't have the background knowledge. They don't have the experiences. Their brain is not elastic enough to have gone from one language to the other.

While Angelica supports bilingual education, initially, she seems to accept some of the images about language development popular through the 1960s and heard in Ilene Gómez's teacher education classes today—that children's brains are not "elastic enough" to accommodate switching between two languages. However, Angelica clarifies that bilingual education is critical for education, cultural affirmation, and family relationships:

> I'm not saying they're not capable or that they cannot aspire. It seems that they're having a really hard time because of the way that they're being brought up; they're not being given a whole language and everything that goes with a language. So, sometimes culturally, they want to detach. They don't want to be looked at like their parents. We all go through that, but I think it's more now. I think that their parents aren't communicating. Then when they become the second generation, the respect is gone.

Students don't have respect for their parents. I don't understand it because I didn't grow up that way. Because my parents were so much older, I was raised like someone who was born in the fifties, even though I grew up in the seventies. When my parents said something, I just did it. I might not have liked it; I just did it because my parents told me to do it. Now I see kids in junior high, they talk back to their parents. God forbid I ever rolled my eyes at my mother. . . . I would never in my whole life ever call a neighbor or an adult by their first name. Yet I see kids call people by their first name and expect that they can. You just don't do that. You would address people respectfully, and you never contradicted your elders, even if you knew they were lying. That wasn't your place. And in a way I'm very grateful for that upbringing.

Perhaps Angelica is especially critical of students whom she believes want to dissociate from their families because they remind them of herself. Just as Angelica's brothers saw her as rude and a snob, she labels today's students as disrespectful. Throughout her narrative, Angelica uses the English word *respect* in her reflection on today's students. However, a review of how she uses the word suggests that she may be referring to the Spanish word *respeto*, which is broader than its English translation. *Respeto* refers to how one interacts with individuals, especially members of one's family, and the attitudes that one has toward the various family roles: mother, father, brother, sister, and others. So when Angelica talks about never "contradicting" your elders because it "wasn't your place," she is referring to an upbringing that emphasized how everyone in the family has certain roles and ways of interacting. If these expectations are transgressed by "rolling your eyes" or "call[ing] people by their first name," children are considered disrespectful, or *irrespetuosos* (Valdés, 1996).

Angelica's family raised her to be "respectful" and "tough." Ironically these qualities enabled her to confront multiple barriers in her pursuit of an education, even if this meant disrespecting her mother and brothers to achieve her goals. Today these qualities are also influencing how she is raising her own children and the critiques she has of some students and parents. She expects the same tough and respectful attitude that her family demanded of her:

> We were brought up that "times are tough, you just need to suck it up; you do what you need to do, you work and you just get over it. There is no time to cry. You just do what you need to do and that's it." Now I see myself with my own children, and I do a disservice to them by overprotecting them and always giving them their way. Sometimes they have to suffer a little bit so that they learn to protect and take care of themselves. Sometimes we overrescue our children. And parents here, for example, it's out of love, they don't want physical education [PE] anymore because their kids are cold. They're not going to die. Put on a sweater. It's going to be okay. The parents were up in arms because there was PE in the morning, and they were too cold.

Among the Latina/o school officials, Angelica has the strongest critiques of parents and students. As we saw in Vivian Sosa's narrative in the previous chapter, Angelica's views on the role of today's Latina/o parents and students are also based on her upbringing. These varied perspectives and life histories suggest how one's "ideological baggage"—personal experiences and memories—can influence one's approach to education (Martínez, 2000). While Angelica is critical of her mother's approach to her children's schooling, she also wants today's parents to be more like her mother: committed to maintaining the Spanish language, tough, and someone who commands *respeto*. Furthermore, although Angelica criticizes some of today's Latina/o students whom she perceives as disrespectful because they want to distance themselves from their families, Angelica's own family may criticize her for the same reasons. Since Angelica had to struggle both at school and in her family to achieve her educational goals, she both admonishes her family and believes that families should be more like hers.

A significant study on Mexican immigrant mothers by professor of education Guadalupe Valdés (1996) found similar patterns to the ones captured in Angelica's narrative. According to Valdés, the parents wanted their children to achieve an education, but they didn't want them to forgo their family's values of *familismo* and *respeto*:

> For the families, then, being in favor of education, caring about education, and wanting their children to go to school in this country did not mean that they wanted their children's values to be different from what their own had been when they were the same age. Of course they were in favor of education. They knew credentials were needed in order to obtain certain kinds of employment. But they also wanted their children to put family first. They wanted them to live nearby, to visit often, and to continue to be part of a network of close relationships and linkages [pp. 172–173].

As was the case with Angelica, children in Valdés's study were expected to be grateful to their parents, unselfish, and willing to look after their parents as they aged by providing for them.

Woven throughout Angelica's narrative are the competing demands of maintaining cultural and familial connections in the context of schooling and educational advancement in the United States. Angelica earned her master's degree in education. However, she is also concerned with what may be lost—the focus on family, *respeto*, and the Spanish language—in a society that emphasizes

she is concerned about these losses because of
ced with a formal education: separation from
ridicule her for not being like them in spite
make them all the same, from their births
as immigrants.

for All

r by Cristina Martinez, Vivian Sosa,
some of the negative ramifications
When formal education requires
, and values of its students, fami-
ituation of "subtractive school-
chers' experiences allow us to
minant notions of success may
be s   ool knowing and feeling and
then   lationships.

To   hared by these teachers are
forgotte   ry discussions on education, bu   tion to the damages that may
occur thr   chooling, we gain new perspectives that
can be app   ed toward improving schools. In particular, school
officials should become familiar with students' cultures, languages,
and experiences and the larger historical, economic, and political
factors influencing them. Doing so will provide a larger context
for understanding students' experiences, help to ward off biased
attitudes and actions, and allow for a greater awareness of how to
redesign exclusionary school practices and course curriculum.

School officials should seek ways to work with and learn from
community members and families. As the narratives in the following chapter convey, one teacher can make a difference. So, the roles
of teachers in adding to—rather than ignoring or minimizing—the
histories, knowledge, and cultural wealth of families is critical in
supporting Latinas/os throughout the educational pipeline.

6

Supporting Latinas/os Throughout the Educational Pipeline

. . . [O]ne teacher, Mrs. Horn, who had the face of a crumpled Kleenex and a nose like a hook—she did not imagine this—asked how come her mama never gave her a bath. Until then, it had never occurred to Estrella that she was dirty, that the wet towel wiped on her resistant face each morning, the vigorous brushing and tight braids her mother neatly weaved were not enough for Mrs. Horn. And for the first time, Estrella realized words could become as excruciating as rusted nails piercing the heels of her bare feet.

(Viramontes, 1995)

Are you coming back tomorrow?" are the last words a student asks me as the class files outside their room toward the cafeteria for lunch. Once in the open air, the first graders chatter about a bird that has just swept down to steal a candy wrapper from the school grounds. Watching the bird, the students walk past the row of twenty pink, black, and blue backpacks hanging outside their classroom. When I had arrived before the start of school, there was just one lone blue backpack. I remember thinking how isolated it looked. These are among my many lingering thoughts as I leave Miguel Elias's first-grade classroom.

The previous morning, Miguel Elias had opened his classroom door to me, and it was not long before the energetic and inquisitive children he was teaching seeped into my thoughts. Among my lasting impressions was the students' exuberance. It was apparent when they bounded into their classroom with their yellow-paged math homework, swung their arms in the air when Mr. Elias asked for volunteers, eagerly touched the steel ball and plastic spoon during their science lesson on solids and liquids, and read aloud about a sleeping pig.

As I think about these first graders, the image of their backpacks returns. How many backpacks will remain hanging as the first graders advance through school? How many will complete high school and college? Will these first graders achieve their dreams? Will they face "excruciating" assaults on their identities, like Estrella in Viramontes's novel, *Under the Feet of Jesus*? As these students progress in life, will they be able to draw on the strengths of their families, communities, and others, or will they be expected to go it alone—to sacrifice parts of themselves to achieve their goals? The pleading question that the young student asked me, "Are you coming back tomorrow?" can be applied to all of them. Will students return to school? Will they get through the educational pipeline or will they be pushed out? As of the 2000, fewer than fifty-four out of one hundred Latina/o elementary school children in the United States will graduate from high school, eleven will graduate from college, and just four from graduate school (Pérez Huber and others, 2006). What about the adults—their teachers, counselors, and other school personnel? Will they have given up on these young children and not support them?

For an understanding of some of the experiences that these six-year-old Latinas/os may encounter as they progress through school, we turn to the voices of their Latina/o teachers, some of whom attended the same or similar schools in other working-class Latina/o communities. Though they were schooled at different times, many of the attitudes, behaviors, and schooling practices that shaped the teachers' experiences persist, and this chapter emphasizes these individual, everyday interactions within schools. In particular, teachers' childhood memories reveal how school officials' gestures of care—encouraging words, reaching out to families, and speaking Spanish—are just as powerful in shaping how students feel about themselves as are the jarring comments that send messages of low expectations and dislike.

Throughout this chapter, teachers' stories of struggling with exclusionary statements by peers and school officials are juxtaposed with their memories of how strong support networks counterbalanced the hurdles that they confronted along their educational paths from kindergarten through college. The significance of social networks or social webs "that connect people to each other and that intertwine groups and communities" into society should not be minimized (Stanton-Salazar, 2001). Networks provide support and resources that may facilitate access through the educational system, but when exclusionary networks are formed along race/ethnicity, class, and gender, systems of power and inequality are maintained. In response to such exclusion, especially in predominantly white and middle- and upper-class spaces, marginalized students have formed "intentional communities" where their experiences are shared, affirmed, and resisted (Martínez Alemán, 1997; Pineda, 2002). Such intentional communities can be critical in enabling academic survival within the educational system (Pineda, 2002).

Along with the importance of caring school officials, supportive networks, and finding strength, a continuing theme that emanates from at least half of the Latina teachers was how "very, very shy" and "quiet" they were—a couple not speaking at all during their first years in school. They attribute this shyness to the actions of their teachers, being English-language learners, or being one of the only Latina/o students in their honors or gifted classes. The literal silencing of some students—even those who eventually become teachers themselves—is a revealing metaphor for the difficulties many students suffer within schools and the losses that we as a society endure from their absent voices. Fortunately, these teachers are making their voices heard.

By listening to Latina/o teachers' stories, we understand multiple patterns that past and present students encounter, learn how these teachers were able to achieve their educational aspirations, observe how they are drawing on their schooling experiences to teach today's students, and hope that their lessons can be applied to future generations.

"He Pulled Me Through That Period": A Story of Struggle and Support

> I went to kindergarten in Compton, California, and I used to cry every day because I was an easy target for students to pick on [Miguel Elias, elementary school teacher].

Months before I sat in on his first-grade classroom, I met Miguel Elias at the elementary school where he teaches. It was December, and the staff had gathered in the school cafeteria for a Christmas party. From the front office where I was seated, I could feel the festive mood of the event. Many were dressed in green and red, and a large gift basket was conspicuously placed in the middle of the room. The smell of cookies and other baked goods filled the air. Demonstrating his musical talents, Miguel was on stage with another male teacher.

As the gathering was ending, Miguel approached me with a warm greeting, and we walked from the school office toward his classroom. During this short walk, we passed several children on the playground who called out his name. He acknowledged each of them with a short salutation in Spanish or English. By the time that he was opening his classroom door, I could feel the memories of elementary school rushing toward me. Maybe it was the small chairs and tables, the colorful artwork, or the boxes of glue and crayons dispersed throughout the room, but Miguel also facilitated this transporting back by vividly recalling his own struggles with school.

Miguel Elias was an undocumented Mexican immigrant, and his schooling in the United States was marked with constant ridicule. He cried throughout kindergarten because his classmates teased him about his immigrant status and socioeconomic background. After his first year of school, his family moved several times across the Mexico-U.S. border before settling in the Los Angeles County city of Norwalk. Schooling in this primarily middle-class area was not any easier for him:

> There were also Latinos there, but they used to put us down a lot because we were more "Mexican." We didn't have roots here. You could ask any student in that school, "How long has your family been here?" They'd say, "Oh, we've been here all of our lives." And me, "Oh, I've been here three months." So they were Latino too, but they used to put us down because of the clothes or shoes that we wore. The kids were really harsh.

The difficulties that Miguel faced as a child escalated, and they reached a point where he had to physically defend himself: "I was in fifth grade, and there was a sixth grader bothering my sister. He just provoked me in a way that I got physical, and I'm not a violent person. He was pushing me and saying things to my little sister, so I punched him and gave him a bloody lip."

Although Miguel fought back against his classmates' attacks, his more established Mexican American peers continued harassing him. Now they were calling him other derogatory names because of his response to their attacks: "Americans who had lived here for many years were prejudiced against us. They used to call me 'the Mexican bullfighter.' They looked at us as newcomers, even though we spoke English."

The ridicule that Miguel experienced throughout his early schooling continued into high school, where white students predominated over Latinas/os by 60 to 40 percent. In most cases, students seemed to get along at this school, but tensions sometimes erupted in the boys' locker room:

> There were still some things that I couldn't believe. I heard comments like, "Hey, where's your green card?" I remember it more from the Mexican Americans. The Anglo coaches would tell jokes, and the Mexican Americans thought some of them were funny. You know, jokes like, "An immigrant went to the border and they said, 'Oh, we're just shooting some cans.' 'What kind of cans?' 'Oh, Mexicans!' " It wasn't humorous.

The intraethnic hostilities that Miguel recounts between Mexican Americans and Mexican immigrants are neither new nor unique, although they are often overlooked (see Matute-Bianchi, 1986; Gutiérrez, 1995; Gonzales, 1999; Valenzuela, 1999; Ochoa, 2004a). Although at first glance, these tensions may be attributed to differences in class position, generation in the United States, and language ability and fueled by peers or school officials such as Miguel's coaches, their origins are much deeper.

Negative perceptions of Mexican immigrants can be traced back to the historical origins of white supremacy and the denigration of Mexicanness. Some of these historical precursors are apparent in today's school practices that fuel divisions among students. For example, in a predominantly Mexican-origin high school in Texas, Angela Valenzuela (1999) found that Eurocentric curriculum and curriculum tracking that places students into different ability groups limited relationships between Mexican Americans and Mexican immigrants. Since the course materials focused on the history and experiences of whites, Mexicanness was devalued, and students who were still learning the English language were removed from their English-dominant peers and placed in English-as-a-Second Language classes instead.

The separation of students by such school practices is often reproduced when students engage in a politics of difference by forming friendships around those who are in their classes and whom they perceive to be more like themselves (Matute-Bianchi, 1986; Gonzales, 1999; Valenzuela, 1999; Ochoa, 2004a). That is, the pervasive and often permanent placement of students in different course levels influences peer networks and how students perceive students who are not part of their classes or peer groups. The results of such school and student practices are that some students may establish a strong sense of being Mexicana/o, Mexican American, *or* Chicana/o as strategies of resistance against the marginalization that they face in schools and in opposition to other students (Matute-Bianchi, 1986; Bejarano, 2005). So those Mexican American students who ridiculed Miguel Elias or laughed alongside their white coaches may have been attempting to minimize their own otherness by distancing themselves from immigrants in their predominantly middle-class and white school.

Recent research captures some of the damaging impacts that such divisions have on students. For students such as Miguel Elias, these divisions can manifest themselves in name-calling where Mexicans born in the United States try to disassociate themselves from Mexican immigrants. Such ridicule can lead some harassed students to withdraw from others and develop a general dislike for school. Collectively, since students possess important experiences, knowledge bases, and support networks, such divisions can deprive both Mexican American and Mexican immigrant students of important forms of social capital (Valenzuela, 1999). That is, when students remain apart and engage in practices of division, they are not able to tap into the resources that each group may possess. The Mexican Americans who ridiculed Miguel may have lost out on acquiring greater knowledge of Mexico and the often positive framework that immigrant students have when they compare their schooling opportunities in the United States with the generally less available opportunities for schooling in Mexico (Valenzuela, 1999). As Valenzuela (1999) describes, "When immigrant youth become unavailable either as friends or as potential sources of academic support, U.S.-born youth are shut off from the pro-school, achievement oriented ethos that prevails among so many of them" (p. 225). For immigrants like Miguel, this separation could hinder the transfer of knowledge that U.S.-born residents may have about U.S. institutions.

While the comments and actions that Miguel encountered from elementary though high school took a toll on his sense of self, he found strength from supportive individuals. Key among them were his parents, who had a dream that Miguel and his siblings would attend a university. Miguel's father passed away when he was just six, but his mother pushed Miguel to do his best at school. She supported him "one hundred percent," even when he was forced to fight back against his classmates' demeaning comments: "I was so scared because of what my mom was going to say, 'Why are you using violence?' But nothing happened. She said, 'That's great. You did what you had to do to defend yourself.'"

Other students supported Miguel too. "One friend from Guatemala had an older brother, and he pulled me through that period. He told me, 'If you ever need any help with these people, let me know.'" In addition, involvement in sports introduced Miguel to greater circles of friends, and when he observed these students excel academically, he became encouraged to do well in school: "By sixth and seventh grade, I met other friends, and I was able to get into sports. Also, I was inspired because there were some very good students. They would always get awards for citizenship and for good grades, and that motivated me."

Although Miguel found support from his family and immigrant friends, he should not have been forced to resort to violence to gain respect from his U.S.-born peers. It is the responsibility of schools to ensure that students are safe from all types of harassment. Schools can do more to counter the anti-immigrant and anti-Mexican sentiment that resurfaces among politicians and others during economic downturns. Several influential teachers in Miguel's life offer some preliminary steps for how teachers and schools might create more inclusive and welcoming environments.

In particular, from his early years of schooling, Miguel fondly recalls the actions of three caring teachers who facilitated his enjoyment of school by talking about Mexico, being encouraging, and expanding the learning process:

> I really liked my first-grade teacher. He would show us the map of the United States with Mexico, and whenever there was a new student, he would ask, "What's the capital of your country?" And if it happened to be Mexico, he'd say, "Where's Mexico City? Wow, see, she knows where Mexico City is." In second grade, I met Mr. Ortega. He was the first male Latino teacher I had, and he was very positive, very caring, and strict. God, help me. I was also with Mrs. Miller, who invited us to her home to spend the night, and she took us to the Pomona Fair. All those experiences really helped me to love education. Also, Mrs. Miller taught the recorder. So that got me into music.

Miguel continued to find caring teachers in high school who offset the negative exchanges he was subjected to by some students and school officials: "The teachers were awesome. They were always pulling for us, and I felt like they were really taking care of me and other ones that had made it that far."

In particular, Miguel felt affirmed by a teacher who presented a critical and inclusive analysis of history:

> In history, Mr. Hino asked us, "Did you know there were Japanese camps here, in America?" And we were all, "What?" That got us into other discussions about Latinos too. . . . Just discussing the Japanese was awesome because I thought, "See, guys, America's not perfect. I'm an American now, but there are some things that have happened in America that I'm not proud of."

Looking through the history books, I would have appreciated if they would have gone over more of the Mexican-American War because a lot of people just said, "Well, see, that's why you guys are enemies." I wish they would have gone deeper into that and explained what happened, and Mr. Hino was the only one who did. He actually said, "Look at this big chunk of land. Do you think that Mexico would have wanted to give it up?" He made us think from different angles.

While Mexico and Mexican Americans are largely absent from course curriculum, Miguel's teacher, Mr. Hino, sought to address these curricular deficiencies by connecting the histories of various racial/ethnic groups and by posing questions. These questions encouraged students to challenge the telling of history, and they conveyed a perspective that Miguel wanted his U.S.-born peers to understand: that "America's not perfect." Miguel believes that teachers such as Mr. Hino who emphasized critical thinking were fantastic. Overall, he remembers his teachers as "very rigorous," helping him when he began college.

In spite of the assistance Miguel received on his path to college, his transition to the University of California, Irvine (UCI), as a first-generation, working-class Mexican student was difficult. As a college student, Miguel had three jobs at one time and no transportation. So it took him eight years, from 1988 to 1996, to earn his bachelor's degree. As he spent hours working and riding buses to his different jobs, his course work suffered:

For many years, I felt lost at UC Irvine. The first quarter was horrible. I got my first English paper back, and it was a C−, which I thought was an A. They said, "I recommend you seek counseling with your writing and at the career center." So I did, and that helped me to develop. It was very tough. I was really struggling. I was failing.

In high school, I was used to being the best in science,
the best in math. But it was a challenge. I had to retake
a lot of classes and at a slower pace. And I started to do
better and understand things.

In addition, as others in higher education have described (see
de la Luz Reyes and Halcón, 1997), college did not shield Miguel
from the overt racism that had haunted him in his early years of
schooling. Miguel still had to contend with his classmates' prejudice and verbal attacks. He recounts one situation where MEChA
(Movimiento Estudiantil Chicano de Aztlán), a national Chicana/o
student organization established during the civil rights movements
of the 1960s, and Mexicanness were the targets of racism: "One time
we had a fundraiser with MEChA, and we had a poster on campus
that was massacred. I don't know who it was, but they put derogatory things on it like: 'You Mexican something.'" This destruction
sent a powerful message to Miguel about the place of politically
involved Mexican American students on campus and how some
were trying to intimidate Mexicans and MEChA into silence.

Another time that Miguel was made to feel unwelcome on his
college campus was when he was walking alone past a group of
fraternity members who were playing catch in front of the administration building, and they yelled something racist at him: "I felt
like, 'Oh my God. Come on. Like, what are you doing? I'm the
only one here. You guys are all together with your friends. Why?
I'm trying my best.'" Experiences such as this one highlighted the
marginalization of Latina/o students at UCI. Latinas/os were among
a small percentage of students in the 1980s, and the dominance of
white students, and fraternity members in particular, was apparent
in classrooms and other spaces on the campus. In this example,
white fraternity members physically and verbally claimed central
parts of the college campus, such as in front of the administration
building. They used their dominance to single out students they
believed did not belong.

As he has done before, Miguel offset some of this hostile campus climate by connecting to several support systems that enabled him to complete his schooling:

> The best support that I got there was from Interfaith. This was a place where people of all faiths used to go, share their beliefs, and do their services. We had mass there, and that's where I ended up meeting some of my best friends that were Latinos. Then I expanded my horizons, and I met a lot of people with my same values, same beliefs, Catholics. They were Asians; they were African Americans. All these different parts of the world; it was very beautiful. But otherwise, it was tough. Also, there were some good counselors. One of them was a Chicana from Texas. She was very helpful; she helped me in a couple situations to think things through, change majors, and stabilize myself.

With support from groups such as MEChA and Interfaith, Miguel drew on multiple networks that facilitated his graduation from UC Irvine and his eventual decision to teach in elementary school to help mitigate the struggles that students encounter in schools. Introduced to teaching by a college roommate, Miguel saw the positive role that he could have in the lives of others:

> When I started to interact with the children, I saw the need for more Latinos in the classroom to teach them about their culture, to show them that it's important, to validate their beliefs and to strengthen them from the beginning. . . . I thought I could be a good role model for them. I lost my dad when I was young. A lot of these kids are from single families. I could make an impact right here. . . . There're not that many male Latinos in the elementary realm. So just to have a male Latino, you don't see it that often.

For Miguel, a role model provides students with whatever they need to succeed: extra help, support from parents, and school supplies, for example:

> I want students to know that education is important and that they can do it. Pay attention, be respectful, and do your best work at all times. Those are the rules of my class, and I think that carries on forever in life. "So if you put in the time and try your best, you will succeed in life. But it comes from you, and I'm here to help you. And I know it's tough, but I'm going to help you through those difficult moments. And if you're not getting how to read, I will come here at 7:30. I will stay after school with you. I will come here during lunch. I will talk to your parents to give you a space in your home. I will tell them to buy you what you need, the literature that you need so you can grow. I will give you homework. I will give you all the tools. All you need to do is come here, and have the desire." . . . I give anecdotes like, "Yeah, I know that you don't have a father, but I didn't have one either. I know that you're a Latino, you don't have a lot of money, but look, I didn't have a lot of money either, and we made it."

Miguel knows some of the difficulties students may encounter because he too experienced them. However, he is optimistic and encouraging. He works to teach today's students about their culture and "validate their beliefs." This approach allows Miguel to nurture students' identities, emphasize the importance of their families' experiences and histories, and demonstrate how doing well in school is compatible with maintaining family languages, cultures, and traditions.

Miguel Elias's narrative powerfully captures many of the experiences shared by the other Latina/o teachers as they made their way from kindergarten through college, and the other stories in this chapter highlight these recurring everyday exchanges within schools.

"One Teacher Can Make a Difference": The Role of School Officials on Educational Outcomes

Other teachers also recounted school officials who shaped their sense of selves and their aspirations. Some remembered teachers who empowered them and worked with their families to enhance their educational outcomes; others recalled teachers who reproduced inequality by privileging the white students in their classrooms and showing their low expectations of Latina/o students. Fortunately, there were friends and others who cushioned these hurtful exchanges. Angelica Vasquez explicitly exclaimed, "One teacher can make a difference," a sentiment shared by most of the teachers.

"She Just Woke Me Up": Teachers and Counselors Who Inspire

Angelica Vasquez remembers the positive influence that two teachers had in her life: one in elementary school and another in high school:

> My fifth-grade teacher made a big difference. He was absolutely amazing. He was a very, very tall man. He must have been almost seven feet tall. He was African American. That was the first time I had ever seen an African American male as a teacher. He taught me all the math that I know. He made a difference by giving me confidence because knowledge gives you confidence. People can tell you you're great, but unless you feel you're great, it doesn't really make a difference. Knowledge gives you that power of being able

to understand; you're not sitting there confused every day. So he helped me a lot by just teaching me a lot of math.

Perhaps capturing a young child's memories of her "amazing" fifth-grade teacher, Angelica remembers the teacher who empowered her as "almost seven feet tall." Among the behaviors that seemed to impress her was how he "stopped all instruction for the first fifteen to twenty minutes of every day until each person learned his or her multiplication." By making sure that all of the students learned, her teacher empowered students with the knowledge of mathematics.

Another teacher who shaped the direction of Angelica's life was a *high school academic decathlon coach*, someone she never actually had in class: "He's Salvadoran and married a Mexican American girl who went to Harvard. And it was amazing having a married couple who had both gone to college. He talked to me and said he knew how I felt. He knew what it was like to be different and to want something different from the people around you and your own family and having the battle within yourself, sometimes."

Angelica's decathlon coach related to some of her own struggles of being the first woman in her family to have college aspirations. By sharing his own schooling and family experiences and modeling how he was part of a college-educated Latina/o couple, he inspired Angelica. Twenty years later, Angelica is still in contact with this teacher, who has left an enduring impression.

For Angelica, two men of color were among the teachers who had the largest impact on her. Both upheld high expectations of the working-class students of color who filled their classrooms, a characteristic that has been found in other research on teachers of color (National Collaborative on Diversity in the Teaching Force, 2004). Furthermore, Angelica's Latino coach could relate to her experiences with family, schooling, and aspirations as the first generation in her family to attend college. In a profession where whites and women predominate, men of color are significantly underrepresented as K–12 teachers (National Collaborative on Diversity in the Teaching Force, 2004), but Angelica's experiences with these two teachers illustrate the importance of diversifying the teaching staff to enhance understandings between students and teachers.

Since teachers such as Angelica Vasquez did not "see themselves in enough teachers," they aspired to enter the profession to share their "funds of knowledge"—their cultural knowledge, immigrant backgrounds, and working-class experiences—with future generations of students, families, and communities (see Rueda, Monzó, and Higareda, 2004). As with middle school teacher Margarita Villa, they wanted to "come back and teach at my school." Angelica explains her desire to teach: "I always wanted to come back to the community because I wanted to make sure that people saw themselves in teachers. . . . I wanted them to see themselves in me, for parents to come and talk to someone." Thus, having related so much to her Latino academic decathlon coach, Angelica hopes that she too can inspire students who may see her as a reflection of themselves.

Although teachers recounted positive memories with teachers of color who influenced their schooling experiences and desires to become educators, most remembered having very few Latina/o educators. As students, some did not always realize how who was in the classroom influenced their schooling experiences. For Vivian Sosa, it was not until our interview that she realized she had had only one Latina/o teacher during her entire K–12 education: Ilene Gómez, who is also included in this book. Vivian reflects on the wonderful time she had in this first-grade teacher's class:

> I remember loving that class because the teacher would sing all the time with her guitar. We kids would speak in Spanish or English, and I would help a lot of the kids. . . .

She would give me books to have them read, and I
would help them and be her assistant. I just remember
having a positive experience because we would sing
lively in Spanish and English.

As our nearly two-hour conversation came to an end, I asked
Vivian if she thought that the racial/ethnic gap that exists between
students and teachers such that 90 percent of today's public school
teachers are white while 40 percent of the students are of color
was significant. She concluded her comments with this outburst
and reflection: "I never thought about that growing up. . . . It was
not until right now where I thought, 'Oh my gosh. I had only one
Hispanic teacher!' Maybe I would have talked more. I don't know.
Looking back and being very objective about it, that was the one
class that I felt comfortable singing, dancing, and talking out loud.
Wow! That was an epiphany."

Vivian's epiphany about how she may have felt more comfortable in her first-grade classroom because of her teacher's background and her use of Spanish and English is revealing, especially
considering that at least half of the Latina teachers described themselves as shy and quiet in the classroom. Maybe individuals like
Vivian Sosa would not have felt so shy if they had teachers from
similar cultural backgrounds.

Although Vivian speculates that maybe she would have been
a different type of student, thirty-five-year-old Lisa Perez, who
entered school speaking Spanish, knows that she would have
participated more in class if she had had additional bilingual and
Latina/o teachers. To help illustrate this conclusion, Lisa contrasts
her experiences with an English-speaking kindergarten teacher
with her second- and third-grade bilingual teachers:

My kindergarten teacher scarred me. . . . I was shy
because I didn't speak English. I was embarrassed
because students would make fun of me. . . . I wouldn't

ask questions, or I'd wait until after school. . . . I didn't talk. . . . My second-grade teacher, I liked her because she spoke Spanish. I thought [she lets out a deep sigh of relief] somebody was going to understand me. With her, I could ask for help in Spanish.

Of all of her early teachers, Lisa remembers her third-grade teacher, a Latina who was Spanish-English bilingual, most fondly. Lisa "loved" this teacher, who was "very nurturing, very caring," and made Lisa feel "comfortable" in the classroom. So great was this teacher's impact that Lisa credits her for "wanting to be a teacher."

The limited scholarship on the role of Latina/o teachers in the classroom supports Lisa Perez's experiences. These studies suggest that Latina/o school officials may possess unique funds of knowledge from their upbringing, their positions in society, and the sociopolitical and historical events that occur during their lives (Moll, Armanti, Neff, and González, 1992; Monzó and Rueda, 2003). These funds of knowledge may be similar to what Latina/o students know and how they interact with the world (for examples, see Rueda, Monzó, and Higareda, 2004), thus ensuring more familiar feelings and connections with the classroom and teacher. Much of this research on funds of knowledge focuses on instructional aides and demonstrates how Latina teaching assistants may encourage collaboration over individualism, integrate community examples into classroom lessons, and interact with students with *cariño* (caring) by referring to them using Spanish-language terms of endearment (Rueda, Monzó, and Higareda, 2004). So, more work is needed to understand Latina/o teachers' styles of teacher-student interactions.

While Latina/o teachers can be important role models who are creating comfortable classrooms, there is nothing inherent about being Latina/o that fosters particular attitudes or actions. Thus, teachers also recalled non-Latina/o educators who were positive influences in their lives. Typically these were teachers who engaged them through critical thinking courses. Thirty-two-year-old Marie Marquez credits some of her English teachers for encouraging her to think: "It was refreshing to be able to think on my own instead of, 'You've got to do this and you've got to do that.'" These teachers challenged her and allowed her to "just break free and really go in depth into the literature and think for myself."

Experiences similar to those of Marie have also led the other teachers to see that while they have much to offer Latina/o students, non-Latina/o teachers who are also committed, caring, and challenging are crucial too. Middle school teacher Lisa Perez explains:

> As teachers, we have an important role, and no matter what nationality you are, you need to validate a student's culture and accept them for who they are, continue to lead them, continue to be role models for them and have high expectations. I believe that Latino teachers have many experiences that Latino students can appreciate, but it doesn't necessarily mean that only Latino teachers can do that.

Retired middle school teacher Diana Cortez adds, "What matters is how you interact with the kids, or if they connect with you, if they respect you, and if they like you."

Although the role of school counselors in shaping schooling experiences, especially in determining course placement, cannot be underestimated, it came up less frequently in the interviews than the impact of inspirational teachers. Marie Marquez's experience best illustrates how counselors can influence a student's academic path:

> In junior high, I just stayed out of the way, and I wasn't a straight A student, but I got good grades. And in my

freshman year, the counselor who knew my family called the house to set up an appointment to come in and discuss school. So we went to her office, and she wanted to go through my future and what I needed. She started discussing it and said, "You know, Marie's doing really well in school. I think she would benefit by going into some honors classes; it would challenge her."

It was fortunate for Marie that her older brothers and sister had graduated from the same high school because this personal relationship between the counselor and her family carried over to Marie. As a result, Marie's counselor "took an interest" in her and scheduled a meeting with her father to discuss college. Following the meeting, Marie was granted access to honors and advanced placement courses, which greatly facilitated her path to college.

Sometimes the special interest that school officials took with these teachers led them to be singled out as "teacher's pet." For Cristina Martinez, who has recounted the sacrifices she and her New Mexican family have made for a formal education, this special attention helped to reinforce her love of school and learning: "When I started getting praised for how well I did, that drove me. . . . I loved that I was always teacher's pet. I got to grade papers for them; I got to come in early from outside and be in the classroom with them."

While Cristina appreciated the special treatment she received from her teacher, even supposedly special treatment and positive labels can result in negative consequences. In some cases, being a teacher's pet may be a stigmatized identity among students and result in resentment by students who detect the favoritism teachers may display to selected students (Luttrell, 1993). In addition, to the extent that being a teacher's pet is correlated with being lighter skinned or more "feminine" and middle class (Luttrell, 1993), teachers' actions may reinforce strict gender expectations and racial and class hierarchies. There may also be social and psychological implications for students who are anointed the favored one. How might the labeling and distinguishing of select students at the expense of others lead to some of the same divisions among students that Miguel Elias experienced between Mexican Americans and Mexican immigrants? And might those students who are labeled pets have a difficult time asserting their own sense of self, or might they come to believe that they are deserving of special treatment while their peers are not?

Overall, these teachers' experiences parallel other studies that have also found that most Latina/o students who complete high school and develop a "school kid" identity have close, personal, and meaningful relationships with a teacher or counselor (Flores-González, 2002). Access to school officials who cared for their well-being was critical in helping them to achieve their educational goals and deciding how to approach their own classrooms and roles as teachers.

Although supportive individuals were crucial in the lives of these teachers, when some students are favored and others are neglected or rejected, the impacts of this inequality can scar. Fortunately, the teachers included in this book found ways to challenge such pain when they were students, and they are inspired to prevent the scarring of future generations.

"He Used to Call the Latino Kids 'Boneheads'": School Officials Who Chip Away at Us

Not all students have teachers who inspire or counselors who take an interest in them. With middle and high school teachers responsible for 180 to 240 students a semester and student-counselor ratios stretching upward of a thousand to one (Romo and Falbo, 1996), it is often difficult for school officials to connect with so many students. In spite of these numbers, we expect teachers, counselors, and principals to create encouraging learning environments that foster growth among students. These expectations are not always met. Too many Latina/o students encounter school officials who impede their movement through school by establishing unequal practices or maintaining low expectations.

These exclusionary attitudes and interactions may stem from larger belief systems and structures of power and inequality. These include dominant ideologies such as the myth that the United States is a meritocracy where one's position in society stems from one's work ethic. Contemporary beliefs and actions also have their origin in biological and cultural deficiency ideologies about Latinas/os, the working class, immigrants, and Spanish speakers. When white supremacy is so pervasive in the United States, it is difficult not to become "smog-breathers," people who breathe in the smog of racism (Tatum, 1997, p. 6). These systems of beliefs are reproduced by institutional practices that privilege wealthier and whiter communities over communities of color, the poor, and those in the working class. The results are self-perpetuating ideologies, institutions, and everyday practices and attitudes where exclusionary ideologies are maintained by unequal institutions and internalized and carried out by some individual school officials.

Despite the self-perpetuating systems of power, privilege, and inequality, there are multiple examples of personal agency and collective resistance among students, teachers, and others who refuse to allow the continuation of racism or other forms of subjugation. As the following examples document, though some of the teachers featured in this book struggled with school officials' low expectations and derogatory beliefs, they also engaged in various forms of resistance by challenging multiple barriers as students and now as teachers—several of them fighting for educational justice.

Dealing with Teachers' Exclusionary Attitudes and Actions

Teachers of all ages recounted school officials' negative attitudes or exclusionary actions. For example, fifty-five-year-old Ilene Gómez, who has taught grades throughout the educational pipeline— primarily in the same community where she was a student— vividly recalls two examples of language discrimination that dramatically shaped her schooling experiences and her approach to teaching.

Similar to several of the other Latina/o teachers, Ilene Gómez described herself as a shy and quiet student. She now knows that her shyness stemmed from her experience of entering an English-dominant school when Spanish was the language of her home. However, the school officials were unaware of how such a transition may influence students' schooling experiences: "I suffered since I was a youngster. Teachers had great difficulties with me in first and second grade because I didn't speak. In kindergarten, I wouldn't speak. They told my mother that I might even suffer from autism because I didn't speak. By second grade, I was on all kinds of speech therapy. I was very, very shy." Rather than seek to understand the experiences of English-language learners and the difficulties in adjusting to an English-only environment, school officials blamed Ilene. They assumed that something was wrong with her, not with the school system.

In high school, Ilene Gómez was again subjected to school officials who undermined the experiences of Spanish-speaking students. This time, a high school teacher implemented a specific school practice that reinforced white privilege and disadvantaged Latina/o students:

> They would not allow any Spanish-speaking individ-
> ual in high school with a Spanish last name who took
> Spanish to get anything higher than a B in Spanish.
> They considered it to be leverage. . . . My husband had
> [the same teacher] for Spanish, and he used to call the
> Latino kids "boneheads." He said, "You have lever-
> age. You bring that language. The Anglo kids have to
> work harder than you." I asked, "Where was my handi-
> cap score when I took English? How come I didn't get
> one? Where was the leverage that you gave them? Why
> did you not give me that extra support?" I had to work

extra hard in my English-language courses because I did not come from a home that practiced English and read English.

While describing this high school teacher, Ilene reflects on the larger implications of such unequal teaching practices and how they minimize the resources of Spanish-speaking students. Rather than emphasizing the language assets that Spanish-speaking students brought to the classroom, these students were punished by the policy of this Spanish-language teacher: "This would have been a wonderful way for the Latino kids to shine to show that they had this gift, and it is a talent. It is leverage, but you take advantage of what you have, and you begin where the kids are. You take advantage of their talents. They didn't." Just as the Spanish-speaking students were unfairly disadvantaged with this policy, the English-speaking students were advantaged because they were not punished in the same way in their English classes.

By criticizing both how teachers labeled her "autistic" and established an unwritten "no A" policy for Latina/o students, Ilene Gómez directly challenges the deficit approach to schooling Latina/o students. Rather than build from where students are by adding to their knowledge, a deficit approach negates or undermines students' resources. Historically, this approach was most apparent in biological and cultural deficiency frameworks where Spanish-speaking Mexican American students were seen as intellectually inferior to white students and lacking English-language skills rather than possessing the potential to learn a second language.

Although the experiences shared by individuals such as Ilene Gómez cause significant hardships for many students, Ilene turned these encounters into a desire to improve the educational opportunities for students in her community. Her schooling experiences also sensitized her to the lives of other English-language learners: "The great thing that happened to me and the reason I became a teacher, I have this understanding for kids whose languages are put into a whole world that's different."

Thirty years later in the 1970s and 1980s, David Galvez encountered similar deficit approaches to the schooling of working-class Latina/o students when he attended Ilene Gómez's alma mater. Like Ilene, since graduating, he has sought to improve the schooling conditions for students. As a student, he observed teachers' negative beliefs, patronizing interactions, and the marginalization of Spanish-speaking students: "I just look back at my experiences with a lot of my teachers, and I realize that a lot of those experiences were negative" (quoted in Ochoa 2004a, p. 148). Part of the reason that David's teachers may have had such low expectations was that most of them were physically, socially, and economically removed from the students and community where they were teaching (see Valenzuela, 1999).

Now, as a teacher at his old school, David continues to see how teachers' low expectations are self-fulfilling: "There are some teachers who aren't motivated, who really don't care about the success of their students. There are teachers who have very low expectations of students. . . . As a result, the students don't perform. They live down to their expectations."

Damaging comments and diminished expectations from school officials can lead to students' negative self-perceptions. However, such comments may also influence how students perceive their own families, cultures, and communities. This was David Galvez's experience. As a child, he could not ignore the negative messages he received from teachers, especially because they were often reinforced by peers and the media. As a result, as early as elementary school, David learned that to be "cool" he should distance himself from his own family's cultural practices. He shunned the Spanish language, Mexican music, Mexican food, and even Mexican immigrants. He explains, "I pretended I didn't know Spanish. I didn't want to speak Spanish to my dad, especially in front of other people. The whole pronunciation of my last name was different. That was a pretty serious identity issue I went through those years" (quoted in Ochoa 2004a, p. 94).

David cannot pinpoint when he began to consciously not want to speak Spanish. However, considering other studies that indicate that as early as the fifth grade, bilingual students have internalized the prestige given to the English language (Orellana, Ek, and Hernández, 2000), it is easy to understand how David may have internalized the belief that "the cool thing was speaking English, being American." He attempted to distance himself from his immigrant family in much the same way that Mexican American students did not want to associate with immigrant students such as Miguel Elias.

Although different students respond differently to the negative messages that they receive in schools, as David's awareness of power and inequality grew, he turned teachers' disapproving comments into incentives to claim a politicized Chicano identity. For him, this meant moving from a feeling of shame for being Mexican to a sense of pride. As part of this process, he became more vocal and tried to prove teachers' stereotyped perceptions wrong:

> "Chicano" was the term I started using in high school when I had these teachers that are pretty conservative. I started realizing certain comments they made and how condescending they were toward Latinos, and then I adopted that term. . . . I kind of turned it into something that brought me satisfaction to throw it in their face. If they want to present being Mexican, being Chicano, as something negative, then I threw it in their face, "Well, you may perceive it as negative, but I perceive it as something that I'm proud of." So, it got me into trouble in high school. They started to look at me as disrespectful. "He doesn't do what he's told." Basically, I was just voicing my opinion. I wasn't going to be

this little kid that just sat and listened to all that they
had to say [quoted in Ochoa 2004a, pp. 94–95].

As David challenged teachers' sentiments by talking back, some
retaliated by labeling him a troublemaker. Fortunately, David was
able to turn teachers' negative messages into motivation to do well
in school, a common strategy of the teachers in this book. This
"defended typification," or trying to prove people wrong when
confronted with a stigmatized identity by race/ethnicity, class,
community, or something else, is not unusual among Latina/o
students who do well in school (Flores-González, 2002). However,
not all students respond to negative exchanges with school officials
in the same way. Those who have been made to feel disconnected
from school may internalize others' low expectations of them and
underperform. With this awareness and a desire to effect change,
David Galvez, like Ilene Gómez, returned to his school district to
become a teacher:

> I was a pretty strong student. You could tell me I wasn't
> going to succeed, and I was going to use that as motiva-
> tion. But, I realize that a lot of students aren't that way.
> When they're told that, they sometimes believe it. . . .
> I wondered how many students they [teachers] held
> back by their comments or sometimes not even their
> comments, but their way of teaching. . . . I just realized,
> "You know what, I want to go back, and hopefully try
> to counterbalance what's going on with a lot of those
> teachers" [quoted in Ochoa 2004a, p. 148].

David Galvez's determination was critical when, as he was
being hired, he encountered a familiar teacher who tried to
constrain his actions yet again. This time it had to do with the
teacher's devalued conception of Chicana/o studies: "The guy
that hired me, the department chair, who's one of my teachers

who told me I wouldn't make it at UCLA, he actually wanted to hire me. One of the comments he told me when he told me he would hire me was "Well, just don't bring that Chicano crap here" [quoted in Ochoa, 2004a, p. 148].

Although some of the members of David Galvez's hiring committee warned him not to apply his Chicana/o studies education and identity to his job, David was not deterred. Instead, returning to his alma mater has made him a more effective teacher because he believes that students listen to him more, and he feels empowered with a sense of ownership over the school. As an insider, he openly expresses himself within the school and district:

> I never really felt like a new teacher. The minute I came in, I was already vocal. I felt like, "This is my school. I don't care if you've been teaching here twenty years. I live right here." So I didn't feel like I was coming into someone's school, so I couldn't step on any toes and I couldn't offend anybody. I said, "This is my community. I have more of a right to say what I want while I'm here than probably you do, even if you've been here twenty years." That really helped me out. It's been four years. I've been really involved. I'm not fully credentialed yet, and a lot of teachers tend to really hold back because they fear that they're not going to get rehired. When we were going through our possible strikes, I was out there. I'm pretty confident in my abilities as a teacher. I feel if a principal isn't going to rehire me, then it's the school that's going to lose. I'll just go somewhere else and find a job, no problem.

Within the classroom, David Galvez is also vocal about educational inequalities between schools. He observed these injustices as a student in his school district, and as a teacher he aims to foster a critical consciousness and a desire among students to challenge such inequalities:

As a high school student, I began to realize the disparity
in our district. . . . It's always the haves and the have-nots.
That's something that the district has helped promote.
Most of the board members represent that side of the district, whether it is because of voter turnout or the fact
that that's where maybe more of the votes come from.
That's always been an issue. I've been exposed to that
now as a teacher where you hear things happening over
there that don't happen here. Why is it that their high
schools have twice as many AP [advanced placement]
classes as the ones on this side? . . . That was one of the
things I saw and realized as a student, and as a teacher, it
just reaffirmed it. It's something that I talk to my students
about today. I tell them, "Look, people see us, and they
think one thing. They see them; they think another." . . .
I used it as a sense of motivation when I was growing up. I
wanted to show them, "Look, I can do it just as much as
you." I try to get that going in my students today.

The narratives of Ilene Gómez and David Galvez reveal the
intergenerational struggles that many Latinas/os continue to
encounter in our schools. Three decades apart, both of these teachers developed a critical awareness of power and privilege at early
ages because of the struggles they endured. Today both are nurturing future generations of students who will also have the strength
and courage to persist in spite of constraints. Fortunately, they are
not alone in their actions. Other teachers are voicing their criticisms too and enacting a politics of resistance.

Resisting Negative Views of an Entire Group or School

School officials' derogatory perceptions of working-class Latina/o
students harm not only individual students. Entire communities,
classrooms, and schools can be the target of negative perceptions,
and the impact may be far reaching. Middle school teacher Lisa

Perez has seen the power of teachers' negative views most recently when teachers at her school espoused anti-immigrant and anti-Mexican sentiment when students and community members were organizing against the federal House Resolution 4437: The Border Protection, Antiterrorism, and Illegal Immigration Control Act of 2005. Lisa describes how such sentiment was voiced to students and faculty:

> There was a student who made a comment, "Viva Mexico." I couldn't believe that a white teacher I work with told the student, "Then you should go back to Mexico." We had a staff meeting and the same teacher sat next to me. . . . She was talking about the immigrant boycott and saying, "Students are not coming to school. What are these people fighting for anyway? If we go someplace else, we're not going to have rights." This other white teacher said, "Yeah, if I go someplace else, I'm not going to get any rights. They're not going to give me rights. So why should they get any rights?"

As the daughter of Mexican immigrants, Lisa knows the impact that teachers' comments and actions regarding Mexicans and immigrants can have on students, and she cannot ignore such sentiments. After waiting a day to consider how to respond to these teachers' comments, Lisa confronted the most vocal one and said:

> Can I talk to you for a minute? I don't know if you realized this or not, but you made some comments yesterday about immigrants and the law. Those are political views. You need to be sensitive of the people who are in your surroundings because I am a Latina. You offended me.... I'm not going to tell you which political view to take, but there's a time and a place, and you need to be careful with what you say because not everyone is in agreement

with you. Do you even know what they're fighting for?
They're not going to take any of your rights. They pay
taxes just like you and me. . . . They pay sales tax.

Lisa concluded her immigration lesson by reprimanding the
teacher about her position: "We are supposed to be role models. If you
don't have anything positive to say, then don't say anything. . . .
You need to be more positive because you made a comment that they
should stay in Mexico, and that's not nice."

As a teacher, Lisa Perez is driven to confront exclusionary
comments and educate students, family, friends, and teachers for
the interests of students and immigrants. Students' interests are her
interests, and she appeals to us all to stay informed about relevant
political decisions that affect education and to be political advocates for students.

When school officials' negative perceptions influence school
practices, the ramifications can be especially insidious. For example,
Spanish teacher Joan Young recalls how a principal's perception
of the worth of students led to the transfer of "good teachers" from
the predominantly working-class high school to the more middle-
class school in the district: "The principal had it in his mind that
certain teachers shouldn't be at that school. According to him, if
you were a good teacher, you needed to be transferred. So many of
us . . . were on involuntary transfers." Such practices maintain a
system that confers privileges and resources to students and communities who are already economically and politically more advantaged; these practices perpetuate larger systems of inequality that
contribute to the cycle of low expectations.

School Officials' Attitudes and Actions Matter

Negative exchanges with school officials are not always explicitly
rooted in race/ethnicity, class, immigrant status, or community.
Nevertheless, the actions of teachers can strike at the core of a
child. Vivian Sosa shared the following experience with her own

third-grade teacher. She prefaced this example by explaining that it was the only negative encounter she could remember. Nearly twenty years later, the details are acute:

> Because I was so shy, I had a hard time dealing with a louder teacher or somebody who was a little bit more aggressive. I had a third-grade teacher who loved basketball, and we would play it for PE [physical education] all of the time. I hate basketball to this day because I was trying to shoot, and I was so shy. I just remember him hitting my hand, "No! That's not how you hold the ball! That's not how you hold the ball!" And I was crying, just because I couldn't hold the ball right. And so I hate basketball. You would think because I'm a little taller I would want to play, but nope. I never wanted to play. For that same third-grade teacher, I had to stand in the corner once, and I remember other kids standing in the corner crying.

Vivian begins this example by blaming herself for how she responded to her third-grade teacher: she was shy; the teacher was loud. However, Vivian did not appear shy or quiet just two years earlier in Ms. Gómez's first-grade class where she danced, sang, and read with her classmates. We are left wondering what happened during these intervening years to change Vivian's classroom personality. What role did teachers play in these transformations, and how might such punishment and humiliation by a teacher have influenced her?

Such experiences by school officials may leave students feeling hurt, angry, apathetic, and disconnected from school (Segura, 1993; Flores-González, 2002). "Feel[ing] unloved by uncaring teachers" has been found to be a factor in limiting students' academic progress, leading some students to leave school altogether (Flores-González, 2002, p. 43). What may have distinguished some of the teachers in this book from other individuals is that as students, they were able to turn hostile attitudes and interactions into motivating factors. Also, there were other people in their lives who encouraged and supported them. Vivian Sosa, in particular, explained how most of her exchanges with teachers were positive, and as we learned from her story in Chapter Four, her parents, especially her mother, strengthened her. Also, at some point in their schooling, most of these Latina/o teachers were among a select group of students who were labeled "gifted," "honors students," or "high achieving." As such, they had access to some of the most rigorous classes in their schools, received other messages that they were special or smart, and were part of a school culture where college attendance was expected.

But what happens to the many students who are marginalized, face multiple exclusionary comments and actions over the course of their schooling, and have no positive relationships with others to counteract such messages? What are the tolls of these attacks? As David Galvez indicated, for some students, teachers' attitudes and interactions with them can become self-fulfilling. Students may begin to see themselves as other people do and respond to their expectations (Cooley, 1922).

A classic study conducted in 1968 by social psychologists Robert Rosenthal and Lenore Jacobson demonstrates the critical role that teacher expectations can have on student achievement. In a California elementary school, Rosenthal and Jacobson tested all first- through sixth-grade students at the beginning of the school year. They told the teachers that the test had identified certain students as having "unusual intellectual promise." Unbeknown to the teachers, these students had simply been randomly selected. At the conclusion of the school year, Rosenthal and Jacobson retested the students. The results were dramatic: on average, the scores of students who were randomly selected and labeled as having unusual intellectual promise improved by about twice as much as the other students. This improvement was most extreme for younger students. Rosenthal and Jacobson concluded that a self-fulfilling prophecy was operating in the classroom. When teachers were told that a particular student would do well, even if there was no basis for such a statement, the teachers treated that student in ways that ensured that the student excelled. Teachers' expectations were met because they acted in ways that reinforced their preconceived notions (Rosenthal and Jacobson, 1968). Thus, we see some of the ramifications of teachers' perceptions and interactions.

When low expectations and discriminatory attacks are linked to students' backgrounds, they can be even more devastating. They strike at the heart of some of the most salient aspects of students' beings—their languages, families, and histories—a time when many are developing their identities. The results can be an attempt to disassociate from community members, a denial of the Spanish language, being ashamed of family members, and a general squelching of self-esteem. These results can drive students away from the critical systems of support—their families and communities—that they need to help with their identity formation and schooling.

Just as Angelica Vasquez claims, "One teacher can make a difference." Each of the examples in this chapter illustrates the ways that teachers both inspired and discouraged students through their beliefs, actions, and course curriculum. However, these attitudes and behaviors do not exist in isolation. First, students who receive encouragement from school officials may be able to tap into teachers' social networks that provide additional support and knowledge. Access to such networks might result in referrals to other individuals who can offer assistance or acceptance into honors and advanced placement courses. Second, school officials' attitudes and behaviors are part of larger ideologies and structures with clearly established policies and practices that often shape and hinder both teachers and students. That is, a teacher's beliefs may emerge from dominant attitudes or stem from taken-for-granted school practices that are unequal and unfair.

Fortunately, students, such as the current teachers profiled here, continue to critique such systems of beliefs and practices.

In this way, they disrupt the status quo, push for change, and foster networks of support that helped them and will aid future generations of students. One area where their resistance is apparent and the possibilities for change are visible is in the support networks that these teachers tapped into as they made their way from kindergarten through college.

"I Think of the Mentors Who Supported Me": Getting Through School with the Help of Others

Almost all of the teachers featured in this book are the children of working-class Mexican immigrants. Most of their parents have less than a sixth-grade formal education. Thus, not only was schooling in the United States a new experience for this generation, but they also encountered unfamiliar terrain with each step toward enrolling and completing college. A couple were fortunate to have older siblings whose footsteps they followed, and others formed familial, cultural, religious, or political support networks that empowered them as they navigated through the educational pipeline. These various forms of social support have been key in providing Latinas/os with the strength, determination, and know-how to contend with new experiences.

Cristina Martinez's experiences with MEChA, a student political organization in existence for over three decades, reminds us of the importance of such support networks. Cristina was among the first in her family to attend college. For her, involvement in MEChA was crucial. It provided a support system where she bonded with other students, developed an understanding of her family's schooling experiences, and established leadership and critical thinking skills. Her experience is an example of the support system that many of the teachers used; it demonstrates the significance of collaboration and the importance of multicultural, power-aware course curriculum.

As a high school student, Cristina began to learn from her mother about the historical and structural inequalities within our educational system. Her mother shared with her that in New Mexico, she and her eleven siblings were often ostracized because of their racial/ethnic and class backgrounds. According to Cristina, her mother, aunts, and uncles "were the kids who got hit in school for speaking Spanish. They were teased because they ate burritos because they couldn't afford to have white bread sandwiches.... When she was in high school, she was never pushed or tracked into going to college. She was told the only two options for her were to get married and have babies or to become a nurse's assistant."

As Cristina learned about her mother's experiences, she became increasingly angry. By connecting with other high school students who had similar family histories, she realized that these experiences were not isolated. They were part of larger systems of inequality. With this knowledge, Cristina worked with her high school classmates to channel their anger of oppression by creating a positive change in their school, their community, and their own lives through MEChA: "We started working in the community and bringing speakers to our school from all over the nation. We held a huge statewide conference. We had the highest number of students come to our high school conference in the state."

Just as David Galvez described earlier, Cristina and her schoolmates quickly realized that their critical awareness of history, inequality, and empowered identity was not well received by all school officials. David Galvez had been labeled a "troublemaker" in high school for claiming a Chicano identity. Cristina and her fellow organizers "were called 'radical' in a negative sense." However, rather than shy away from this label, they used it to their advantage: "We said, 'If they're going to call us radical, let's make it positive. Let's be radical. Let's take on our education and what we want to learn.' At that time, we were upset. We had a paragraph about our culture in history class. We had nothing culturally in our school, and that's crazy because it's a predominantly Hispanic/ Latino community, but it was very, very Anglicized."

The positive results of working with MEChA were many:

> We impacted a lot of people's lives throughout the three
> and a half years that we were together in MEChA. That
> also provided a lot of opportunities for me to be that
> speaker, to be up in front of crowds, to see my friends
> doing it, to see, "Wow, we can actually be achievers in
> the ways that we want to be." Then when I got to col-
> lege, it helped knowing about my family because that
> was one of the things that we said: "You can't ever really
> go forward unless you have a strong base and know
> where you come from."

MEChA and other systems of support contributed to Cristina's
strong base that enabled her to grow and achieve her educational
goals: "I think of the mentors who supported me, whether it was
in MEChA, our people, or being a Girl Scout, and having really
strong women. Those things provided a lot of strength when I got
to college."

As Cristina's experience demonstrates, student-initiated organizations such as MEChA are critical for developing students'
leadership skills, support networks, awareness of power and inequality, and connections to schools. Furthermore, in situations where
performing well in school requires learning the histories, cultures,
and traditions of middle- and upper-class whites, MEChA provides
a space for students to adopt a bicultural identity (Bettie, 2003).
As Bettie also found from her work with Mexican American high
schoolers, through MEChA, students are able to "do well in school
and yet maintain a political-cultural racial/ethnic identity" (p. 89).
Given these multiple benefits, student involvement in such social,
political, and cultural student organizations may be seen as an
ethnic strategy that does not require complete replacement of one's
family values, norms, and traditions with dominant expectations.

Instead, it allows "accommodation without assimilation" (Matute-Bianchi, 1991; Gibson, 1988; Bettie, 2003).

Despite the benefits of such student-initiated systems of support, we as a society cannot rely solely on these sources of support to assist students through the educational pipeline. Schools and policymakers have a responsibility to do more for all students and communities. Today Cristina still sees the importance of working collectively to improve educational outcomes. She and her fellow colleagues offer several avenues from which to work for change, and these avenues involve more than just the actions of individuals and support groups.

Effecting Change at Multiple Levels

No student should have to face the hostile treatment and attacks on identity that some of the teachers in this chapter remember. School officials should create inclusive learning environments and must work to name, interrogate, change, and eliminate their biases by race/ethnicity, immigrant status, gender, class, and sexuality. Not all students can be expected to turn negative exchanges into positive motivators, and students should not be required to prove people's stereotypes wrong. Without proactive responses to changing attitudes and actions, we risk scarring more students to the extent that their voices are muffled, they scale back their aspirations, or they drop out of school.

Part of caring for students is treating them with respect and dignity and transmitting high expectations to all of them. For school officials to exhibit genuine care for all students more effectively, the ratio of teachers and counselors to student must be reduced. Fewer students to be responsible for will provide school officials with more time and energy to work with individual students. Teachers and counselors cannot effectively know and work with the large number of students who currently fill many public school classrooms. However, we cannot wait until policymakers see the importance of reducing these ratios. For now, we can learn from the actions of teachers who are facilitating students' academic and social development. Teachers in this chapter fondly recall school officials who connected with them by speaking Spanish, reaching out to families, sharing their similar experiences, or integrating multicultural curriculum. Such everyday actions are meaningful and should be encouraged.

The significance of supportive networks was another thread woven throughout these teachers' lessons. As students, some formed intentional communities in opposition to the negative sentiment they encountered by their peers and adults. For Miguel Elias, such communities helped to offset the anti-immigrant and anti-Mexican ridicule he faced at every stage of his schooling. Cristina Martinez became empowered through such inclusive and affirming spaces as the ones formed through MEChA. However, as other scholars have described, having to form intentional communities is a burden that adds to the stress that many working-class students of color already face in schools as they try to navigate new arenas (see Pineda, 2002). It is the responsibility of schools to do more to provide support for students. To overlook the many changes that are needed at both the individual and institutional levels is to ignore the eager first-grade students in Miguel Elias's classroom and the futures that lay before them.

Middle school teacher Cristina Martinez knows the importance of making change at multiple levels, and as her interview ended, she reflected on the overall difficulties in improving educational experiences: "There's always that positive thing that you tell yourself, 'Oh, I'm making a difference.' And I really do hope that the children I touch do feel something, do get something out of it that's positive for them. I definitely know that I come in every day, and I give them 110 percent." Regardless of how much she gives students, Cristina questions whether the actions of individual teachers will lead to overall change: "The dropout rate, do I think it's going to change very much? This way that education is set up, this way that curricula is disseminated to students, no."

To some, Cristina's response to changing the dropout rate or the rate of students who are pushed out of schools may seem harsh and overly critical, but all of our emphasis cannot be placed on changing individual teachers or students, no matter how much of a difference one person can make. The possibilities for change within schools involve not just altering teachers' actions. Instead, improving the number of students who advance through the educational pipeline requires working collectively and at multiple levels to change school practices. Teachers are important in this process, but they are not alone. As Cristina charges, we must consider "this way that education is set up, this way that curricula are disseminated to students." Like Cristina, the other Latina/o teachers were very aware of the school practices that influence students' movement through the educational pipeline. The following chapters shift the focus away from the microdynamics in schools to some of the institutional practices shaping education for students and teachers.

Part III

Improving Outcomes for Latina/o Students

7

Detracking Inequality

*Tracking seems to be one of those well-intended pathways
that . . . has some pretty hellish consequences.*

(Oakes, 1985)

When I asked twenty seniors enrolled in a non-college-preparatory English class to describe their high school experiences to me, they initially responded with a mixture of moans and giggles. However, slowly they shared:

"It's friends that have made school good. It's seeing and spending time with friends," Hector begins.

Several Latinas vehemently disagree. "It's all about the drama. It's mainly girls gossiping. It's jealousy. It's spreading rumors. I think that girls are worse about this than the guys. It's about picking fights," Marisela explains.

According to Celia, this drama hurts school performance: "We can't think about school; we're worried that we're going to get beat up."

Shifting topics, Mona bursts, "We should have less homework."

"And nicer counselors. They're always calling my home when I'm not in school, and they were telling my parents that I wasn't going to graduate even though I am," Tom interjects.

"And nicer teachers," Martin chimes.

"We have teachers who try to be our friends. They're all into our business. They need to be our teachers and not our friends," Marco clarifies, and several students nod.

Suddenly from the front of the room, Albert pounds his fist onto his desk. The class is still, and all eyes are on Albert. Slowly, as if for effect,

Albert turns around in his chair, glares into the faces of his classmates, and scolds, "Hey, I don't know if you've noticed, but we've been together all four years. It's almost like this is the Mexican class."

Albert named the problem that no one would, and the carefree tone of the discussion is now tense. After a long pause, a few chuckles break the silence, and students try to understand the magnitude of the problem. Why, in the year 2000, have they been confined to a segregated, non-college-preparatory classroom and removed from their Asian American and white schoolmates?

From the second row of the classroom, Priscilla whispers, "It's because of the Chinos." While Priscilla blames Asian Americans for this segregation, other students blame themselves. They rationalize, "We're different. We might be slow readers. We don't read as well. We like to party and have fun more than the honors students; we don't like to work as hard. We're lazy."

Shifting from individual explanations to school factors, Sam interjects: "They've given up on us. They pay more attention to the honor students than to the students who are not college prep. like us. They get all the awards and the attention."

At Grant High School, Latinas/os comprise 40 percent of the student population, but they are 96 percent of the students in this non-college-preparatory English class. The school principal reports that less than 5 percent of all Latina/o students at the school are enrolled in honors and advanced placement courses.

The dynamics here are not unique; Albert's observations are replicated in schools across the nation. In general, Latinas/os are significantly underrepresented in honors and advanced placement courses and overrepresented in non-college-preparatory classes, limiting their access to critical thinking courses, higher-level learning, and attendance at four-year colleges and universities (Oakes, 1985; Segura, 1993; Ginorio and Huston, 2001). In Los Angeles County, where Grant High School is located, only about one in four (26 percent) of all 2004 Latina/o graduates had completed the necessary course work with a grade C or better to attend California State University (CSU) or University of California (UC) immediately after high school. The percentages for other groups were not much better: 31 percent of African Americans, 32 percent of Native Americans, 43 percent of whites, and 60 percent of Asian Americans had completed the required classes to attend a CSU or UC (California Department of Education, 2005). These patterns reveal that many high school students are not prepared to enter four-year colleges, but on average, Latinas/os, African Americans, and Native Americans are most likely to be shortchanged of the opportunity.

Standing in front of the group of Grant High School seniors while they tried to understand their schooling experiences by blaming Asian American students, themselves, and school officials, I felt my heart sink and my anger rise. Why were the students quick to blame themselves, especially when it was their school that confined them to a noncollege preparatory course labeled Transitional English? The students were kept in this class for their four years of high school, transitioning to nowhere. Why did they blame Asian American students? How does such scapegoating reinforce stereotypes that pit Latina/o families who are believed to not care about education against Asian Americans, the assumed model minority? How might such scapegoating camouflage the long history of inequality detailed in Chapter Two? Finally, what role do such school practices as curriculum tracking have in maintaining stereotypes and inequality, and what might be done to remedy these injustices?

Although it is surely true that one teacher can make a difference, these high school seniors' experiences reveal how school practices undeniably influence students' lives. Practices such as curriculum tracking are not neutral policies unrelated to race/ethnicity or class. Just as such practices disproportionately disadvantage Latinas/os, African Americans, and working-class families, they also affect other students. Institutionally, white, Asian American, and economically advantaged students are more likely to gain access to the most challenging college-preparatory courses. Nevertheless, they too lose out from these practices. Their physical separation from their classmates may exacerbate racial/ethnic stereotypes and tensions, and those in the honors courses may develop an inaccurate sense of self and believe that they deserve the best resources and the most attention.

Turning to the experiences of teachers who encountered such school practices as students and now as instructors, this chapter does what little previous research has done: it focuses on the perspectives of Latinas/os and teachers. Too many people are quick to blame Latinas/os and teachers for not doing more to improve today's schools. Others attempt to implement new school programs under the pretense that they know best how to remedy educational outcomes. Missing in many of these public debates and top-down educational programs are the perspectives of teachers—how teachers understand and attempt to work within schools today.

In their interviews, the Latina/o teachers echoed the Grant High School students' observations about curriculum tracking. They also challenged Eurocentric and test-driven course curriculum as additional school practices that are hindering many Latina/o students and exhausting teachers. Curriculum tracking and course curriculum are linked to the past century of scientific management with its emphasis on standardization, scientific methods of assessment, control over workers, and efficiency. Today such school practices are maintained by neoliberal policies that focus on accountability, privatization, and the "free market." These school practices and their legacies perpetuate racial/ethnic and class inequality, and teachers see and feel their devastating impacts.

By focusing on these school practices, this chapter centers the teachers' perspectives and their challenges to unequal schooling. Given their educational experiences, many are trying to subvert various school practices or shield students from their damaging effects. However, teachers' lessons reveal how additional voices of dissent are needed to push for institutional changes.

The Legacy of Tracking

Most of the teachers remember being tracked when they were students. They and the other students were placed into groups or classes based on their academic performances and their perceived intellectual abilities. These took the form of distinct reading groups in elementary school, special programs for students labeled "gifted and talented" based on intelligence tests, and designated vocational, college preparatory, or honors and advanced placement courses in high school.

This practice of selecting and sorting students into different courses based on perceived capabilities can be traced to the changing demographics at the turn of the twentieth century, the growth of factories, and prevailing ideologies (Oakes, 1985). In particular, tracking emerged during a period when access to public schooling was increasing and growing numbers of poor, immigrant, and second-generation children from southern and eastern Europe were entering school. During this period, the ideologies that shaped the formation of schools and the system of tracking included social Darwinist assumptions about the biological superiority of white Anglo Protestants, cultural deficiency perspectives that justified Americanization programs for immigrants, and scientific, management-based models of the factory as the most efficient way to educate a mass citizenry (Oakes, 1985). Thus, tracking has its origins in racist and classist assumptions, hierarchies, and ideologies. The history of allocating students to distinct educational and career paths by race/ethnicity and class position has reproduced inequalities and maintained the capitalist system by ensuring a ready-supply of laborers, managers, and owners (Bowles and Gintis, 1976; Gonzalez, 1990).

School officials have a long history of channeling Mexican American students into slow-learner ability tracks and vocational courses (see Gonzalez, 1990). Biological and cultural deficiency arguments have been used to justify the placement of Mexican American students into these courses. Despite landmark court cases, including the Civil Rights Act of 1964, which provided protection from discriminatory practices under the Fourteenth Amendment, Latinas/os and African Americans are still overrepresented in low-ability tracks and vocational classes and underrepresented in honors and gifted courses (Oakes 1985).

Today tracking is pervasive and ingrained in how schools are organized. As the status quo, it typically goes unchallenged or is rationalized—often by the teachers, students, and families in the top courses—as the best way to teach students (Oakes, 1985; Lee, 1996). Tracking is believed to allow students to progress at their own pace without hindering the advancement of other students.

Underlying the acceptance of tracking are the beliefs that the United States is a meritocracy, educational policies are unbiased, and students are accurately placed in the courses and tracks commensurate with their abilities. Thus, the underrepresentation of Latinas/os and African Americans and the overrepresentation of Asian Americans and whites in the most rigorous courses remain largely unquestioned. The assumption is that students are in the courses they deserve.

Most of the Latina/o teachers disagree with the uncritical acceptance of tracking. They believe that tracking reinforces asymmetry within schools and society, and they criticize the fact that some students are being prepared to enter occupations that require higher levels of learning and critical thinking while students in non-college-preparatory courses are being tracked into low-wage occupations with limited opportunities. The teachers' criticisms are connected to their own K–12 schooling; inequalities by race/ethnicity and class are fundamental to their critiques.

Given their experiences and current positions within schools, the teachers possess what Patricia Hill Collins (1991) describes as an "outsider within" perspective on the educational system. That is, the teachers have a unique angle of vision that enables them to see the contradictions and complications within schools. Although they personally know the damaging impacts of tracking, they are caught in a double bind: they find themselves working within an unequal system that hurts the very students with whom they often identify—working-class Latinas/os. Detailed in the following three sections on tracking are the teachers' schooling experiences and the ways that they are both subtly and explicitly contesting the system of tracking. Their experiences offer critical insights for those of us concerned about schooling against inequality.

Challenging Track Selection and Allocation

> In junior high school, there were quite a few counselors. They never came to me and said, "You know what, you're doing well; maybe for high school we should put you into these honors classes." No one ever approached me about that. So I honestly never thought about that until my counselor in high school— she knew my family, and she took an interest in me and saw how well I was doing. So she decided, "This kid needs to go into these classes." Looking back, it makes me mad. How come those counselors never came to me and said, "I think these are the classes you should be taking." It wasn't until the end of my freshman year that they decided, "Okay, sophomore year you're going to be in this, this, and this class."
>
> —Marie Marquez, middle school teacher

One high school counselor who knew Marie's family changed the direction of her education. This counselor took a special interest in Marie and facilitated her entrance into honors and advanced placement (AP) courses that challenged her academically and aided in her advancement to college.

This example illustrates how seemingly individual behaviors, such as the one taken by her high school counselor, are part of established school practices that influence educational outcomes and life opportunities. After all, Marie's counselor would not have needed to recommend her for honors courses if all students had access to a rigorous curriculum where gatekeepers such as school counselors or teachers did not regulate course placement and avenues for college.

Among the factors that angered Marie was that she was not recommended for the top classes until later in her schooling. Teachers were also late in recommending Miguel Elias: "I didn't get into the honors and the AP courses until I was a junior in high school. In tenth grade, my English teacher recommended me to honors, and that's how I started on that track, and I took honors language arts and honors history. I took AP English and Chemistry." Access to such classes widened Marie and Miguel's college options. However, since they were both identified as honors students late in their K–12 schooling, questions arise as to what would have happened if their counselors or teachers had not recommended them for advanced classes. How would their path to college and teaching have been more difficult? Would they have become teachers? Maybe they would have had an easier time in college if they had access to the most rigorous courses throughout high school? Furthermore, how many students slip through the cracks and are never deemed worthy of honors courses? These are some of the questions that haunt teachers as they see the pernicious ways that tracking affects students.

Typically students' course placements and life trajectories are determined by their performance on standardized tests and school officials' recommendations, and the teachers critique all of these criteria. For example, Grant High School teacher Ana Camacho denounces the unfair tracking that begins at such an early age and is linked to economic factors. At her school, curriculum tracking is compounded by economic inequalities in the two schools that feed into Grant High School. The students at the wealthier school have educational advantages over the students coming from the more working class and typically Latina/o school:

> The big significance is the tracking that begins even before students set foot onto this campus. There are students who have attended a junior high that had a little bit more affluence and had an honors program, whereas the other junior high with a low socioeconomic area doesn't have those programs. Automatically, the students are already tracked, and breaking out of those is very difficult. Once they get here, the student really has to push and the parent has to push, and they have to go to the counselor's and do a lot of things that they shouldn't have to just to try to get themselves into an honors program.

High school teacher Emily Saldana also challenges the ways that students' futures are predetermined by track placement. She believes that middle school teachers have too much control over the life chances of students. They select which students are placed in integrated or non-college-preparatory courses and which gain access to the highest-ranking courses at Grant High School: enrollment in the International Baccalaureate Program (IB):

> When a kid comes in from junior high, that is the most significant turning point if that kid is going to go to college or not. . . . I think that they are categorized early on without knowing their abilities because we don't know the students. We just go off of what the junior high teachers tell us. . . . That is bad because you are now tracking a student saying, "You are now going to be in an integrated class" [a non-college-preparatory course]. It's

> going to be very hard for you to go from an integrated course to an AP course. . . . If you are AP/IB, you are what we call a pre-IB student; you are going to be put into the best classes with the best teachers.

With the stakes of track placement so high—access to privileged resources and preparation for college—a couple of teachers argue for lessening or eliminating not only the role of teachers as gate-keepers in determining track placement but also the overreliance on tests. Ana Camacho challenges the use of standardized tests, specifically California's SAT 9, for track placement on at least two principles:

> We shouldn't have to give them a test based on the SAT 9 to decide [track placement]. Rather, just allow the student to [enroll in advanced classes]. If they can do the work, then have them there. If their writing is bad and needs improvement, then help them improve. That's what the role of the teacher is. The SAT 9 doesn't represent students, especially Latino and African American students. It doesn't do them justice, and so automatically they don't get into those classes. We need to give students the benefit of the doubt and have them there and then work with them if they're willing to do the work.

Ana argues that teachers are responsible for enabling all students to do well in advanced classes. She believes that teachers should do more to develop students' skills so that struggling students can receive the benefits of a challenging education that widens their life options. In addition, Ana references the extensive literature documenting how standardized tests are biased against working-class, Latina/o, and African Americans students and in favor of middle-class, English-speaking white students whose backgrounds, experiences, and cultural references tend to reflect those designing the tests (see Oakes, 1985). In particular, for the multiple-choice and norm-referenced SAT 9, California students are compared to a national group of students who may be very different from the Latina/o and African American students in Ana's classes. Overall, rather than basing courses and life trajectories on test performance, Ana favors providing open access to honors courses, encouraging hard work, and emphasizing improvement.

Emily Saldana supports Ana's critique of tests as a determining factor in track placement:

> To get into any honors class, you need to be tested. The thing that was very troubling was, in English, you are tested once in the ninth grade. You are in ninth-grade English honors. Therefore, you go into tenth-grade English honors, eleventh grade. You are tested just once. What if you had a bad day? What if it just wasn't a test for you? What if you didn't make tenth-grade English and you would like to get into tenth-grade honors? How do you get in? There aren't too many spots because all of the spots are filled by the other kids.

Not only may students be tracked out of more rigorous courses early in their high school careers because of poor performance on standardized tests, but they may also be prevented from moving into honors courses after ninth grade. That is, the number of classroom slots in honors and advanced placement courses may be too filled with continuing students to accommodate any more students, or nonhonors courses may have deprived students of the equivalent knowledge and skills provided to their classmates. For example, in her extensive study of twenty-five high schools, Oakes (1985) found that students in the high-track courses were exposed to "high-status" knowledge necessary for college (p. 76). These courses encouraged students to think critically, solve problems, evaluate information, and draw conclusions. In comparison, rote memorization, comprehension, respect, and discipline were expected of the students in the lower track courses. Given such different expectations, it is easy to imagine how the knowledge gaps between nonhonors and honors students would increase with each passing year in school, impeding students' abilities to excel in more challenging courses.

Students typically know whether they are in the honors courses. Thus, not only may students realize how they are labeled "talented and gifted," "honors," "regular," or "remedial," but to the extent that school officials and peers respond to students differently and give them access to unequal knowledge, course placement may become self-fulfilling (Oakes, 1985). Students placed in the honors courses may be treated as more intelligent, influencing how they see themselves and students not enrolled in honors courses. The teachers criticize how such unequal course placement can then influence students' levels of motivation. While some negatively labeled students may be motivated to prove people wrong, this is certainly not the case for all. High school teacher Ana Camacho explains what she has observed: "If they are not honors students or AP students, they seem to not have as much of the spotlight on them. So just for that reason, they don't try as hard. They figure, 'I'm never going to be an honor student, so why even try hard.'"

At her middle school, teacher Vivian Sosa is trying to counterbalance the detrimental impacts of tracking and labeling for the students who are not considered the academic elite or the preacademy students: "I feel like my students just perceive that as, 'Oh, then I'm dumb because I'm not in that class.' That bothers me, so I tell them, 'There's no difference here. You're in my class, and I'm going to teach this class like an honors class. So expect it.'"

Contesting Racial/Ethnic Isolation, Profiling, and Their Ramifications

By high school, most of the current teachers were recommended for and placed in the top classes. However, several remember the isolation that resulted from the separation of students. For Ilene Gómez, this negative experience intensified her shyness at school:

> I was recommended for the gifted program in the eighth grade from a teacher in math. . . . That meant that all students who were in this program for all four years, unless you left it on your own, were segregated. . . . We were very academically oriented, so everything we took was together, and it was the same group that got into the twelfth grade together. . . . I was the only Latina . . . in the program, they were all Anglo. So I was not comfortable all the time. I was very shy, extremely shy.

Similarly, Marie Marquez recalls that curriculum tracking at her school fostered student cliques that were often based on race/ethnicity:

> They put me in honors classes. It was kind of difficult because at that time, there weren't a lot of Latinos in those honors classes; there were a few of us, but it was mostly white or Asian. . . . It was a little intimidating because I really didn't know some of those kids. They all were tracked into the same classes, so they all knew each other. It was hard to get involved with some of those people; they weren't very friendly, and they had their own little cliques.

For Ilene and Marie, relating to their classmates was difficult because not only were they admitted into the top classes late in their schooling when peer groups had already been established, but they were in classes with very few Latinas/os or even none at all. Such skewing where racial/ethnic groups are not equally distributed throughout the curriculum tracks is similar to what the Grant High School seniors described in 2000. Several of their teachers at Grant also criticize such racial/ethnic disparity, especially in the school's renowned IB program.

Established in the 1960s for students in international schools, the IB program has expanded in high schools throughout the United States. The four aims of the program are (1) to provide internationally qualified courses to students seeking acceptance into higher education, (2) enhance international understanding, (3) educate the whole person, and (4) develop critical thinking skills (International Baccalaureate Organization, 2002). These are wonderful goals that could form the basis of any education, but this type of education is not provided to all students.

The IB program is an honors college preparatory program, and in the high school materials where several of these teachers work, it is described as "offering an academic challenge to bright, motivated students." By focusing on what Latina/o teachers have to say about this program, we better understand the differential institutional factors influencing students' experiences in schools. In particular, teachers reveal how at their school, this program magnifies and reinforces racial/ethnic stereotypes and inequalities. Key to their critique is what twenty-six-year-old high school teacher Manuel Cadena calls "academic profiling." He describes this as the tendency for "teachers and counselors to place an Asian student into biology or a college prep class over a Latino student."

This academic profiling that assumes that Asian American students should be placed in more rigorous classes than Latinas/os is part of a long history of unfounded beliefs about race/ethnicity, diligence, and academic ability. Too many school officials have accepted dominant constructions and tracked students by such biased criteria as race/ethnicity, language, appearance, and behavior (see Oakes, 1985; Valenzuela, 1999; Lopez, 2003; Conchas, 2006). For example, teachers and counselors may accept inaccurate assumptions that African American and Latina/o families do not value education or that students are lazy. Media images maintain and reproduce these constructions of youth by depicting African

American and Latino males as criminal and hypermasculine individuals who are uninterested in education and more engaged in gangs, drugs, sports, or music. Though depicted less often, African American and Latina females are seen as hypersexual and teen mothers (Lopez, 2003). As a result, school officials may expect little of African American and Latina/o students and place them in less challenging courses.

In contrast to these images, school officials are often bombarded with messages casting Asian American students as the model minority. Dominant images construct Asian American students as intellectually gifted or culturally predisposed to working hard. On the surface, these stereotypes may positively influence school officials' perceptions of Asian Americans and lead to the disproportionate placement of Asian American students into high track classes. However, along with lumping all Asian Americans together without regard for within-group heterogeneity, the model minority myth pits Asian Americans against African Americans and Latinas/os, deflects attention away from structural inequalities, and creates "an imagined yardstick" that is impossible for many Asian Americans to achieve (Kibria, 2002, p. 136). An assumption underlying this myth is that we live in meritocracy and that African Americans and Latinas/os are to blame for their positions in society. Theories of biological and cultural deficiencies persist.

While dominant conceptions of African American, Latina/o, and Asian American students are often unidimensional, this is not typically the case for white students. The overall predominance of whites in power and in the media translates into more complex and heterogeneous images of whites. Furthermore, although there are stereotyped constructions of working-class whites and white females, these images are typically not as menacing as the images and stereotypes of African Americans and Latinas/os. White teachers, who are the majority of educators, may also possess higher expectations of white students and more sympathetic understandings of white families.

Overall, studies find that these competing images of African American, Latina/o, Asian American, and white students parallel teachers' expectations and students' perceptions of their peers (Kao, 2000; Lopez, 2003; Conchas, 2006). Thus, the racial/ethnic isolation, segregation, and profiling that the teachers describe can be attributed at least in part to the ways that racialized constructions are self-fulfilling and reproduced through the system of curriculum tracking.

To the extent that track placement is correlated with race/ethnicity, student segregation into different tracks can result in entire groups of students who feel that they do not belong in the school. High school teacher Manuel Cadena describes how Latinas/os are often the "forgotten" students and that this may have a negative impact on their levels of motivation:

> It's an academically divided school. It's a school that excels in academics, but it's a school that's only one-sided. The Asian population excels, and there's nothing wrong with that. They should excel. They're supposed to. Everyone should excel, but it's very one-sided, and I think that Latino students are unfortunately forgotten about. . . . Nobody wants to teach the classes where it's mostly Latino students, because unfortunately they're not as motivated.

According to Manuel, this feeling of being forgotten has also translated into limited school involvement and governance by Latina/o students: "I consider this an Asian school. Our student government is all Asian except for one senior senator, I think. . . . A lot of the Asians are involved in the most noticeable groups on campus. I don't think that the Latino students feel like this is their school because I don't think that they're recognized enough." Although this school is about evenly divided between Latina/o and Asian American students, Latinas/os are underrepresented in the most academically challenging classes and in student leadership positions.

The ramifications of such racial/ethnic divides as perpetuated by curriculum tracking and racialized constructions extend beyond feelings of belonging and include cross-racial/ethnic resentment and conflict (Valenzuela, 1999; Ochoa, 2004a). Rather than fault their schools or the system of tracking, some Latina/o students scapegoat Asian Americans and express resentment toward the attention and awards that they receive. High school teachers Joan Young and school counselor Marcos Padilla have observed this resentment:

> Overall, the Asian kids are still doing much better than the Latino and the white kids, and I think there is a jealousy there. When it comes at the end of the year, when they announce all these scholarships, I hear these comments afterward. "Gee, it's not fair. They got all these scholarships" [Joan Young].

> The kids do see a difference between the groups. They do see that, and comments are made. In fact, when we had the senior assembly, several kids said, "I don't want to go to that stupid thing. All we're going to see are Asians getting awards" [Marcos Padilla].

Such resentment does nothing to address the root causes of curriculum tracking and dominant ideologies about various racial/ethnic groups. Instead, it pits groups against each other, and it allows tracking and prevailing perceptions to persist. How students have different access to school resources remains unnamed, and some teachers may come to accept that Asian American students are just better students and that Latina/o students do not want to work hard. Such teachers may then treat students differently, and the self-fulfilling cycle, stereotypes, and inequality continue.

In extreme cases, student segregation and resentment from curriculum tracking at Grant High School have resulted in fights among Asian American and Latina/o students. Ana Camacho describes: "They don't get to interact with students from different races, and that kind of falls throughout. In the social level, they're separated that way. I think the only place where they get to interact a little, maybe sports and PE [physical education], some of the extracurricular activities. That's a very big problem because I think we've had a number of fights that have dealt with racial tension." Manuel Cadena has also observed this tension: "We have a small problem right now where a group of students, some Asian and some Latino, keep fighting. So they bump heads a little bit. But other than that, the kids get along. They know each other. They'll say 'Hi.' But they don't hang out with each other that much because they're not in the same classes."

Several Grant High School teachers explain how this separation between students in tracks inhibits students from experiencing one of the unique aspects of their school: the large and diverse Latina/o and Asian American student populations. Ana Camacho explains:

> I've also heard a lot of discouraging comments from teachers saying that we place so much emphasis on IB classes and students are losing out on interacting with other students from different cultures. The IB, AP, and honors consist mainly of Asian students, and if they're not involved in extracurricular activities, that interaction with other groups is not there. We place a lot of value on academics, which is great, but I think there also has to be more value on that social level and having students know each other, especially if they're different races and cultures.

As long as curriculum tracking and an unequal distribution of students in tracks by race/ethnicity, class, or other salient factors persist, peer groups are going to tend toward homogeneity, and students are going to limit their social capital by interacting with people who are like them. All groups lose out by being segregated from their peers who bring different experiences and perspectives that can enhance social skills and peer networks (Valenzuela, 1999). However, the predominance of Latina/o and African American students in less challenging and non-college-preparatory courses has significant societal ramifications for continual inequality. Even the IB Program—with its commendable goals of enhancing international understanding, educating the whole person, and developing critical thinking—may be critiqued because it too may foster racial/ethnic and class segregation and reproduce inequality by providing only some students with such a valued education.

Denouncing Disparities in Resources

What is perhaps most pernicious about curriculum tracking is that different students, classes, and schools are provided with unequal resources. As tracking expert and professor of education Jeannie Oakes (1985) explains, "Those children who seem to have the least of everything in the rest of their lives most often get less at school as well" (p. 4). Too many times at Grant High School, Ana Camacho has observed how students in the higher tracks receive more college information and attention:

> A very big problem that I have is with the counselors. The counselors go in and visit the honors classes and the AP classes and give them more information about college than they do the regular classes and the remedial classes. I don't think I've ever seen a counselor come in and talk to my kids who are in remedial classes. It's very sad because when I ask my students, a lot of them raise their hands; they want to go to college. They just don't know how to get there; they are struggling. If there were more services for them—tutoring, maybe a home period where they can get some homework done.

Students who could benefit from more assistance and resources become what high school teacher Manuel Cadena labels the "forgotten" ones, whom, says high school senior Sam, teachers have "given up on."

Grant High School teachers Emily Saldana and Joan Young are also critical of how school resources and teacher energies are unequally distributed, and the IB program is the target of much of their criticism:

> There is a lot of opposition to IB because of the amount of money that goes into it, and what are the results for the few students who are already high achievers? We keep saying, "What are we going to do with the bottom kids? Why don't we spend the money for the kids on the bottom?" [Emily Saldana].

> I bet you at least a million dollars has been spent already on this IB program, and this year, at the graduation, seven people graduated. So for seven people, they're spending all this money; now you tell me, Is that equitable? I mean how about the 50 percent of the campus who are sitting there, not learning anything and they're closing the auto shop. There's no money for that, for these lower-economic kids, right? But for the few elite at the top, they are spending these hundreds of thousands of dollars on a yearly basis [Joan Young].

Emily and Joan believe that the students enrolled in the IB program are already on the way to top universities. They are concerned with the students who are experiencing cuts in vocational courses at the same time that more money is being spent on the academic elite at their school. Emily Saldana continues:

> So much time is invested for just seven kids. That's not allowing all kids to be part of it. . . . Guess what? Those seven kids, they are going to make it to Stanford.

They're going to make it to Harvard anyway, even without the IB program. . . . We are so high academically that we are losing the bottom half of the kids. We have now lost wood shop [and] . . . we now do not teach home economics or auto shop. We have no technical things for kids who are not academically bound. . . . It's like we're doing a disservice to kids by not offering classes like that, and the high demand of having AP and honors classes is taking away from the kids at the bottom.

Not only are a select number of students at this school privy to the wealth of academic resources and challenges provided to the IB students, but courses that could provide interested students with vocational training are being slashed. Emily Saldana and Joan Young condemn such disparity in funding and programs, and they link this discrepancy to socioeconomic class. In their estimation, the IB students receive educational opportunities at the expense of more working class students. Perhaps if public schools had more resources to provide stellar educational opportunities to all students, regardless of race/ethnicity or socioeconomic background, teachers such as Emily and Joan would be less skeptical of programs that serve only an elite group of students.

Resource disparities by race/ethnicity and socioeconomic position are also apparent between schools within the same school district, and middle school teacher Marie Marquez denounces these injustices too:

When I look at the high school where a lot of our students will go, I am amazed and shocked that they don't have honors and AP classes for some of these kids. Why is that? That's totally unfair. Some of the kids are not going to the local high school. They say, "I'm going to another one in the district because the classes are better for college." And I'm like, "Are you kidding me?" This is a school district that has to be equal all the way through. Why is it that the other high school has these AP, honors

classes, college-prep classes, and our high school doesn't?
There are kids who need to be in those classes there too.

Marie's school district has an unequal distribution of honors
and advanced placement courses among the high schools. The high
schools, including Grant High School, in the middle- and upper-
middle-class communities offer more honors courses than the primarily working-class and Latina/o high school that serves Marie's
students. According to education scholar Gary Orfield (1996), such
disparities are a national phenomenon: "Not only do white and
wealthy schools offer more high-ability classes—two to three times as
many AP courses per student as low-income, predominantly minority
schools—but a larger share of the students take such classes" (p. 68).

Although most of the teachers emphasized the salience of race/
ethnicity in curriculum tracking, class disparities underlie many
of their discussions. The significance of class in track placement
is well documented (see Oakes, 1985; Gonzalez, 1990). Poor and
working-class students are often placed in tracks where they are
prepared for vocations. In comparison, middle- and upper-class
students are typically provided access to courses that require the
higher-level thinking and decision making necessary for managerial
and professional careers (Oakes, 1985; Gonzalez, 1990). As Marie
observes, schools serving middle- and upper-class students tend to
offer more honors courses than poor and working-class schools,
which also tend to be predominantly Latina/o and black (Ochoa,
2004a). Such a class-based tracking system reproduces capitalism
by ensuring future generations of workers and professionals, divid-
ing and fostering tensions between different groups of students, and
restricting opportunities for class mobility.

Sharing Their Lessons for All

The teachers' critiques of curriculum tracking suggest the importance of detracking or untracking schools by making classrooms

heterogeneous. The perpetuation of curriculum tracking where the students in the highest tracks receive the most and other students are ignored or dismissed is a civil rights issue. All students should have access to challenging curriculum that prepares them for fulfilling lives with multiple opportunities.

One of the changes that must be made is a rethinking and restructuring of which students receive most of the schools' resources, energy, and attention. Not only should all students have access to school resources, but schools should devote more of their attention and resources to students who are struggling. In our current system, many of the same students receive the most from their schools: the challenging classes, school officials' positive attention, and academic awards, regardless of how hard they have to work. Instead, Romo and Falbo (1996) recommend rewarding students not just for being the most able but also for working hard. Thus, they advocate that "the highest rewards should be given to students who work the hardest" (p. 68). As insinuated by the high school seniors who began this chapter, this revised rewards system has the potential to inspire, motivate, and foster feelings of belonging and hope for all students.

Class-size reduction should accompany the abolition of tracking. Overcrowded classrooms with thirty to forty students make connecting with students and providing them with individual attention very difficult. To improve student learning, the factory model of education that focuses on efficiency and educating students in large classrooms must be reconsidered.

A shifting of exclusionary ideologies and stereotypes must also occur. The biological and cultural deficiency perspectives that are used to justify preparing students for unequal opportunities by race/ethnicity, class position, and other factors need to be buried. These ideologies pit racial/ethnic and class groups against each other and camouflage the structural and institutional inequalities that make categories and differences by race/ethnicity, class, gender, and other divisions seem normal and natural. Finally, to the

(Wood, 2004). Thus, as well as diverting public funds away from schools in need, these sanctions fuel the movement for school vouchers, school choice, and charter schools (Hursh, 2005), all policies long endorsed by the conservative agenda. These educational policies under NCLB are part of a larger movement that emerged in the 1980s during the Reagan-Bush era and should be seen as a result of the neoliberal agenda to control the curriculum, evaluate teachers, and ultimately privatize public education.

An underlying assumption of NCLB is that standardized tests are neutral, fair, and accurate measurements of student and teacher ability. When analyzing test results, little consideration is given for how external factors, such as the construction of the tests, school and societal inequalities, and students' diverse backgrounds, skills, and experiences, influence test performance (see De León and Holman, 2002).

Initially NCLB had wide bipartisan support. However, over the past few years, school officials, parents, and legislators have become increasingly critical of its impacts on public schooling (Wood, 2004). Given this growing criticism, it is not surprising that nearly all of the teachers featured in this book challenge the provisions of NCLB. Those who have the least to say about NCLB are the high school teachers whose curriculum and pedagogy has been less directly impacted by it. By listening especially to the K–8 teachers, we see firsthand how a group of teachers is responding to the growing emphasis on testing and how they believe that NCLB is actually leaving many Latinas/os behind.

Students Are Not Examination Machines

A first-grade teacher of primarily working-class Latina/o students, Miguel Elias finds many faults with NCLB:

> Now we have No Child Left Behind. It's so much paperwork, and I feel like: "Wow, do they want us to fall more behind?" I could understand pushing students, but so

many tests. It's like we're testing every other week. In the first and second grade, there is so much testing. I mean kindergarten is not kindergarten; it's more like first grade. First is more like second. Everything is pushed quicker. We're writing paragraphs so early. Everything comes down to that one test score. Like, "Well, you're not meeting these standards, so you're not showing any growth, so you're failing at this point."

In particular, Miguel is concerned that the policies of NCLB disregard how language and socioeconomic class position influence test performance. All students are given the same test and evaluated similarly, but not all students have equal experiences or resources:

The language experiences, the trips, they don't happen in all of the Latino families. Students can't relate to, "Yeah, I went to Catalina." Or, "Yeah, we went for a weekend in San Diego," or, "My family in San Francisco." Those are all experiences that strengthen children and make them feel more successful or more confident. I don't think that the way NCLB is set up that we're going to have more successes. It seems like you're suppressing students more. Now that Latinos are starting to improve, they're like, "Okay, well, guess what, we're going to push you down a little bit more. Let's see if you can make it through this one." To me it seems unfair, because I don't think Latino students have all the language experiences, all the economic advantages that other students have. NCLB doesn't help the immigrant. It puts a barrier, a ceiling.

Miguel wonders:

Where are they going with this, testing every month? Now we get observed here three times a year. Are they going to do it weekly? That could cause stress, for the students and the teachers. I don't see where this is going. It seems like it's just breaking everyone down in America and especially the immigrants. In the end, those are the ones who, "Well, sorry. You didn't have those nighttime stories. You didn't have all those rich learning opportunities. Your uncles or aunts didn't expose you to the correct type of cultural experiences."

While working-class Latina/o and immigrant students enter school with important familial and cultural resources, such as speaking another language and working collaboratively, this is typically not the type of cultural capital that is valued in U.S. schools. As Miguel highlights, students who have access to middle- and upper-class experiences are more likely to perform well on standardized tests because those constructing the tests often share their cultural background and reference points. And with tests administered in English to students who have been in the United States as little as one year, English-language learners as well as all students who have been exposed to a language or dialect other than English are placed in unfair positions. Knowledge of the English language, including syntax and semantics, is critical in performing well on standardized tests (De León and Holman, 2002). As De León and Holman remind us, "For students who have been exposed to a language other than English or who speak a dialect of English, 'every test administered in English becomes, in part, a language or literacy test'" (American Educational Research Association, American Psychological Association, and National Council on Measurement in Education, cited in De León and Holman 2002, p. 187). Overall, with decades of research demonstrating the racial/ethnic, gender, class, and regional biases in standardized tests (see Gonzalez, 1990; Haney, 1993; De León and Holman, 1998), an accountability system that relies extensively on testing results in more inequality and an increasing educational gap.

Miguel Elias's final thoughts on NCLB are, "I feel overwhelmed." He is not alone in his feelings. Several other teachers used this same phrase to characterize their reactions to increased testing. Eighth-grade math teacher Vivian Sosa also feels overwhelmed and worries most about the deadening of students through constant testing:

> I don't like the pressure that is on my students. I think assessments can be positive. We definitely need to have assessments to see if the kids are understanding or learning. As a professional, I need assessments to see if I'm a decent teacher or not. But it's overwhelming for my students, and we're starting to get a generation of students that is freaked out about tests. It's every day. I feel like I'm turning these kids into machines, computating all this stuff, bubbling in the answer. And I never thought it would get to a point where it's this bad. For us, we have four district assessments, plus the state testing, plus the tests that we give them, and this is not just my class. They have them in history, science, and language arts. These kids come to my class, "Ms. Sosa, I don't want to take another test. We just took one last period." Are we really doing these kids a service? Is this just paperwork? Data are helpful, but I'm sensing that the kids are starting to become a little bit more unmotivated with school. Why would you want to come to school if it's driven by tests? We're teaching them to take tests. I want to teach kids to expand their minds, be critical thinkers, and learn life skills; that's going to help them in the long run.

As Vivian expresses, students respond emotionally to so much testing, especially when it is high-stakes testing and their performance is linked to school funding, teacher rewards, and student opportunities. Such pressure is not conducive to fostering school enjoyment, and Vivian believes that it is eating away at student motivation. She worries that rather than developing critical thinkers, she is helping to create a generation of robots who are programmed to fill in predetermined answers.

Compounding Vivian's critiques of NCLB are the competing messages that she is receiving about the abilities of students. On the one hand, she has to prepare students for generic, one-size-fits-all state expectations that require all students to be enrolled in algebra in eighth grade. However, despite these high state expectations, she finds that school district officials have limited confidence in the largely working-class and Latina/o students at her school. These officials seem more concerned about enforcing state and federal policies than about educating students:

> The vision for this year is that these kids pass algebra I. This is the first year that the kids have to take algebra I. It's mandatory by the state. The expectation level for my students is definitely getting higher, and their knowledge and their skill level are not very high. So we have to bring them up to the bar, and it's really hard. For me, the frustration lies in comments I'm getting from the district. I don't feel that their intention for eighth-grade algebra is for these kids to pass. I hear, "If they don't pass, they can have next year. And if they still don't pass, they have the following year. At least they have five years to pass, so they can graduate from high school." I feel that the expectation level is minimal, and that frustrates me.

It is aggravating that some educational bureaucrats emphasize enrolling in algebra in eighth grade just to meet state requirements, not because of a concern for student achievement. It is not surprising that students who are required to reenroll in algebra I year after year because they have not passed it may eventually give up on school altogether. In fact, with the increased pressure on test performance, schools are losing students both figuratively and literally through boredom, grade retention, and dropping out (see McSpadden McNeil, 2005).

All students are hurt by federal and state mandates and the growing emphasis on testing, but the impacts on Latina/o students, in particular English-language learners and working-class students, are especially significant. Not only are students leaving school early, but they are being pushed out by school officials. In her analysis of Texas schools, education professor McSpadden McNeil (2005) reports, "The accountability system itself is creating incentives for principals to 'lose' low-performing students, more frequently their Latino, African American, Limited English Proficient, and immigrant students, to make sure that the *school's* scores are high" (p. 74). In McSpadden McNeil's analysis, this pushing out of Latina/o and African American students in Texas often occurred before the tenth-grade test.

Fortunately, there are teachers such as Vivian who find the strength to work against such appalling practices and district officials' low expectations by structuring their courses along students' interests:

> My class is an algebra I class, and I will teach my class as an algebra I class. And whoever passes with an A or B will have passed an algebra I class. I truly believe in these kids. And I told the kids the first day of school, "There are a lot of people who are not for you. But I'm for you. And my perception is this is meant for you to fail. You can do this. Don't prove them right. I believe in you."

However, even for inspired teachers such as Vivian Sosa, the increased emphasis on testing and meeting state and federal standards is also felt in course curriculum.

No More Teaching to the Test

At a time when Latinas/os are beginning to achieve some educational success, Miguel Elias believes that the system of testing is becoming a hurdle, and he sees the price that testing is having on young students and on course curriculum:

> The kids are getting stressed, and we're getting stressed. There're days in the week where you just have to stop and say, "This is not part of the curriculum, but we need this music time right now, or we need to go outside and do PE," because I don't see those activities emphasized anymore and that's a problem too. We need more PE time. We need time to incorporate music. I try to do it through the program, but sometimes you have to dream up things so they'll say, "Okay, you're going by the standards. Yes, you're doing PE, but you're also coordinating math into it or language arts into it." You always have to tie it to something. Sometimes I think that the kids need to have those parameters, but they need to go outside for a while because they're kids. Right now, I feel bad for these kids. So many tests all the time; it breaks them down. They get frustrated bubbling in answers.

During tests, Miguel observes students' frustration, and he feels badly when they ask him, "Teacher, what does this mean?" Sometimes it's the phrasing of the sentence. You're like, "Ugh. If they had phrased it like this, we could have modeled that more. But then, yikes—is that teaching for the test?"

High school teacher Manuel Cadena concurs with Miguel and fears that he is teaching to a test. He also sees how these tests are wasting two to three weeks of school:

> You also worry about all these new state regulations. You got your SAT 9 tests. Are they going to hold you

accountable to that? Now, it's almost like you're not teaching to teach and nurture a student's intrinsic learning, but you're almost teaching to a test, and this testing ends up taking up to two to three weeks of the school year, and then you also worry about what's going to happen to some of these kids. It could be very overbearing if you let it, but you just have to take the punches as they come.

Researchers have also documented the faults that Miguel and Manuel describe (see Meier and Wood, 2004; Valenzuela, 2005). Their research findings suggest that the pressures to teach to the test may narrow the course curriculum to the extent that "non-tested areas (art, music, social studies) and 'frills' (field trips, naps, even recess) are eliminated" from the school day (Wood, 2004, p. xii).

Teachers' approaches to teaching may also shift. Growing numbers of teachers are required to follow scripted curriculum that is adopted by school districts and sold by textbook companies that are making huge profits. Such canned curriculum provides little space for teachers or students to shape the direction and content of learning. In extreme cases, teachers' lessons are highly monitored by school principals, who expect to walk into any classroom and know that all of the other teachers in the same grade are following the same lesson. Maybe Vivian Sosa's concern that NCLB is turning students into machines is so strong because she sees that teachers' curriculum and pedagogy are also so regimented and controlled by others.

Students' cultures, experiences, perspectives, and interests are often lost within such top-down constructions of curriculum. In such an environment, there may be limited time to incorporate student voices, family histories, and community experiences. Teachers may be pressured to employ exercises that are more conducive to multiple-choice tests such as test practice, memorization, and drills. Combined, the mandated inflexible curriculum and pedagogy often bores students and inhibits their critical thinking skills and engagement with school. The focus on the impersonal or technical aspects of test performance over "authentic caring" where students' backgrounds are affirmed is a form of "subtractive schooling" that divests students from what they know and experience (Valenzuela, 1999). An effect of such subtractive schooling can push some students further away from school.

Not all schools, classrooms, teachers, and students are equally affected by the policies of NCLB and high-stakes testing. These negative impacts are greatest for students in non-college-preparatory courses and in working-class areas with large percentages of English-language learners because students in these schools tend to perform less well on English-only standardized tests. Therefore, under NCLB, teachers in these schools are pressured to improve their test scores for fear of losing money and closing schools. However, schools in wealthier communities and those serving more privileged students typically have the luxury of continuing with business as usual, making few curricular or pedagogical changes (Robles, 2002). Since Latina/o students are overrepresented in non-college-preparatory courses and poorly funded schools, their curriculum and classrooms are often the first targeted for regressive change. Thus, with each passing year in school, the educational gap for students by race/ethnicity, community, and class position may actually grow (McSpadden McNeil, 2005).

One poignant example of how a testing-centered education is fostering disparity is Texas, whose educational policy was used to shape the national policy of NCLB. In Texas, student performance on state tests has increased. However, the number of students who complete high school has declined, and scores on the SAT remain near the bottom of the nation (McSpadden McNeil, 2005). Thus, with increased emphasis on tests, fewer students are remaining in school, leading to accusations that some students are actually being pushed out of high schools to provide the illusion that schools are improving scores on standardized tests. In reality, schools have lower rates of high school completion (see McSpadden McNeil, 2005). Also in Texas, studies suggest that students from poor schools where tests are emphasized seem to be improving their test scores. However, preparing K–12 students for tests does not translate into college success, and many of these students are placed in remedial courses during their first year in college because their high schools failed to prepare them adequately (Robles, 2002).

The Toll of Testing on Teachers

Teachers see that NCLB is hindering students; they also worry about the effects that it is having on them. Teachers such as Cristina Martinez, who sacrificed to receive her master's degree and become an educator, feel more pressure and less autonomy in the classroom. For Cristina, the mandates of NCLB are taking the joy out of learning, and she is now questioning whether she should stay in the profession:

> I've been here three years, and there've been plenty of days, even this year, where I say, "I don't know if I'm going to teach next year." The reason is that my kids come to me ill equipped. They don't get to me at sixth-grade level. But I am to give them sixth-grade level material, test them at sixth-grade level, have them succeed at sixth-grade level, and then earn these points for No Child Left Behind, plus meet an overwhelming amount of information. When we're talking about every student deserves an equal education, yes, my kids here should get the same information that's being taught over there, regardless of the color of their skin or how much money their parents make. Yes, that's true; that's what my students deserve, but my students don't deserve to be stressed out, tested nonstop. They feel really stressed out. As a teacher, you feel stressed out. It's not a fun

environment. Learning should be safe—strenuous, but fun. Now kids are doing back-flips like, "Where am I today?"

Cristina is not alone; Marie Marquez also has days when she questions whether she will continue teaching. She faults the school district and other bureaucrats for making her job "really frustrating":

> This school district is all about business. They don't really do anything to help us. They give us these expectations and give all kinds of tests to these kids. We feel overwhelmed; how are we supposed to be teaching the kids if this is what we have to do? It feels like they don't really value us as teachers and just say, "Here, this is your job, and you're going to work until it's over." So by the end of the year, a lot of us are burned out. Last year was a horrible year for me. I was deciding whether to come back. And this year, it's not as bad, but it's pretty bad.

The emphasis on testing is leading some to claim that we live not in a democracy or a meritocracy but instead in a testocracy where individual worth is increasingly measured by performance on tests. We are educating students to perform on tests, and the aspects that inspired these teachers to join the profession—to be role models, for the love of learning, with a passion for teaching—are being undermined and pushed to the side.

Miguel Elias says this about these detrimental impacts: "No Child Left Behind restricts us, and I don't see it as a breakthrough. I don't think any teacher would see it as, 'Wow! Yeah, that's fantastic!' Teachers need to take care of the system instead of the government. We need more input. They need to let us help out in that aspect because it can't be from the top down, from the governor's office, from President Bush, or whoever's in office."

Marie agrees with Miguel. She believes:

Politicians have gotten involved with schooling, and they don't know what they're talking about. It's all about the money to them—how much money they could get from the school, and how much money they could earn in their high jobs. They're not thinking about the kids. They're so detached. That's what I hate. And teachers are trying, but it's very difficult. I know there's a lot of money out there, but is it getting spent the way it should? It's really hard to help these kids achieve sometimes because of all these people saying, "You have got to do this, you have got to do that."

It's a trickle-down theory. You have these laws that are being passed, like No Child Left Behind. Yet you have no federal money to help with this. And it's absolutely ridiculous. And then it comes to the state, and the state has these requirements. And you're thinking, "Do these people know the students who are coming to our schools? Have they ever stepped foot in a classroom? Do they know the makeup of our school? Do they realize that some of the kids have very little education and then are coming here and are expected to be at the level? Are they serious?" Then you get the superintendents who don't set foot on our campuses and don't know what we're about, yet they are getting raises. And last year, our principal was so into technology he was gone half the time at these meetings, and some kids remarked that they didn't know who the principal was, or they thought one of our vice principals was principal.

In this situation of No Child Left Behind, the situation I work in, it's impossible; it's really impossible. There're rumors out there, and I don't know whether they're true about testing. If your students don't perform well, it's all going to come back to you. And it's just difficult, because I'm thinking, "Am I going to have a job?" Well, I do the best I can for these kids. I'm not a perfect teacher. I'm hoping one day I'll be one of those really good teachers like some of the teachers I work with. I think that I do my best to try to help these students. But there's so much; it's so demanding. They're putting a lot on us. And I know they put a lot on the higher-ups, but by the end of the year, I feel this weight on my shoulders. It's like, "Did I help them? Did they learn anything?"

Miguel and Marie are among the teachers who forcefully indict the bureaucratic structure of schools. They perceive education as a business where teachers are expected to implement policies and practices that are dictated by principals, superintendents, and policymakers who perhaps have never "stepped in a classroom." These same people expect teachers to educate students in overcrowded classrooms and to "miraculously" complete more school-, district-, state-, and federal-level student assessments in addition to their already extensive workloads. No wonder many of the teachers feel overwhelmed and devalued.

Among the top-down policies that are wearing down teachers is the narrow definition of "highly qualified" teachers detailed under NCLB. One of the provisions of NCLB is that "highly qualified" teachers are required to have majored in the subject that they are teaching or they must complete competency tests and be fully credentialed or working toward certification. However, as Miguel argues, these requirements, as important as they are, say little about the quality of teachers and their commitment to students:

Even for the new teachers who are coming in, all the tests that they have to go through. I feel bad for all of the tests that I had to take, but there are even more tests for the new teachers. I don't know if that's really helping us.

Teaching is a special field, and at the core of it is, Do you have the heart for teaching? Do you enjoy working with the students? If you do, then you have a structure for learning, and the children will pick up on it. I don't see that so much testing is necessary for the kids or for the teachers.

For Miguel, being an effective teacher extends beyond credential or performance on a test. It means loving to learn and caring for students or "hav[ing] the heart for teaching." However, these critical aspects of teaching are lost within the federal designation of "highly qualified" teachers.

Like Miguel, eighth-grade math teacher Vivian Sosa also disagrees with the measurements used to determine teacher quality. Additional testing requirements are keeping her from teaching and accomplishing her educational goals:

Sometimes the federal legislation creates these amazing hoops that I need to jump through just to prove that I am qualified enough. Those are the things that frustrate me because I just want to teach. I went through the credential program, and now, with the pressures of No Child Left Behind, I need to go back and take another test. I was an undergraduate with a liberal studies degree. Why do I have to go back and take another subject test to prove it? At the time, that was enough. I took classes. To me, that's more important—taking classes and getting that done—than studying for a test. It's stressful for me. I want to finish my master's, but having to go back and study for yet another test, that's more time. I'm not opposed to learning. I definitely love it. But I just don't see that I need to prove myself again.

For teachers such as Vivian, the testing focus is the antithesis of learning. Both students and teachers are expected to jump through various hoops with little regard for how they experience schooling and what they can contribute to the learning process. As with the tests required for students under NCLB, these teacher education tests emphasize test taking and rote memorization over critical thinking skills. They do not measure whether teacher candidates understand how to learn or how to teach (Au, 2004). Just as students may become deadened by testing and bubbling, teachers' creativity is also undermined. NCLB seems to be emphasizing an education in which people submissively learn to work within the system—jump through the hoops—and not to question it.

Also lost in the federal conceptualization of "highly qualified teacher" is how biases in standardized tests that inaccurately measure student ability persist in the use of standardized tests required for teacher certification. Studies suggest that the Praxis, a test commonly required for teacher certification and produced by the Educational Testing Service, favors white candidates (see Au, 2004). Since these tests are racially and class biased, they also hinder the number of first-generation, Latina/o, and African Americans candidates who may wish to become teachers. Thus, the racial/ethnic gap between students and teachers continues, and some of the benefits of a diverse teaching staff are also diminished with more testing. Wayne Au (2004), a former high school teacher and current editorial associate for *Rethinking Schools*, clearly captures the ironies of defining qualified teachers only in terms of credentials and tests: "The real folly, however, is that NCLB, with its rigid imposed definitions and mandates, is actually so focused on keeping track of 'highly qualified' teachers' credentials that it has very little to do with keeping track of quality teaching" (p. 13).

Sharing Their Lessons for All

Together, the teachers' narrative reveal the many ways that the No Child Left Behind Act is actually leaving some children and teachers behind. This legislation is fostering testing as big business.

Tests are shaping curriculum, pedagogy, and the school day. They are putting undue stress on students, dictating their futures, and removing the joy of learning and teaching, especially in working-class communities of color where the pressure to improve test performance is greatest. Under the current high-stakes curriculum, teachers have reduced autonomy and little opportunity to engage students in critical thinking assignments, employ critical pedagogy, and integrate multicultural, power-aware curriculum. Likewise, students and families may experience school officials as impersonal and uncaring because teachers are limited in how they can tailor the course content. The strict standards are inflexible and impersonal. Tests are dramatically lessening the role of school officials in assessing student performance. Instead, student, teacher, and school performances are evaluated through unfair tests that are constructed by large businesses removed from classrooms, schools, and sometimes even the state where the tests are being administered.

In addition, under NCLB, college degrees, performance on standardized tests, and teaching credentials determine whether teachers are considered "highly qualified." This focus solely on technical aspects undermines the importance of recruiting and retaining teachers who demonstrate high expectations for all students, a commitment to teaching, a love of learning, and knowledge of the students' backgrounds. The growing use of standardized tests to enter and exit teacher education programs is having a negative impact on the percentage of teachers of color in the profession because of various test biases (Au, 2004; National Collaborative on Diversity in the Teaching Force, 2004).

Some individuals, such as middle school teacher Lisa Perez, are finding ways to subvert high-stakes testing and scripted teaching to include multicultural and relevant course content:

> . . . I teach the standards, but I also teach, "Okay, today is el Día de Los Muertos." I still touch on different cultures . . . Kwanza, Black History Month. . . . We have pacing guides

that we have to follow. We have to be here by a certain point, and I veer off because it's important that we cover certain aspects of our history and make students more culturally aware. That's what makes you a better person.

Challenging the pacing guide by veering off of it is one way of resisting the policies of NCLB, but individual subversion is not enough. People need to hear from school officials about how high-stakes testing and canned curriculum are negatively influencing teaching and learning. Through letter writing and dialoguing with other teachers, parents, and community members, school officials can raise the public's awareness of these damaging school practices. We all have a stake in eliminating ineffective top-down, one-size-fits-all policies.

Policy changes are needed now. However, we must proceed with caution and critical eyes. Questions of power, privilege, race/ethnicity, class, gender, and inequality must be at the forefront of any discussion of education. Without these crucial considerations, we risk designing new programs that reinforce old injustices, as was done with NCLB.

In a society that preaches liberty, equality, and justice for all and has an educational policy that promises to leave no child behind, it is a travesty how much inequality exists within and is perpetuated by our educational system. Not only are these policies damaging to students and families, but they are also stifling teachers' creativity and autonomy. There is much work to be done. Fortunately, as I describe in the next chapter, there is no shortage of recommendations for change.

9

Strategies for Effective Teaching and Learning

It is impossible to teach without the courage to love, without the courage to try a thousand times before giving in.
                                                              Freire (1998)

This chapter draws on the collective knowledge of the Latina/o teachers, college students, high school students, and various community activists whom I have interviewed, taught, and observed. Together, their ideas illustrate the power of our wisdom and the importance of listening to teachers, students, and community members. They also provide multiple recommendations for how teachers, students, families, communities, and students might collaborate to improve schools along a vision of love, justice, and humanity over competition and inequality. There is too much at stake not to listen and learn from these many lessons.

When asked to describe what makes an effective teacher, elementary teacher Angelica Vasquez confidently exclaims, "Basically, very effective teachers give the kids what they need, when they need it, and how they need it." There is no step-by-step formula that teachers must adopt to be effective. To prescribe one would be as stifling as prescribing a canned curriculum that all teachers must follow. Both disempower teachers, squelch their creativity, and hamper the learning process for students. Besides, as Angelica Vasquez says, "Kids can feel when things aren't genuine, when things aren't real. When you're forced to do something, kids don't respond to it. There's no flow to it."

Different teachers can be effective in the classroom by using various techniques. To illustrate, Angelica Vasquez compares herself with Gloria, another teacher at her school:

> There's Gloria. We taught next door to each other for a couple of years; she is a fabulous teacher, and she gets good results. I would tell her, "You give your kids filet mignon, and I give my kids hamburger helper." I have young kids [at home]. I don't have the time to spend here until 10 o'clock at night, but I gave the kids what they needed, and I made sure I talked to parents. And at the end of the year, they did okay. But we were different; I did what worked for me, and the kids felt that I was giving them [what they needed]. And she gave them what was right for her.

Like Angelica, when I asked teachers what they believe makes one effective, they tended to give general responses, such as "open to change," having "thick skin," being "committed" or "devoted." However, when they described their own teaching philosophies, their responses were much more detailed. Their intentional and self-reflective teaching philosophies broaden the conception of education and create inclusive school environments for students and parents. With the hope of fostering dialogue and reflection among all those concerned about achieving educational justice, students and I also add several recommendations to the teachers' philosophies. Students tell us not only what they need but what they want.

Expand the Curriculum

For teachers like Miguel Elias, "go[ing] outside of the curriculum" entails adopting the concept of *educación* over education. *Educación* is a broader concept than its English translation. It means focusing on the whole person—how one behaves and interacts; it also includes being respectful and well mannered (see Valdés, 1996; Valenzuela, 1999). For some of the teachers, expanding the curriculum also includes incorporating multicultural materials and perspectives that integrate students' histories and experiences.

The high school and college students whom I held discussions with in fall 2004 and April 2006 expanded on these recommendations. They believe that if we are to foster agents of change, schools must be willing to listen to students and educate them about systems of power, inequality, and privilege. I concur and believe that our current narrow focus on testing and structured curriculum is limiting the full potential of teachers, students, and communities. Although some teachers and schools already adopt a broad curriculum that includes respect and multicultural content, the following collaborative philosophies and recommendations are offered to school officials and educational policymakers who are constraining today's curriculum by making it inflexible and canned.

Foster Self-Confidence, Kindness, and Respect

In a racially/ethnically and class-stratified society such as the United States, the Latina/o teachers featured in this book are keenly aware of the stigma that Mexicans, the poor, immigrants, and Spanish-speaking people face. They know it because they have experienced the ramifications of these stigmas in their own lives or witnessed them among their family members. Based on these experiences and their family's teaching of being *bien educado*, many teachers are committed to teaching students the required subject material but also to instilling self-confidence, kindness, and respect.

Marie Marquez's reflections parallel the goal of many of the teachers:

> I hope that the students will get some self-respect, encouragement, and will in them so that they will be able to accomplish anything they want out of life.

It doesn't necessarily have to do with language arts, but I hope that they will get the encouragement so that they won't be held back by anything. I want them to be able to have good lives and to hold their heads up high and not feel like they're inferior to others. But I want them to respect others too. Because one of the things that I tell them in my classroom, "It's not just about being Mexican. Look around; there are students in this classroom whose parents are from Central America and South America. Some students are African American. Guys, you have got to respect each other and learn about each other."

In schools where competition and individual achievement so often predominate, Marie is emphasizing building self-esteem, community, and respect.

Similarly, middle school teacher Erica Burg believes that working together and building students' self-confidence is key to improving academic performance. Since she finds that many students lack self-esteem, she is constantly giving them positive feedback, reassuring them with phrases such as "I knew you could do it. I told you." She also encourages students to work as a class to review material. In this way students can share what they know with their peers and become accustomed to receiving praise and feeling proud. Learning is not an individual endeavor:

We had a quiz today, and I reviewed all of the material right before the quiz. We went through all of the questions and answers, but they didn't know that those were going to be the questions and answers for the quiz. But I was quizzing them, and they were raising their hands like crazy trying to answer. They had to put everything away and then take their quiz. The quiz had almost the same questions, and they knew them; they got so excited just because they knew them. They get excited when they can do something. So it's important to make sure that material is at their level, or I just adjust it to their level so that they can do it and feel proud of themselves for doing it.

Where Manuel Cadena teaches, Latina/o and Asian American students are often divided racially and by class position into distinct curriculum tracks. The Latina/o students tend to come from working-class families, and they are often placed into the nonhonors or non–advanced placement courses. In contrast, the Asian American students are often second-generation college-bound students from more privileged class backgrounds, and they comprise the majority of students in the elite academic courses. Given these patterns, Manuel encourages confidence in the Latina/o students and collaboration, awareness of privileges, and a sense of social responsibility among the Asian American students:

I have a pretty good understanding of what life is, with all the things that I've experienced. . . . So, what I tell my students, mostly my Latino students, is I try to give them the real picture. I don't just teach them science because that's not all that I want them to learn. If anything, I could care less if they remember a specific part of an atom. I would rather they had some common knowledge and understanding that when they leave high school there's a world out there that is different, that's not structured. . . . I try to get them to believe in themselves, have confidence, and understand that they need confidence in order to survive. The kids that are way at the top, above the clouds, I try to bring them back down to realize that there are other people whom they can help because they're better off than other people. Like in this school, I tell Asian students that most of you are wealthy and it's your responsibility as citizens to inspire individuals who are not as well-off as you because that's a good human thing to do, help those who don't have as much as you.

While one must not assume that all Latinas/os and all Asian Americans are from particular class positions, by not denying how race/ethnicity and class privileges influence school opportunities, Manuel is teaching students powerful lessons about how to recognize and attempt to address inequality.

Going beyond the curriculum, instilling self-confidence in students, and conveying that "there's a world out there that is different" is also achieved by diversifying the curriculum and making learning relevant to students' lives.

Integrate Multicultural, Power-Aware Curriculum

Middle school teacher Marie Marquez remembers that it was the teacher in her senior AP English class who "woke me up":

> She's the one where my Mexican heritage just popped out. . . . She had us read a novel by Gabriel García Márquez. Up until that point, I had never read anything about Latinos. And I was like, "Oh my God! This could have happened in La Palma, Mexico, where my parents are from." And I thought, "Well, this is cool. I like this." And then I got into literature in college, and I really enjoyed it.

Marie's response to the inclusion of Latino novelist Gabriel García Márquez in her English literature class is not surprising. Students learn best when their backgrounds are affirmed by school officials and multicultural curriculum (Ladson-Billings, 1994). A multicultural, power-aware curriculum is inclusive course content that does not center the histories, perspectives, experiences, and literatures of middle- and upper-class European American heterosexual men. It is neither assimilationist nor is it based simply on a diversity model that touts cultural differences by celebrating holidays, food, and styles of dress. Instead, it combines analyses of power, privilege, and inequality with multiple histories, perspectives, experiences, and voices. Such an approach helps students see themselves and their families in what they learn; affirms their families' histories and knowledge; encourages students to understand how all of our lives are interrelated and influenced by similar historical, political, and economic factors, though experienced differently; and allows students to envision possibilities of change (Anderson and Collins, 1995). With all of these advantages, a multicultural curriculum also reduces grade retention because students are more engaged and interested in materials that are relevant to their lives (see Nelson, 1992). Given these benefits, if all of Marie's classes were based on a framework of multiculturalism where power and inequality were centered, she would not have had to wait until her senior year to be woken up with curricula relevant to her family history.

Despite the benefits that accrue from the use of multiculturalism, course curriculum on Chicano/Latinas, derogatorily referred to by a fellow teacher at David Galvez's school as "Chicano crap," remains largely excluded from K–12 classrooms (Segura, 1993). Thus, Miguel Elias "would have appreciated" more information on the Mexican-American War—often the one time that Mexico is discussed in school—and Marie Marquez had to wait until her senior year to "read anything about Latinos." Twenty-three-year-old Geraldo Romero does not "remember having teachers who really talked about identity and about just being Latino in a predominantly Latino community." He "never had an idea of what [working class] was, growing up" (quoted in Ochoa, 2004a, p. 94). To him, it was "almost like an oxymoron" that he had to leave his working-class Latina/o community and attend an elite institution like UCLA to finally "learn about my culture and to learn about myself" (quoted in Ochoa, 2004a, p. 94).

Once in college, many of the teachers were finally able to explore their identities and study the histories of Latinas/os in the United States by enrolling in courses such as Chicana/o Studies, politics, and sociology. Access to this knowledge was empowering. Middle school teacher Lisa Perez, who described herself as "quiet" and "shy," changed in college because of her course work. She "became more empowered: It was through reading, my classes in sociology . . . that I broke free. . . . They talked about education. They talked about politics, what had happened with Cesar Chavez, all of the struggles. I was just in awe of everything that we had fought and struggled for, and it really captured my attention."

Some teachers, such as Lisa Perez, are now applying the knowledge they acquired in college to their classrooms. Elementary teacher Miguel Elias is also an ardent supporter of integrating culturally relevant material into the curriculum. He believes that

> it's a responsibility of the teachers to expose students to many experiences and to go outside the curriculum. You have to bring in extra literature and experiences from your own life, or if not from your life, from Mexican American history, Chinese American history. A teacher has to accommodate to the students. And yes, you give students the standards, you give them the curriculum, but they need to have the backbone of their identity also. This really helps to validate their experience in school and to show them that their background is important. It's part of the American culture. How do you fit into this puzzle? It's important; I don't care what race you are. Like if I went to a mostly Asian school, then I better read up on Asian history from all corners of the earth. You better have a background, and you have to expose the kids to this daily, daily, daily. I do it in my reading groups. I try to always make that connection with them. . . . You have to validate students daily.

According to Miguel, this validation of students and knowing their histories and experiences is important work that must be done:

> Just because you're a Latino doesn't mean you're going to automatically bring in all of the culture into your classroom. You have to work at it. You have to bring not only Cesar Chavez, but also Gary Soto, the children's literature. Develop your own literature. I'm already talking to my friends and saying, "We have to write books. We have to develop a curriculum that goes side by side with all the diversity that we're having in America, or in [this school district]." Students have to be able to relate to those stories, and so that's my next step, literature, so we'll see how that goes. A teacher needs to be responsible for all the kids, regardless of their background or socioeconomic or social circumstance. You just need to be there for them and accommodate yourself and empathize with everyone.

Many of the high school and college students agree with Miguel Elias. During a 2006 session I co-facilitated for one hundred high school students who had walked out of their schools in opposition to anti-immigrant legislation, students expressed a desire to learn more about the issues influencing their lives, including the histories and cultures of different racial/ethnic groups. To foster this learning, students recommended spending time discussing these topics in class, establishing more student clubs, and implementing a schoolwide food festival. Students hoped that these learning opportunities would help foster cross-racial/ethnic alliances and raise student awareness.

Across racial/ethnic backgrounds, college students enrolled in a course with me in 2004 on Latinas/os and education emphasized that schools should teach multiple histories as well as the dynamics of power, inequality, and privilege as they are linked to race/ethnicity, class, gender, and sexuality. In freewrites directed toward K–12 teachers, they highlighted how such courses are critical for all students to better understand and change society. Three students' freewrites best capture some of the benefits of diversifying the curriculum:

> I had some fantastic teachers in my K–12 years, even with overcrowded classrooms of 40+ and often not enough chairs for everyone, but there could have been a broader curriculum that includes students of diverse backgrounds. I remember novels featured white heroes/heroines almost exclusively, and we primarily studied the history of Western civilization, as if it were the only one that mattered. Even I, a white student, was taught nothing about my Eastern European Jewish roots. So, I can imagine that students of color were even more disenfranchised. As far as literature classes, I strongly identified with the likes of Henry David Thoreau and Holden Caulfield, but I don't know how universal these men (and characters) are in their appeal, as they are white men with individualistic values. There needs to be a more diverse cultural representation in class readings.

> Schools need to actively and explicitly address issues of race, gender, class, and sexuality. These are often issues that are heavily present in social interactions, and the failure of schools to acknowledge them keeps them underground. In some way, it also invalidates them. By talking about them in school, teachers legitimize students' feelings. It can also act as an avenue for expressing genuine interest and care for students.

> I wish that I had been told how privileged I was when I was in high school. . . . I was given special privileges and made to feel that I somehow deserved them because

of some superiority in intellect or character. On a very basic level, I wish I was taught about the prevalence of racism in our society now. It is not a historical structure but one that continuously comes up in the literature we read and government policies we learn about. I wish I had been made to feel uncomfortable about the privileges I have as a white middle class girl.

When schools do not provide a critical framework for understanding contemporary forms of discrimination and inequality, students are likely to accept the idea that we live in a meritocracy and that some people are deserving of privileges while others are not. Not only may this message foster a sense of entitlement and an incomplete understanding of society, but when students find out that the privileges they received may have been linked to factors beyond their control, such as their skin color, place of birth, or class origin, they might feel deceived. Knowledge of discrimination and privilege is crucial for helping students know how to bring about change.

The struggle for relevant and inclusive curriculum is long standing. Among the many demands of the 1968 Chicana/o high school walkouts was access to course curriculum on Chicana/o history and experiences; decades later, the struggle persists. For example, in 1996, two Chicanas in New Mexico were fired for teaching Chicana/o history in high school, though they were teaching a range of other subjects, including the Jewish Holocaust. Opponents of their curriculum, including the school board president, argued that "teaching Chicano history was racist" and "anti-American" and was "teaching stereotypes of Anglos." Instead, the two teachers, who did not learn about Chicana/o history until their mid-twenties, aimed to teach "tolerance" and "self-respect" (Haederle, 1997, p. E2). However, because they were presenting a critical analysis of U.S. history and society—one that challenges dominant perceptions and frameworks—they and their Chicana/o studies curriculum were targeted.

Most Latina/o students never attend college or have the opportunity to take courses that present these topics. Instead, they are left sitting in classrooms where their identities, communities, and histories are ignored or misrepresented. It is easy to imagine the psychological impacts of such absences on individual students, as well as the larger ramifications for our society. Besides feeling disconnected or discouraged, students are often left with incomplete histories and knowledge bases that reinforce larger systems of inequality and hinder effective policy. For example, how can we understand Latin American immigration, address racial/ethnic tensions within our changing communities, or improve educational outcomes without courses and knowledge on Latinas/os?

Look Beyond the Classroom

Students say teachers should help students envision possibilities for change. Students need to see themselves as change agents and to learn how they can become politically active. Teachers who share examples and discuss strategies for transformation help students envision themselves as knowledge producers and change makers and bring course material to life. Students are then better able to interact with the course curriculum and think critically about how they fit into history and contemporary society. Helping students see themselves as change agents is especially important when multicultural, power-aware material is presented because discussions of oppression, though important, may weigh heavily on students. Students may feel that they are powerless to transform institutions, let alone the conditions of their own lives (Ochoa and Ochoa, 2004). In her freewrite, one college student wrote about a Chicana teacher she had in high school: "When people learn how the world works, they realize that it is oppressive to people of color, people of low socioeconomic status, queer people, and women. I think that as a Chicana teacher, she should . . . let students know they can challenge the way the world works."

Schools and teachers can adopt various models to help students see themselves as active agents. For example, service-learning assignments, where students tutor, mentor, or provide other forms of assistance to nonprofit organizations, schools, or community groups, help bring course materials to life; encourage students to become active participants in local struggles; and enable them to see the connections between course materials and local communities. Such experiences can also help students develop leadership and communication skills that they can apply to other arenas of their lives.

Value Student Knowledge

According to both high school and college students, part of "go[ing] outside the curriculum" means seeing students as teachers who also possess knowledge and experiences that can be shared in the classroom. While some school officials paternalistically believed that the protesting students did not know why they had walked out of school in March 2006, students' comments reveal that they knew more than these adults assumed. During the session we had with students, they linked immigration policies to labor demands, questioned the impact that deporting immigrants would have on the U.S. economy, and equated the increased militarization of the U.S.-Mexico border to imprisoning U.S. residents. While discussing the section of House Resolution (HR) 4437 that would require building a double security fence along parts of the U.S.-Mexico border, a high school junior perceptively asked: "Do they want to keep us in or them out? It's almost like we're in jail." Students had been watching and listening to Spanish-language media and learning from their families about HR 4437 and immigration. However, since the English-language media initially spent little time on the bill or immigration in general, many of the students' school officials were disconnected from students' concerns and uninformed about the bill and the plans for the walkout. So, ironically, it was many of the school officials, not necessarily the students, who were ignorant of HR 4437.

Instead of maintaining low expectations of students and what they know, effective teachers should be willing to learn from students and build on students' knowledge. An important step is creating spaces and opportunities where students are allowed to teach others. Various techniques include integrating Spanish and English in the classroom and providing opportunities for family-community input. Other strategies emphasize creative thinking, cooperative and collaborative learning, and hands-on assignments over rote memorization, individual assignments, and competitive environments. All of these alternative approaches draw on diverse ways of learning and conveying information. They also allow students to demonstrate and affirm their families' knowledge, histories, and cultures.

All knowledge does not emanate from teachers or textbooks. There are multiple ways for learning to occur, and it does not always happen in the classroom or from teachers. The walkouts excited many students precisely because they were thinking for themselves, shaping the direction of their activities, and sharing their experiences and perspectives. Students were actively engaged in learning about immigration, student rights, and community organizing. And by gaining the attention of the media, politicians, and school officials, many students felt that adults were finally listening to them.

Know That Everybody Can Learn

Several teachers and students adamantly declared that "everybody can learn," and all school officials need to know this. The comments by sixth-grade teacher Margarita Villa were explicit: "I want the kids to like to learn. Basically I'm a language teacher; I want them to be able to speak English better. I want them to be able to write. . . . I think all kids are able to learn. So everybody learns at a different rate. Some kids are going to take longer than others, but everybody can learn." For some teachers and students, underlying this sentiment is a critique of labeling students as "bright," "gifted," or "dumb" because these labels often become self-fulfilling. As middle school teacher Lisa Perez argues, "When a teacher has high expectations, and you continue to be positive, the student feels more confident." All students should be held to high expectations.

Know and Care About Students

Both high school and college students expressed a desire to be known and understood. In particular, the high school students appealed to their teachers to know that "we are not all Mexican. We are Brazilian, Venezuelan, Nicaraguan, Salvadoran, Puerto Rican." Several college students also conveyed that they want their teachers to be more informed about Latinas/os and to have a better understanding of students as individuals. One college student wrote: "Understand the role my family plays in my life. Understand that they come first, no matter the circumstance, and don't punish me for that. . . . Also, understand the resources many Chicanos/Latinos lack in comparison to their Anglo classmates."

This theme of wanting to be known is a common one in the literature on Latina/o students. Studies indicate that these students may feel that their teachers do not care about them (see Segura, 1993; Valenzuela, 1999). In some of the examples described in this book, it is easy to see why students might feel this way. However, students may express this sentiment even when teachers do not make overtly exclusionary comments. As Valenzuela (1999) found in a Texas high school, students want teachers to exhibit "authentic caring," where they are concerned not simply with how students perform in their classes but with students as whole people, including knowing about their family and community. Part of caring for students means treating students with respect and dignity (Flores-González, 2002).

Don't Play Favorites

The following two freewrites from college students indicate that students see the privileges that accrue to favored students:

> Create equal relationships with students, instead of having favorites. Students know when other students are favored in classes, and although some teachers tend to relate to or want to help the high achieving students, this has a negative impact on the rest of the students.

> Stop privileging the "highest" academic achievers. Look at relative gains, and celebrate them.

One college student identified the consequences of this differential treatment:

> Though most of my years in K–12 were spent in honors classes, even in these classrooms there existed a difference of treatment between students. Distinctions varied by teachers. Sometimes I was treated better because of my gender, sometimes worse. Sometimes I was paternalized because of my race and sometimes ignored. It was always up to the teacher to decide what dictated his/her attitude toward me, and this influenced my reaction to the class and my performance.

Accommodate Different Learning Styles

Several students emphasized that they all learn differently, so there should not be one way of teaching. One college student wrote in his freewrite that teachers should alter their pedagogies depending on their students and the classroom dynamic: "They should be open and flexible in their teaching methods because a student might not be doing well in a class because of the teaching style not because they are 'dumb.' Different styles of teaching might work for some and not for others."

One student explicitly advocated for student-centered classrooms because he believes students possess important knowledge and insights that should be shared: "Classrooms should be more student-centered. Teachers can and will learn as much as students, and I am almost positive that more students will respond positively to this process."

Student-centered classrooms foster an active exchange of ideas, and they reposition teachers as learners, too. These classrooms challenge the banking system of education, in which teachers are positioned as knowers who deposit bits of information into students, who are expected to passively receive, digest, and recite knowledge (Freire, 1970). In classes where students are encouraged to take more active roles, students may develop a sense of ownership of the class, feel more committed to learning, and realize that knowledge is not static or objective. Part of the process of creating student-centered classrooms can start with restructuring the classroom space, or as one college student pleaded in his freewrite, "Put desks in a circle, please."

Another approach that has been used to decenter the teacher, especially in heterogeneous classrooms, is cooperative learning, with groups of students working together. Cooperative learning groups provide opportunities for students to work across racial/ethnic, class, and generational boundaries. These groups allow students to demonstrate and share their differing strengths and knowledge bases. Also, they can develop their social skills and cross-racial/ethnic relations, and they have the potential to expand peer networks and the social capital that come from a wider network of friends (see Valenzuela, 1999).

If teachers are to structure their classrooms more creatively, they need fewer students or more teaching assistants. With classes of thirty to forty students, it is difficult to engage all students in student-centered activities. However, even in these situations, with time and experience, students and teachers might work together to design classrooms that work for them.

For some of the same reasons that the teachers, students, and I advocate going beyond the curriculum, we also see the tremendous benefits that emerge when schools are transformed into inclusive and welcoming spaces. Such schools can become models for how communities and society may also be transformed.

Create an Inclusive School Environment

High school teacher Ana Camacho notes that schools can be "very intimidating" places, "especially if parents don't know the language." With gates and security guards increasingly greeting visitors as they enter campus, schools are not always inviting. Their cold and impersonal environments can be magnified by their size, and since many Latina/o students attend urban schools, their campuses are typically large. On entering the school grounds, visitors may be interrogated as to the purpose of their visit. Afterward, they may have to find the main office, which is not always clearly marked. Finally, the school may not have enough Spanish-speaking receptionists, teachers, or administrators to communicate effectively with Spanish-speaking visitors. Feelings of exclusion may be exacerbated if school officials are inpatient or intolerant or possess stereotypical attitudes about Latinas/os (see Shannon and Lojero Latimer, 1996).

Even Latina/o families who just want to enter their children's schools and classrooms to drop off and pick up their children may see schools as uninviting. Family members may be greeted with suspicion, seen as distractions, or questioned because they do not appear to belong; teachers may not want family members in their classrooms, and principals may avoid having them on campus (for examples, see Ochoa, 2004a).

Realizing that schools in the United States can be intimidating, impersonal, and cold, several teachers and other school officials have adopted the philosophy and practice of inclusion in their classrooms and campuses. They affirm the Spanish language, maintain an open-door policy, involve parents, and challenge racist comments. From their important vantage point, students add recommendations for how teachers might better relate to them.

Find Ways to Connect with Families

Knowing the community that their schools serve and realizing the significance of speaking Spanish to foster more comfortable spaces for Spanish speakers, most of the school officials in this book are challenging English-only efforts by using Spanish throughout their schools: in classrooms, at parent-teacher conferences, in front offices, and during assemblies. High school teacher Manuel Cadena echoes the sentiment of most of the other teachers in this book: "Just being a teacher, I want to be able to provide the best service to my students and to their families and the best way of doing that is by speaking to them in their native tongue, their language."

Elementary school principal Lourdes Fernandez concurs with Manuel. She sees the positive effect that speaking Spanish can have on students: "Seeing their faces when you speak to them in Spanish and they understand, that makes your day. When we get [students] that have gone to other schools, they really hurt when they say, 'Oh well, they didn't like me over there. The teachers were real mean to me. I didn't know what they were doing. They were teaching in English.' So, they come over here and they know that they are treated with respect" (quoted in Ochoa 2004a, p. 167).

Just as students feel respected when they are spoken to in a language they understand, so do their parents. Teacher-parent relationships change when teachers hold conferences and other parent meetings in the parents' languages. Sixth-grade teacher Cristina Martinez explains:

> A lot of parents don't feel comfortable at school. A big reason is when you have to use a translator; that's already uncomfortable, and you lose the meaning. Everything

doesn't get translated. I'm so thankful for my broken ability to communicate with our parents in Spanish. When I've had Asian students, that has been my biggest frustration, that I couldn't talk to those parents, that I couldn't explain or ask questions of those parents. When a parent knows I speak Spanish, it changes 90 percent. When they come in and think, "Oh, we're just going to hear it all in English and then the kid's going to translate it," the parents see I'll talk to their kid in Spanish.

If schools expect Latina/o families to participate in school events such as parent-teacher conferences, back-to-school nights, and other activities, it is crucial that material be provided in Spanish as well as in English. With this awareness, school principal Lourdes Fernandez holds some parent meetings entirely in Spanish; if there are any people who do not speak Spanish, she will make the meetings Spanish-English bilingual. She also ensures that Spanish-speaking visitors feel welcomed in the school office by "speak[ing] their language" and doing anything else "to help them out" (Ochoa, 2004a, p. 167).

Open Lines of Communication

Elementary school principal Denise Villarreal believes that schools belong to the community and parents should be able to freely enter their children's classrooms and schools. Her experiences have convinced her that "Mexican mothers take their kids to the [classroom] door and say, 'Ms. Ochoa, this is Alfredo. He is yours for the year. Take care of him for me'" (quoted in Ochoa 2004a, p. 169). With this belief, Denise Villarreal has struggled to change some teachers' reluctance to allow parents on the campus or in classrooms. She advocates "making compromises" with parents to enhance teaching, learning, and understanding. For her, the way to make compromises is to literally have an open-door policy.

Although he teaches at another school in the district, Miguel Elias agrees with Denise Villareal. He tries to leave the classroom door open for parents and students. Parents visit his classroom before and after school to pick up their children, ask questions, and talk with him.

Students also appreciate Miguel Elias's open door:

> I always try to leave the door open; it's never closed. I have a student from last year who comes here every morning. So it's an open-door policy forever. I tell them, "Whatever you guys need, I'm here. Whatever it is. Somebody's bothering you on the campus, you have to tell me. I've been there. Don't worry." The same thing with the parents. I tell them, "I have been there. It has happened to me. I take it seriously." And we have meetings. There were some kids who were being bullied here. I talked to both sides, and we ended it. I just want to empower them, show them it's possible, and I'm right here. "I'm behind you all the way. You're here for eight years," because this is a K through eighth. "Whatever it is, you could always come."

The benefits of Miguel Elias's philosophy and practice are many, including greater student satisfaction and a stronger connection to school:

> A lot of kids come here early in the morning, before school starts, and they ask, "Mr. Elias, what can I do?" And I reply, "Let's get on the computer. Let's work on some math problems, or help me begin the day." It really helps them to feel like school is important, that they are needed, and that this is their school. They're part of the preparation; they're part of the building. It makes it more tangible for them. I try to give them all

the kindness and motivation that I can. And they leave with that, and they're always very happy.

While speaking parents' languages and having an open-door policy facilitates teacher-parent relationships, several Latina/o teachers describe other strategies for making schools more welcoming and connecting with families. For example, elementary school teacher Gabriela Muñoz visits every student's home at least once a year:

> Sometimes I ended up going at a time when a student did something really good and would say, "I came by to see how you're doing, to give you some tips on how to help your child, and to congratulate you for having a wonderful kid." Sometimes I went to their house because I could not get hold of their parents. If you can understand where they're coming from and what situations they had, then you can accommodate each student.

Sixth-grade teacher Erica Burg knows the importance of communicating with parents. However, her school is hampering full teacher-parent interaction. As she describes, if schools are going to connect more effectively with parents and be inclusive spaces, they must rethink the times for parent conferences and meetings:

> There are some parents who are very involved, who write us notes almost every single day, "How is he doing?" Some parents are just like that. They'll call or e-mail us all the time. There are a lot of parents whom we try to get hold of and can't because they're at work and they get home too late. . . . Communicating with some of the parents is tough just because of jobs. But parent-teacher conferences are one time that we get to see and talk to them. We have fifty-three sixth-graders, and we're scheduled to see about thirty-eight of them,

which is good. Conferences are scheduled this whole week from 12:15 to 2:30. Wednesday's the only nighttime one. So on Wednesday from 4:30 to 7:30, we were jam-packed with parents because a lot of them are working. That seems strange to me that a school like ours schedules conferences during the day. Today, I had only two parents come in from 1:00 to 2:30, because they can't come in at that time. I think the school could probably do a better job of accommodating the parents.

For Marie Marquez, part of accommodating parents is to assist them in helping their children achieve their goals. Marie believes that schools need to start disseminating information to students and their families about college and financial aid as early as elementary school:

I don't think parents know how to approach going to college. If it wasn't for my counselor saying, "We need to do this, this, and this for you." My dad was shocked, "You're already thinking about college?" A lot of the parents want their kids to succeed. I hear in the conferences parents asking their kid, "Do you want to work twelve hours a day like your dad and I do?" or "your mom and I do?" The kid's like, "No." "Well then you got to do well in school." But at the same time, the parents need more guidance from the school district: "This is what your kid needs to do. This is how you can accomplish it. This is how your kid can go to college." They need that information. I think in high school they do it more, but they need to start doing it in elementary school. They don't prepare the parents. It's not just the kid; they have to prepare the parents. And sometimes the parents think, "I can't afford it. How can my kid go to college? We can't pay for it." They need to know what's out there for them.

Although Marie is optimistic that students and parents are receiving information about financial assistance, national studies suggest otherwise. A Tomás Rivera Policy Institute report released in 2004 found that 75 percent of young Latinas/os who never attended college or did not complete college would have been more likely to had they known more about financial aid; most of their parents did not receive financial aid information when their children were in high school (DiMaria, 2006). With such staggering percentages, it is crucial that schools do more to inform families about financial aid.

Another strategy for strengthening teacher-parent connections is for more schools to establish family-community centers that are truly community centered. These should be safe spaces for families to gather, seek support and information, and organize meetings and other events that are endorsed by the school but determined by community members. To the extent that these spaces are community determined, community activists agree that such spaces are critical for increasing parent and community engagement without the constraining oversight of school officials (Ochoa, 2004a). Currently parents are typically invited to participate only in school-defined meetings through the school site council, bilingual advisory committee, or the parent-teacher association (PTA). Since these meetings and committees are structured and controlled by school officials, there is little opportunity for parents to determine the agenda, thereby limiting their full participation and input.

An open-door policy must be broadly applied. This includes opening up the physical structure of schools so that family members do not have a difficult time gaining entrance in the building and welcoming the perspectives and ideas of students, families, and other community members.

Support Efforts to Diversify Schools

This diversity should be reflected at all levels of the school—not just in school personnel but also in school practices and policies. To take full advantage of a diverse staff that extends beyond diverse instructional assistants and cafeteria workers, schools must critically analyze and restructure their school policies, curriculum, and culture. For example, as the teachers' lessons have revealed, without changing narrow conceptualizations of education or assimilationist practices such as Eurocentric curriculum and antibilingual education movements, who is in the classroom becomes less salient. Latina/o school officials may enter schools with important funds of knowledge, but if they are prevented from sharing their perspectives and approaches to learning and teaching, the full benefits of a diverse staff can be lost (see Monzó and Rueda, 2003; Rueda, Monzó, and Higareda, 2004).

When diversity is at the core of how schools are structured, individuals of color or from the working class are less likely to feel that they are tokens who are responsible for bringing all of the diversity to the school. High school teacher Ana Camacho's experience captures the problems of this form of diversity where school structure and politics remain intact and only personnel are changed:

> The administration is playing politics. They may be using the fact that I am Latina on paper to cover up some of the things that are not happening here. For example, there are not enough Latinos in the honors and AP courses. So, next year, I've been told that maybe I should teach an honors course. This is great, but this is also a way to show on paper that the school is trying to make changes. I think that the school needs to change some of the politics instead of just changing the staff. Sometimes I feel that I'm being used as a puppet or a token. They just had a report that they wrote for the state, and the school used a lot of the things that we have done as MEChA to make the campus look good. But it was the students who made these changes; it wasn't so much the school.

Author and social critic bell hooks (1992) supports Ana Camacho's warning about tokenized diversity. She warns that we must avoid the current fashion in which "ethnicity becomes spice, seasoning that can liven up the dull dish that is mainstream white culture" (p. 21).

Advice for Students

Just as school officials should demand that schools work for all students, we should not forget the important roles that students play in this struggle as well. Too often students' perspectives, experiences, and feelings are forgotten within our educational system. They may be blamed for their supposed "failures" or "laziness." They may be acted on by policymakers who claim to know what is best to "leave no child behind," so they instill structured, boring, and top-down school practices that stifle students' critical thinking and active engagement. However, students are thinking about current issues and their own schooling experiences. Some engage in various forms of resistance within their schools, and despite the many schooling practices that may objectify, alienate, or disengage students, students are actively navigating through the educational pipeline. As today's students make their way through school, they may draw inspiration from the following recommendations that emerged from the Latina/o teachers' memories of their K–16 schooling.

Develop and Maintain a Strong Identity

Become familiar with the expectations of U.S. schools, but do not forgo your identity or your family's values and cultural practices. Another way of describing this recommendation is "accommodation and acculturation without assimilation" (Gibson, 1996). Being bicultural or multicultural and bilingual or multilingual is associated with improved school performance and higher ambition among immigrant students (Portes and Rumbaut, 2001). In addition, being bicultural or multicultural and bilingual or multilingual will help to enlarge your perspective and understanding, facilitate racial/ethnic interactions, navigate different institutions, and establish a wide support network. In Chapter Five, Angelica Vasquez's description of how she combined the individualist approach to education in the United States with helping her family is a perfect example of accommodation without assimilation. She justified receiving her education by realizing that it would allow her to help her family better.

Maintain or establish an identity that is linked not only to being a student. While some may encourage you to wrap your entire identity around school, especially in college and graduate school, I could not do this. It would have meant distancing myself from other aspects of my identity. Since I enjoyed working with students and valued learning from community members, stripping myself away from these populations would have been detrimental to my sense of self. My connections with these communities and family sustained me as I progressed through school.

Do not let how you perform on standardized tests define you. Know that you and your school are more than statistics and that various factors influence test performance, including unequal school resources and test design.

Seek Support

Surround yourself with people who encourage and support your goals. These individuals should counteract negative stereotypes and the prevailing beliefs of a meritocracy that assume individuals are entirely to blame for their "successes" and "failures." Internalizing such beliefs can become immobilizing. So keep in mind the role of institutional injustices and ideological processes in influencing opportunities, and remember as well as your own agency.

Seek out institutionalized systems of emotional, academic, cultural, political, and financial support. Meet with and ask counselors and academic advisers for the support and information that you need. If you find that they are limiting your goals, let them know or seek the advice of peers, coaches, family members, or others who are able to be more supportive.

Finally, search for supportive organizations. There are established organizations that have been working to improve educational outcomes for decades. For several teachers in this book, MEChA provided them with the strength to pursue a critical education and work for the greater good of their communities. Others found support in religious organizations. Sports can be an important avenue for affirmation, establishing a healthy lifestyle, and uniting with other students across the boundaries of year in school, curriculum track, and social positions.

Search for Additional Bodies of Knowledge

At all levels of the educational pipeline, try to augment the information that is disseminated in your classes with materials that inspire, challenge, and engage you. I found this to be especially important in college and graduate school, where students have more control over what they learn. Seeking out additional bodies of knowledge and perspectives was critical for me in completing graduate school in sociology.

My first year of graduate school when I had to take the required courses in sociology was a practice in learning the traditional or classic theories in the field. At UCLA in 1990–1991, this still meant a Eurocentric curriculum that focused on middle- and upper-class white men and white women. This was also the case in a feminist theory course that looked at women of color only in the last week of class using just three assigned articles.

A group of us who had similar perspectives and expectations quickly realized that we were not going to be given or even encouraged to read the theories and topics that drew us to graduate school. We had to seek them, and in some cases we had to demand them. So we did what we could to educate ourselves beyond the narrow traditional sociology that characterized our classes. For me, this included learning from my family and community members by completing interviews and seeking teaching experiences in women's studies and Chicana/o studies and reading materials from Asian American studies and Black studies. These disciplines and spaces were critical for providing me with what Emma Pérez (1993) refers to as *un sitio y una lengua*—a space and a language—that was lacking in my department. This space and language "rejects colonial ideology and the by-products of colonialism and capitalist patriarchy—sexism, racism, homophobia, etc." (pp. 47–48).

Those of us who sought knowledge and community outside our department because of its exclusionary curriculum often had easier times getting academic jobs because we could cross disciplinary boundaries and were raising new questions and offering unique perspectives.

Advice for Families

Teacher Vivian Sosa realizes that parents have different ways of showing love, but she is concerned that too many students may not realize this:

> For many parents, the lack of communication between students and them is a lot. Sometimes students don't realize that their parents love them. I've come across this many times in parent conference; they just don't realize it. For many of my kids, that's one of the reasons they're coming to my classroom in deficit of something. On a presurvey for my master's, I asked the kids, "Do you feel your parents support you?" A lot of my students said, "No, I don't think my parents care at all. I don't feel my parents support me. I don't think they care if I do well in school." My follow-up question was: "What would make your parents proud of you?" Students said, "If I got good grades, if I was successful at school, I think they would be proud of me. I want them to be proud of me." I know if I asked the parents, they care. I think that the communication is not happening. If it did, some of my students might turn around. I think they don't understand that mom and dad might have

something personal, might have grown up in a certain way, might have some other struggles that they're trying to deal with, or might have to work.

For high school teacher Ana Camacho, loving children entails being involved in their lives. She explains that parents sometimes think that once their children turn age sixteen, seventeen, or eighteen, "they know what to do." Instead, she believes, "That's not the case. Especially at seventeen or sixteen is when we lose a lot of these kids." She encourages active parental involvement, especially as children age, because this is when they may need even more guidance.

Remember to support and encourage students, especially as they enter new environments. As we learned from the teachers, this support is critical for first-generation college students who may face unfamiliar, uncomfortable, and even hostile classrooms and campuses.

Finally, within homes and communities, convey family and community histories, cultures, and traditions. These knowledge bases provide a crucial supplement to course material and help to foster self-confidence, pride, strength, and awareness. They may also inspire curiosity, a critical consciousness, and a desire for social justice.

As we turn to the following section on creating schools that work, we see how the more schools and society move toward a vision of love and justice the easier it is for students and teachers to achieve. We cannot expect all change to come only from teachers, students, and families. Most of the philosophies and recommendations offered throughout this book about effective teaching and learning require transforming school practices and rethinking how we view education.

Creating Schools That Work for All Students

Mexican immigrant mother and long-time activist Raquel Heinrich asserts that the only way to work for children is collectively: "Which way is the right way to approach education? What programs are good? How can we help with something that is going to benefit the community and the children?" (quoted in Ochoa, 2004b, p. 116). She advocates that parents, teachers, schools, and community members work in partnership to "maintain and sustain the quality education for our child[ren]" (Ochoa, 2004b, pp. 116–117). Raquel's collaborative ethos removes the blame from any one group; she does not point fingers at teachers, students, or families. Instead, she challenges capitalist constructions that emphasize individualistic concerns. She calls on all of us to work together for the community and the children. The following recommendations are premised on this collaborative ethos. Our schools and communities benefit when we work for the collective good of students, not for the individual benefit of select students. Rather than abandoning local public schools in the search for supposedly better schools for individual students, we must seek opportunities to work with others to improve the conditions of education. This must include increasing the amount of funding provided to students and schools as well as eliminating unequal school practices.

Increase College Financial Aid

Since the 1980s, programs designed to increase rates of college attendance have been reversed across the nation, and students rather than taxpayers are increasingly covering the costs of higher education (Adam, 2006). As the government has moved away from grants to loans and costs of higher education exceed costs of living (Allen, 2006), attendance at a four-year college or university is becoming less of an option for poor and working-class families. Using 2002 data, journalist Michelle Adam (2006) exposed vast socioeconomic gaps in college completion rates. Although more than half of all those eighteen to twenty-four years old from families making over ninety thousand dollars a year had obtained a bachelor's degree, only 6 percent of their counterparts from families making less than thirty-five thousand dollars had graduated from college.

Among the teachers who attended college in the 1980s and 1990s, several explain the damaging impacts that inadequate financial aid had on their schooling and health. Thirty-year-old Gabriela Muñoz attended a Los Angeles–area college that covered her tuition for the first two years. However, she received no financial assistance her last two years, and unlike many of her middle- and upper-class peers, she could not rely on her parents to pay for her expenses. She found two jobs, but they quickly took a toll on her grade point average (GPA), her health, and her options for graduate school:

> I paid for my last two years because they gave me nothing. I took out loans. I paid for some of it because I had two jobs while going to school full time. I was juggling everything. My GPA was so low. I was taking twenty-one units, practically working full time with the two jobs. . . . I was on probation for I don't know how many semesters because it was too much, and my mom was like, *"Te vas a matar."* [You are going to kill yourself.] I had lost so much weight . . . I went from a 3.8 to barely a 2.5 when I graduated. I had to take classes after I graduated to bring up my GPA. I couldn't get into any graduate programs because my GPA was so low.

The lack of sufficient financial assistance provided to working-class students should not be overlooked. It is one of the most important factors influencing college attendance and rates of completion (Vasquez, 1997), especially as college tuition continues to increase while federal financial assistance declines. As Gabriela Muñoz's example plainly illustrates, without sufficient financial assistance, students' course work, personal health, and academic dreams suffer.

For several teachers, this lack of financial assistance was compounded by the fact that counselors or administrators never explained the workings of financial aid to them, even though they were the first members of their families to attend college. Because they lacked this knowledge, the system of financial aid became a catch-22: the more money they needed, the more they worked, and consequently the less money they received in assistance, which meant the more they had to work. Angelica Vasquez's comments are illustrative:

> Ever since I graduated from high school, even though I was going to college, I was expected to pay rent and utilities. So I had to work. And so I got financial aid, but the financial aid wouldn't be enough, and something awful happened. So I would work. The more I worked, the less financial aid I would get, which would mean more work, because I didn't know how to work the system. I guess I should have just said, "Hey, don't work at all." But I didn't, and I worked. I would work anywhere from thirty-two to forty hours a week. I worked about an average of thirty-two hours a week, which is almost a full-time job. And I would take the bus to and from work for two or more hours. It was more hours than I'd spend in class.

Not only does lack of financial assistance require students to dip into their already scarce study time to work, but it may also diminish feelings of belonging in college. Vivian Sosa compares her college experiences with that of her more economically privileged classmates who seemed not to recognize that by cleaning up after them, she made their academic lives easier and hers more difficult:

> I needed a job, and I was definitely going to work and go to school. I wasn't going to be playing Frisbee out in the back like some of the other students during off time. I had to work. And my parents did what they

could to give me enough money, but I didn't want to
burden them with my costs. . . . They raised me for this
long. I didn't want to continue burdening them. So I
worked as a housekeeper in the dorms, cleaning girls'
and boys' bathrooms every day. Girls were walking in,
seeing me, and I just thought, "I wonder what they're
thinking? Do they appreciate what I do, or is it just what
they expect?"

At a time when a college education is more important than ever
before, these patterns are detrimental to all working-class students
and families, but especially to Latinas/os because of their lower-
than-average family incomes and unequal access to financial aid.
According to a 2005 report by *Excelencia*, for the past ten years,
Latinas/os have received the lowest average financial aid award of
any other racial/ethnic group in the United States (Allen, 2006).
On average, the financial aid packages of low-income students
actually leave more need unmet than the packages provided to
other students (Martínez and Martínez, 2006). The results are that
poorer students, especially Latinas/os, are not attending college,
or they are enrolling in community colleges where retention and
transfer rates remain low (Adam, 2006).

As the cost of colleges and universities becomes increasingly
prohibitive for poor and working-class students, we must push for a
redistribution of resources that provides assistance and information
to those students who are in the most need economically to receive
state and federal scholarships and grants. The growth in merit-
based over need-based state grants should be reversed to allow more
opportunities for poor and working-class students to attend college. Also, it is critical that financial aid opportunities be extended
to undocumented students who, through Assembly Bill 540 in
California, are able to pay in-state tuition if they have completed
at least three years of high school in California. Although this legislation is an important step in making college more accessible to

all California's residents, the lack of federal and state aid provided to undocumented immigrants makes college attendance extremely difficult or impossible for many.

It is equally important that school officials inform themselves, students, and families about scholarship opportunities and how financial aid works. High schools, colleges, and universities should organize bilingual and multilingual workshops for students and their family members on how to apply for financial aid and scholarships. These workshops should occur early in students' high school careers, so they have time to plan and prepare for college.

Redistribute Funding

Teacher and author Jonathon Kozol (1991) has charged that schools in the United States are savagely unequal by class and race/ethnicity. This inequality is transparent in school grounds, classrooms, libraries, bathrooms, textbooks, and equipment. Students and school officials see these differences, which lead to differences as well in teaching, learning, and opportunities.

The U.S. Supreme Court has done little since 1954 when its ruling in *Brown* v. *Board of Education* overturned the doctrine of "separate but equal" established in *Plessy* v. *Ferguson* (1896) to address these underlying injustices. For example, in *San Antonio Independent School District* v. *Rodriguez* in 1973, the U.S. Supreme Court ruled against a case charging that the Texas policy of relying largely on local property taxes to fund public education violated the Fourteenth Amendment's equal protection clause of the U.S. Constitution because it did not distribute funding equally to all school districts. The Court held that in the U.S. Constitution, "there is no fundamental right to equality in public school education" (Hirji 1999, pp. 587–588). As a result of such rulings, federal case law on inequality in public schooling has shifted to the state courts, where state constitutions form the basis of such litigation (Hirji, 1999). Thus, school funding systems vary across states. Some states continue to rely heavily on local property taxes to fund public schools, while a few states such as California and Michigan are funded through state revenues (www.edsource.org).

California has not been immune to the funding inequalities that plague schools nationwide, and several landmark court cases magnify such disparities. One of the most important and earliest cases challenging states to ensure equitable school funding was *Serrano* v. *Priest* (1971) in California (see Oakes and Rogers, 2006). The plaintiffs charged that by relying on local property taxes, California public schools violated the equal protection clause of the Fourteenth Amendment. Among the examples cited in the argument was that Baldwin Park Unified spent only $577 per pupil during the 1968–1969 school year while Beverly Hills Unified spent $1,232. The court ruled in favor of the plaintiffs that the school funding system discriminates based on the wealth of school district residents. Under the direction of the court, the California legislature developed a formula that would reduce the gap in spending among school districts to no more than $100 per student. In 1976, the California Supreme Court reconsidered *Serrano* in *Serrano II* and affirmed the court's earlier decision (see Hirji 1999).

Despite such victories by working-class and communities of color, school funding disparities persist. For example, in the 1996–96 school year, "Revenues per ADA [average daily attendance] of the Beverly Hills District were 150% higher than those of Baldwin Park District" (Hirji, 1999, p. 598). An Associated Press analysis of per pupil spending in California during the 2003–2004 school year was just as staggering: spending ranged from $4,806 to $34,279 per pupil, with the state average of $6,857 per student. The results of such disparities are apparent in teachers' salaries and school resources from toilet paper to computers (Williams, 2006).

Various factors account for these persisting discrepancies, and they must be addressed if we are committed to educational equity and excellence. Among the most devastating impacts to *Serrano* and the possibilities of school funding equalization was the antitax movement of the 1970s epitomized in California's Proposition 13.

In 1978, the same year that the California state governor was to implement Assembly Bill 65, which under *Serrano* would have redistributed some of the property taxes garnered from wealthier school districts to poorer ones, California voters approved Proposition 13. This proposition rolled back property assessments to 1975–1976 values, limited property valuation to 2 percent per year unless property sold, and restricted property taxes to 1 percent of their assessed value (Odden and Picus, 2004). The year after it was implemented, Proposition 13 resulted in about $7 billion less to local governments (Green, 2005). Overall, local property tax revenues were reduced by 60 percent.

As a result of Proposition 13, California has had less funding for education. There are fewer property tax revenues generated by all districts, "causing many school districts to become dependent on state aid" (Hirji, 1999, p. 601). Furthermore, California has less money relative to almost all other states. For example, from the 1960s to 2004, California slid from fifth in per pupil spending in the nation to forty-third (Karp, 1997; Williams, 2006). Moreover, home owners are paying a growing percentage of California's property tax than businesses are because commercial and industrial property is sold and reassessed less frequently than homes (Odden and Picus, 2004). As members of the community that also benefit from well-educated students, businesses have a stake in contributing more to our schools.

Proposition 13 has also severely hampered the ability to change California's tax system. As part of the proposition, statewide property taxes—among the suggestions proposed under *Serrano* for funding equalization—are not permitted, and special nonproperty taxes can be adopted only if they are approved by a two-thirds majority (see Hirji 1999).

At the same time that Proposition 13 has decimated school financing and the possibilities of great equity, disparities between families and schools are perpetuated when wealthier schools are more financially able to raise extensive amounts of money from local fundraising, parent donations, and grant writing. These funds are then used to provide teachers and students with additional staff support, educational resources, sports equipment, and learning opportunities (Hirji, 1999; Oakes and Rogers, 2006).

Along with a radical rethinking of taxes, including the abolition of Proposition 13, we must demand greater spending in public education at local, state, and federal levels. With a growing percentage of state budgets going to corrections, schools, communities, and students are losing (Sides, 1997). In fact, the California Department of Corrections and Rehabilitation had a budget of $9.8 billion, surpassing the state's spending on higher education (www.lao.ca.gov). A 1999 article in *Color Lines* reported that California "spends $60,000 a year to incarcerate a young person, but only $5,000 per year to educate one" (Della Piana, 1999, p. 13). These statistics indicate that we must rethink spending priorities.

Finally, federal spending on education remains extremely low. Only 3 percent of the total federal budget is allocated to education (Sadker and Sadker, 2005). As a country, we must be willing to invest in the education and future of our youth. Doing anything less maintains the current system of inequality.

Eliminate Unequal School Practices

Within individual schools, we must work to eliminate practices that privilege some students at the expense of others. Curriculum tracking, for example, is shortchanging students, families, and communities by inhibiting the full development of all residents. This has significant implications in the context of our changing economy and increasingly diverse cities. Not only may students who are tracked into non-college-preparatory courses or vocational classes feel as though they do not belong in school or that they are overlooked, they are being cheated out of college opportunities or occupations in our changing economy (Romo and Falbo, 1996). Students in advanced placement and honors courses are also disadvantaged in the current system. They may have limited opportunities to learn from and interact with a cross-section of the student population, and they may internalize school officials' messages that they are "the best and the brightest" and deserve by birthright special treatment. These experiences and sentiments hinder community building. We must work together to ensure that all courses are available to all students. This requires eliminating the role of gatekeepers in determining which classes and life opportunities are available for which students.

Finally, we must resist media and school reports that define students and schools based on performance on standardized tests. By using performance on these tests to determine a school's quality, we are overlooking other aspects of our schools that may be more important for living in a diverse and just society: the number of students who are bilingual; the racial/ethnic and class diversity of students, teachers, and administrators; and the integration of multicultural, power-aware curriculum and critical pedagogy. If we start demanding that schools be evaluated along these dimensions where higher rates of bilingual students, diversity among faculty, inclusion of courses on power and inequality, and a commitment to community are praised over test performance, what types of changes might we see in our schools and society?

Part of this work must include redefining the relationship between schools and communities. Schools should be envisioned as community spaces that are held accountable by all members, not simply by how students perform on standardized tests. When we collectively restructure our schools into community spaces where all children are challenged and valued, we demonstrate the love that the teachers in this book model.

10

Conclusion
Love and Justice in Our Schools

We need mass-based political movements calling citizens of this nation to uphold democracy and the rights of everyone to be educated, and to work on behalf of ending domination in all its forms—to work for justice, challenging our educational system so that schooling is not the site where students are indoctrinated to support imperialist white supremacist capitalist patriarchy or any ideology, but rather where they learn to open their minds, to engage in rigorous study and to think critically.

hooks (2003)

Teachers often say that they want "the best for children." The general population also wants what is best, and many people rank education as a top governmental priority. Politicians know this, and during elections, political candidates spend millions of dollars trying to convince us that they are "the education candidate." With education touted as the key to success, it is hard to be opposed to it. However, often lost within sound bits and pro-children rhetoric such as No Child Left Behind are the more substantive questions about education, students, and success. What is really best for children? Who determines what is best? Why is it perceived as best? What type of education do teachers, politicians, and the general population endorse? These are critical questions, and depending on one's position within the educational system, responses may vary.

Story of a Lost Teaching Moment

These divergent perspectives were magnified during March 2006, when over forty thousand students walked out of Los Angeles area schools in opposition to the anti-immigration bill: House Resolution 4437: The Border Protection, Antiterrorism, and Illegal Immigration Control Act. Many students and school officials clashed over their conceptualizations of education and what is best for students. Large numbers of students wanted to demonstrate their support for immigrant rights by participating in mass demonstrations. However, many school officials attempted to keep students in class by locking down schools and punishing students with detention and truancy tickets.

As an observer of the student walkouts in my community and a co-organizer of a session on immigration with nearly one hundred high school students who participated in the walkouts, I learned that students walked out for immigrant family members and friends and in opposition to anti-Latina/o policies. Walking out and marching made them proud, allowed them to affirm their identities, and was a way for them to talk to students from other schools and learn more about HR 4437. Students were emotionally, politically, and intellectually engaged with a contemporary issue and with one another.

Unfortunately, many school officials responded negatively to this unique learning opportunity. Most students were given tickets that required them to appear before a judge for being "truant"; others faced detention and even suspension, and some received both tickets and detention. Coupled with this punishment, some teachers ridiculed students and dismissed the walkouts by declaring that "illegal immigrants should go back where they came from" and that students were "stupid" or "delinquents who just wanted an excuse to get out of school." Many teachers and schools opted not to use class or school time to talk about the proposed legislation, students' rights, the legislative process, or political participation. Instead, students were portrayed by some as wasting time and money. Placed on lockdown, many schools continued with the curriculum as usual. They claimed that they were "protecting" the students and were concerned that schools were losing money for each student who was out of school. Some schools were in the middle of test preparation or were administering tests and saw the walkouts as hurting school performance on tests.

During the walkouts, what was "best for the students"? Should the administrators alone decide what is best? What role should teachers, students, and families play? Why did many schools fail to connect the student activism and awareness with learning and education? Why are there few spaces for school officials, students, and families to come together to engage in dialogue around education—its meanings, forms, and purposes? It is clear from the walkouts that students and school officials have opinions on these pressing topics. How might we learn from them in hopes of moving toward more just schools and communities?

Listening and Learning from These Lessons

Despite the clarity of recommendations and the recurring negative school and work experiences presented by Latina/o teachers, educational problems persist in U.S. schools. These problems are many, and the experiences delineated in these teachers' narratives provide a glimpse into how school practices are manifested in the lives of too many students, teachers, families, and communities. During their years in school, it is likely that Latina/o students will encounter damaging school practices such as curriculum tracking, high-stakes testing, and biased school officials. Among the results is that over 40 percent of Latina/o students are not completing high school, and those who remain often encounter what Valenzuela (1999) has described as "subtractive schooling," where monolingual and Eurocentric course curriculum and practices prevail. Within institutions of higher education, cuts in financial aid and increases in tuition are further limiting poor and working-class Latina/o students from pursuing an advanced education so critical today.

Even teachers who enter the profession with a love of learning and visions for creating socially just classrooms and schools may find that the structure of schools is overwhelming. Additional testing, paperwork, and standards-based teaching are constraining already time-strapped teachers. This busywork is detracting from time that could be better spent meeting with students and families; learning more about the histories, cultures, and experiences of students; refining pedagogies; and thinking about the state of education.

Teachers, especially those in government-defined "low-performing-schools," find that they have less autonomy under programs like No Child Left Behind. With more classroom observations, reviews of lesson plans, and requirements for structured instruction, teachers face greater surveillance by school administrators, who are pressured to improve scores for threat of government takeovers and school closures.

Since the federal government under No Child Left Behind defines "highly qualified" teachers as those who are state certified and have demonstrated mastery of their subject area, other qualities that students and families seek in teachers, such as care, commitment, and cultural awareness, are deemed less salient. In the fight to raise test scores to prove the proficiency level of students and the quality of their schools, the voices of students, families, and communities are being pushed out of many public discussions and policy debates.

Inequalities in school resources remain hidden in current educational debates and policies. From differential access to courses and curriculum tracks within school to insufficient financial aid to students and unequal funding by schools and states, the ramifications of these inequalities on the lives and opportunities of students, teachers, and communities cannot be dismissed.

Although these problems and inequalities within the educational system are not new, they are not the ones that typically make headlines. Instead, newspapers rant about "underprepared students," "out-of-control teens," "unqualified teachers," or "wasteful school spending"—headlines that dramatize myths about public education begun in the 1980s during the Reagan-Bush era of cuts in social spending and moves toward privatization (Berliner and Biddle, 1995). These inflammatory headlines persist under No Child Left Behind and camouflage and reproduce many of the real problems that plague our schools and society.

What Is at Stake

The stakes of today's educational practices are higher than ever before. In our current period of neoliberalism and the push for market-based reforms such as standardized and controlled curriculum, accountability through high-stakes testing, and privatization, public education is under attack. Resources and attention are being diverted away from our public schools, and under NCLB, more schools are threatened with government closure and takeover. The movement toward privatization intensifies, and the racial/ethnic and class gaps increase.

Students who are pushed out of schools face decreasing opportunities within the economy. The unionized high-wage durable-goods manufacturing jobs that provided previous generations of working-class families with opportunities for job stability, health benefits, and economic advancement without a college or high school degree have dramatically disappeared. In their place are jobs in light manufacturing such as electronics and garments and in the service sector as salespeople and custodians. Many of these are part-time jobs with low wages, few benefits, and limited advancement possibilities. With just 11 percent of today's Latina/o students receiving college diplomas, most are excluded from the higher-paid service jobs of this new economy.

Not only are many Latinas/os being excluded from the possibilities of college and careers, but many find that the assets they enter school with are often ignored or depleted—even though Latinas/os represent a growing percentage of our student population and nation. For example, rather than build on the Spanish-language skills of many Latina/o students, states and schools are adopting regressive antibilingual education practices. These practices hearken back to the era of Americanization when Mexican schools and classrooms focused on transmitting the English language as quickly as possible. With Spanish as the second most common language in the United States and the one most used in the Western Hemisphere (Gonzalez, 2000), all would benefit if schools embraced learning and teaching Spanish and other languages.

In our increasingly diverse communities and nation, all students must be educated about the histories and experiences of the groups that comprise the United States. Without these broader perspectives and understandings, we risk perpetuating exclusionary beliefs and practices. Also, given the transnational connections by individuals, communities, and nations, greater global awareness is more important than ever before. The United States cannot continue to perceive itself as the center of the world and remain uninformed about other communities, practices, and countries.

Not only do we risk losing additional students within our current economic and educational systems, but too many teachers are finding that tests, stress, work, and oversight are threatening the passion and joy that drove them to the classroom. And although U.S. schools and communities are becoming increasingly diverse, low salaries and additional hoops for teachers in training are hindering teacher diversity.

For families and communities, the emphasis on the technical aspects of schooling and the push toward assimilation through English-only instruction can be equally as damaging. As students progress through the educational system, some may be forced to make critical sacrifices and risk forgoing the Spanish language and familial connections. Thus, individuals, families, and the nation may lose out on the wealth of resources that exist in the diverse forms of cultural and social capital that students of color and first-generation students possess.

Hope for Change

Amid what appears to be a bleak story, we find much hope for change. All around us there are forms of resistance, though they are not always transparent. In homes, resistance is apparent in the actions of mothers who are augmenting a deficient school curriculum by sharing their individual stories, family cultures, and group histories with their children. Just as these stories inspire a future generation of youth, so do other forms of family encouragement, as in the philosophy of Marie Marquez's father to do "whatever you want" or in the admonishment by parent activist Raquel Heinrich that we should work together for the community and all children.

Within schools, we find examples of working-class Latinas/os returning to their communities and schools to help raise the next generations of students. Many are committed educators who are modeling the possibilities that exist for students, challenging exclusionary school practices, and refusing to succumb to external pressures that distort their vision of an education. These teachers are maintaining their beliefs that education is much more than standards and high-stakes testing; for them, education means putting students first and fostering self-love, confidence, kindness, and an awareness of others.

Also, there are the students who took to the streets in 2006. Collectively, they raised their voices and fists in opposition to regressive immigration policies and sent strong messages to the U.S. Senate and others. Although their activism was not well received by all school officials, it instilled pride among many and fostered a desire to learn more about students' rights and immigration policies.

Much work needs to be done to address the vast inequalities that persist. However, as the students who walked out of their schools demonstrated, the power of the people cannot be underestimated. By envisioning love and justice for all of our communities' children and working together for the students, communities, and schools that typically receive the least, we can improve our schools and communities for all.

References

Acuña, R. F. *Occupied America: A History of Chicanos*. (5th ed.) New York: HarperCollins, 1988.

Adam, M. "Who Can Afford to Pay for College?" *Hispanic Outlook*, Jan. 2006, pp. 9–11.

Allen, K. "Show Me the Money: The Latino Search for Financial Aid." *Hispanic Outlook*, Jan. 2006, pp. 20–22.

Almaguer, T. *Racial Fault Lines: The Historical Origins of White Supremacy in California*. Berkeley: University of California Press, 1994.

Amott, T. "Shortchanged." In M. L. Anderson and P. H. Collins (eds.), *Race, Class, and Gender*. Belmont, Calif.: Wadsworth, 1995.

Anderson, M. L., and Collins, P. H. *Race, Class, and Gender: An Anthology*. Belmont, Calif.: Wadsworth, 1995.

Anzaldúa, G. *Borderlands/La Frontera: The New Mestiza*. San Francisco: Spinsters/Aunt Lute Foundation, 1987.

Apple, M. W. *Educating the "Right" Way: Markets, Standards, God, and Inequality*. New York: RoutledgeFalmer, 2001.

Apple, M. W. *Ideology and Curriculum*. (3rd ed.) New York: RoutledgeFalmer, 2004.

Au, W. "The NCLB Zone." *Rethinking Schools*, Fall 2004, pp. 11–13.

Baca Zinn, M. "Feminist Rethinking from Racial-Ethnic Families." In M. Baca Zinn and B. Thornton Dill (eds.), *Women of Color in U.S. Society*. Philadelphia: Temple University Press, 1994.

Baca Zinn, M., Weber Cannon, L., Higginbotham, E., and Thornton Dill, B. "The Costs of Exclusionary Practices in Women's Studies." In G. Anzaldúa (ed.), *Making Face, Making Soul Haciendo Caras: Creative and Critical Perspectives by Feminists of Color*. San Francisco: Aunt Lute Books, 1990.

Baldarrama, F. E., and Rodríguez, R. *Decade of Betrayal: Mexican Repatriation in the 1930s*. Albuquerque: University of New Mexico Press, 1995.

Barrera, M. *Race and Class in the Southwest*. Notre Dame, Ind.: University of Notre Dame Press, 1979.

Bejarano, C. *Qué onda? Urban Youth Culture and Border Identity*. Tucson: University of Arizona Press, 2005.

Berliner, D. C., and Biddle, B. J. *The Manufactured Crisis: Myths, Fraud, and the Attack on America's Public Schools*. Cambridge, Mass.: Perseus Books, 1995.

Bettie, J. *Women Without Class: Girls, Race, and Identity*. Berkeley: University of California Press, 2003.

Bloom, G. M. "The Effects of Speech Style and Skin Color on Bilingual Teaching Candidates' and Bilingual Teachers' Attitudes Towards Mexican American Pupils." Unpublished doctoral dissertation, Stanford University, 1990.

Bogardus, E. S. *The Mexican in the United States*. Berkeley: University of California Press, 1934.

Bourdieu, P., and Passerson, J. C. *Reproduction in Education, Society, and Culture*. Thousand Oaks, Calif.: Sage, 1977.

Bowles, S., and Gintis, H. *Schooling in Capitalist America: Educational Reform and the Contradictions of Economic Life*. New York: Basic Books, 1976.

Brown v. Board of Education of Topeka, Kansas. 347 U.S. 483 (1954).

Buriel, R., and De Ment, T. "Immigration and Sociocultural Change in Mexican, Chinese, and Vietnamese American Families." In A. Booth, A. C. Crouter, and N. Landale (eds.), *Immigration and the Family: Research and Policy on U.S. Immigrants.* Mahwah, N.J.: Erlbaum, 1997.

Calavita, K. *Inside the State: The Bracero Program, Immigration, and the I.N.S.* New York: Routledge, 1992.

California Department of Education. "Grads & Grads with UC/CSU Required Courses by Gender & Ethnicity, 2004–05." Educational Demographics Unit, Sacramento, 2005.

Camarillo, A. *Chicanos in a Changing Society: From Mexican Pueblos to American Barrios in Santa Barbara and Southern California, 1848–1930.* Cambridge, Mass.: Harvard University Press, 1979.

Chavez, L. *Out of the Barrio: Toward a New Politics of Hispanic Assimilation.* New York: Basic Books, 1991.

Collins, P. H. *Black Feminist Thought: Knowledge, Consciousness, and the Politics of Empowerment.* New York: Routledge, 1991.

Conchas, G. Q. *The Color of Success: Race and High-Achieving Urban Youth.* New York: Teachers College Press, 2006.

"Confronting the Graduation Rate Crisis in California." Harvard University: The Civil Rights Project, March 24, 2005.

Contreras, F. E., and Gándara, P. "The Latina/o Ph.D. Pipeline: A Case of Historical and Contemporary Underrepresentation." In J. Castellanos, A. M. Gloria, and M. Kamimura (eds.), *Abriendo Caminos: The Latina/o Pathway to the Ph.D.* Sterling, Va.: Stylus, 2006.

Cooley, C. H. *Human Nature and the Social Order.* New York: Scribner, 1922.

Cummins, J. *Negotiating Identities: Education for Empowerment in a Diverse Society.* Los Angeles: California Association for Bilingual Education, 1996.

Darder, A. *Reinventing Paulo Freire: A Pedagogy of Love*. Boulder, Colo.: Westview Press, 2002.

De León, J., and Holman, L. J. "Standardized Testing of Latino Students." In M. L. González, A. Huerta-Macías, and J. Villamil Tinajero (eds.), *Educating Latino Students*. Lancaster, Pa.: Scarecrow Press, 2002.

Delgado Bernal, D. "Using a Chicana Feminist Epistemology in Educational Research." *Harvard Educational Review*, 1998, 68(4), 552–582.

Delgado-Gaitan, C. "Involving Parents in the Schools: A Process of Empowerment." *American Journal of Education*, 1991, 100(1), 20–46.

Delgado-Gaitan, C. "School Matters in the Mexican-American Home: Socializing Children to Education." *American Educational Research Journal*, 1992, 29(3), 495–513.

de la Luz Reyes, M., and Halcón, J. J. "Racism in Academia: The Old Wolf Revisited." In A. Darder, R. D. Torres, and H. Gutiérrez (eds.), *Latinos and Education: A Critical Reader*. New York: Routledge, 1997.

Della Piana, L. "Reading, Writing, Race, and Resegregation: Forty-Five Years After Brown v. Board of Education." *Color Lines*, Spring 1999, pp. 9–14.

Dill, B. T. "Fictive Kin, Paper Sons, and Compadrazgo: Women of Color and the Struggle for Family Survival." In M. Baca Zinn and B. T. Dill (eds.), *Women of Color in U.S. Society*. Philadelphia: Temple University Press, 1994.

DiMaria, F. "ABCs of Educational Loans." *Hispanic Outlook*, Jan. 2006, pp. 24–25.

Education Data Partnership. "Enrollment by Ethnicity, 2002–2003." September 2004a. http://www.ed-data.k12.ca.us.

Education Data Partnership. "Students by Ethnicity, 2002–2003." September 2004b. http://www.ed-data.k12.ca.us.

Education Data Partnership. "Teachers by Ethnicity in Public Schools." September 2004c. http://www.ed-data.k12.ca.us.

Eitzen, D. S., and Baca Zinn, M. "Structural Transformation and Systems of Inequality." In M. L. Anderson and P. H. Collins (eds.), *Race, Class, and Gender.* Belmont, Calif.: Wadsworth, 1995.

Flores, L. A. "Reclaiming the 'Other': Toward a Chicana Feminist Critical Perspective." *International Journal of Intercultural Relations*, 2000, *24*, 687–705.

Flores-González, N. *School Kids/Street Kids: Identity Development in Latino Students.* New York: Teachers College Press, 2002.

Foster, M. *Black Teachers on Teaching.* New York: New Press, 1997.

Frankenberg, R. *White Women, Race Matters: The Social Construction of Whiteness.* Minneapolis: University of Minnesota Press, 1993.

Freire, P. *Pedagogy of the Oppressed.* Trans. M. Bergman Ramos. New York: Seabury Press, 1970.

Freire, P. *Teachers as Cultural Workers: Letters to Those Who Dare to Teach.* Boulder, Colo.: Westview, 1998.

Fuentes, M. A. "Keeping Our Children in High School: We Know What Works—Why Aren't We Doing It?" In J. Castellanos, A. M. Gloria, and M. Kamimura (eds.), *Abriendo Caminos: The Latina/o Pathway to the Ph.D.* Sterling, Va.: Stylus, 2006.

Galguera, T. "Students' Attitudes Toward Teachers' Ethnicity, Bilinguality, and Gender." *Hispanic Journal of Behavioral Sciences*, 1998, *20*(4), 411–428.

Gándara, P. *Over the Ivy Walls: The Educational Mobility of Low Income Chicanos.* Albany: State University of New York Press, 1995.

Garcia, A., and Martínez, E. "What Is Neoliberalism?" In B. Bigelow (ed.), *The Line Between Us: Teaching About the Border and Mexican Immigration.* Milwaukee, Wis: A Rethinking Schools Publication, 2006.

Gibson, M. A. *Accommodation Without Assimilation: Sikh Immigrants in an American High School.* Ithaca, N.Y.: Cornell University Press, 1988.

Gibson, M. A. "The School Performance of Immigrant Minorities: A Comparative View." In E. Jacob and C. Jordan (eds.), *Minority Education: Anthropological Perspectives*. Norwood, N.J.: Ablex, 1996.

Gimenez, M. E. "Latino/Hispanic—Who Needs a Name?" In A. Darder, R. D. Torres, and H. Gutiérrez (eds.), *Latinos and Education: A Critical Reader*. New York: Routledge, 1997.

Ginorio, A., and Huston, M. *Sí, Se Puede! Yes, We Can: Latinas in School*. Washington, D.C.: American Association of University Women Educational Foundation, 2001.

Glazer, N., and Moynihan, P. *Ethnicity: Theory and Experience*. Cambridge, Mass.: Harvard University Press, 1975.

Glenn, E. N. "From Servitude to Service Work: Historical Continuities in the Racial Division of Paid Reproductive Labor." *Signs: Journal of Women in Culture and Society*, 1992, *18*, 1–43.

Gonzales, M. D. "Crossing Social and Cultural Borders: The Road to Language Hybridity." In D. L. Galindo and M. D. Gonzales (eds.), *Speaking Chicana: Voice, Power, and Identity*. Tucson: University of Arizona Press, 1999.

Gonzalez, G. G. *Chicano Education in the Era of Segregation*. Philadelphia: Balch Institute Press, 1990.

Gonzalez, J. *Harvest of Empire: A History of Latinos in America*. New York: Viking, 2000.

Gordon, M. *Assimilation in American Life: The Role of Race, Religion, and National Origin*. New York: Oxford University Press, 1964.

Grant, G., and Murray, C. E. *Teaching in America: The Slow Revolution*. Cambridge, Mass.: Harvard University Press, 1999.

Green, L. "Don't Be a 'Girlie Man.'" *Los Angeles Times Magazine*, Apr. 2005, pp. 12–13, 30.

Guba, E. G., and Lincoln, Y. S. "Competing Paradigms in Qualitative Research: Theories and Issues." In S. N. Hesse-Biber and P. Leavy (eds.), *Approaches to Qualitative Research: A Reader on Theory and Practice.* New York: Oxford University Press, 2004.

Gutiérrez, D. G. *Walls and Mirrors: Mexican Americans, Mexican Immigrants, and the Politics of Ethnicity.* Berkeley: University of California Press, 1995.

Haederle, M. "Culture Clash." *Los Angeles Times,* Nov. 21, 1997, pp. E1–E2.

Hamilton, N., and Chinchilla, N. S. *Seeking Community in a Global City: Guatemalans and Salvadorans in Los Angeles.* Philadelphia: Temple University Press, 2001.

Haney, W. "Testing and Minorities." In L. Weis and M. Fine (eds.), *Beyond Silenced Voices: Class, Race, and Gender in United States Schools.* Albany: State University of New York Press, 1993.

Harrison, L. E. "How Cultural Values Shape Economic Success." In F. L. Pincus and H. J. Ehrlich (eds.), *Race and Ethnic Conflict.* Boulder, Colo.: Westview Press, 1999.

Helfand, D. "Nearly Half of Blacks, Latinos Drop Out, School Study Show." *Los Angeles Times,* Mar. 24, 2005, pp. A1, A26.

Heller, C. S. *Mexican American Youth: Forgotten Youth at the Crossroads.* New York: Random House, 1966.

Herrera, R. "Notes from a Latino Graduate Student at a Predominately White University." In J. Castellanos and L. Jones (eds.), *The Majority in the Minority: Expanding the Representation of Latina/o Faculty, Administrators and Students in Higher Education.* Sterling, Va.: Stylus, 2003.

Hirji, H.S.P. "Inequalities in California's Public School System: The Undermining of *Serrano v. Priest* and the Need for a Minimum Standards System of Education." *Loyola of Los Angeles Law Review,* 1999, *32,* 583–610.

Hondagneu-Sotelo, P. *Gendered Transitions: Mexican Experiences of Immigration.* Berkeley: University of California Press, 1994.

hooks, b. *Black Looks: Race and Representation.* Boston: South End Press, 1992.

hooks, b. *Teaching to Transgress.* New York: Routledge Press, 1994.

hooks, b. *Teaching Community: A Pedagogy of Hope*. New York: Routledge, 2003.

Howard, G. *We Can't Teach What We Don't Know: White Teachers, Multiracial Schools*. New York: Teachers College Press, 1999.

Hunter, M. *Race, Gender and the Politics of Skin Tone*. New York: Routledge, 2005.

Huntington, S. P. "The Hispanic Challenge." *Foreign Policy*, Mar.–Apr. 2004, pp. 30–37.

Hursh, D. "The Growth of High-Stakes Testing in the USA: Accountability, Markets, and the Decline in Educational Equality." *British Educational Research Journal*, 2005, *31*(4), 605–622.

Inouye, A. "Standing Up to Military Recruiters." *Rethinking Schools*, Spring 2006, pp. 52–55.

International Baccalaureate Organization. "A Basis for Practice: The Diploma Programme." 2002. http://www.ibo.org/.

Kao, G. "Group Images and Possible Selves Among Adolescents: Linking Stereotypes to Expectations by Race and Ethnicity." *Sociological Forum*, 2000, *15*(3), 407–430.

Karp, S. "Equity Suits Clog the Courts." In S. Karp, R. Lowe, B. Miner, and B. Peterson (eds.), *Funding for Justice: Money, Equity, and the Future of Public Education*. Milwaukee, Wis.: Rethinking Schools, 1997.

Kennelly, I., Misra, J., and Karides, M. "The Historical Context of Gender, Race, and Class in the Academic Labor Market." *Race, Gender, and Class*, 1999, *6*(3), 125–155.

Kibria., N. *Becoming Asian American*. Baltimore: John Hopkins University Press, 2002.

Kochhar, R. *The Wealth of Hispanic Households: 1996 to 2002*. Washington, D.C.: Pew Hispanic Center, 2004.

Kozol, J. *Savage Inequalities: Children in America's Schools*. New York: Crown, 1991.

Ladson-Billings, G. *The Dreamkeepers: Successful Teachers of African American Children*. San Francisco: Jossey-Bass, 1994.

Landsberg, M. "Alumni Go to the Head of the Class: Bishop Amat is Among Many Southland Schools the Welcome Graduate Back—as Teachers." *Los Angeles Times*, May 31, 2005, p. A1.

Lareau, A. "Social Class Differences in Family-School Relationships: The Importance of Cultural Capital." *Sociology of Education*, 1987, 60(2), 73–85.

Lareau, A. *Home Advantage: Social Class and Parental Intervention in Elementary Education*. Bristol, Pa.: Falmer Press, 1989.

Lee, S. J. *Unraveling the "Model Minority" Stereotype: Listening to Asian American Youth*. New York: Teachers College Press, 1996.

Levy, J., Wubbels, T., Brekelmans, M., and Morganfield, B. "Language and Cultural Factors in Students' Perceptions of Teacher Communication Style." *International Journal of Intercultural Relations*, 1997, 21(1), 29–56.

Lewis, O. *La Vida: A Puerto Rican Family in the Culture of Poverty—San Juan and New York*. New York: Random House, 1966.

Lindholm, K. "Theoretical Assumptions and Empirical Evidence for Academic Achievement in Two Languages." In A. Padilla (ed.), *Hispanic Psychology*. Thousand Oaks, Calif.: Sage, 1995.

Lopez, A. C., Scribner, J. D., and Mahititvanichcha, K. "Redefining Parental Involvement: Lessons from High-Performing Migrant-Impacted Schools." *American Educational Research Journal*, 2001, 38(2), 253–288.

Lopez, D., and Stanton-Salazar, R. D. "Mexican Americans: A Second Generation at Risk." In R. G. Rumbaut and A. Portes (eds.), *Ethnicities: Children of Immigrants in America*. Berkeley: University of California Press, 2001.

Lopez, N. *Hopeful Girls, Troubled Boys: Race and Gender Disparity in Urban Education*. New York: Routledge, 2003.

Luttrell, W. "'The Teachers, They All Had Their Pets': Concepts of Gender, Knowledge, and Power." *Signs*, 1993, 18(3), 505–546.

Madrid, A. "Missing People and Others." In M. L. Anderson and P. H. Collins (eds.), *Race, Class, and Gender*. Belmont, Calif.: Wadsworth, 1995.

Madsen, W. *Mexican-Americans of South Texas*. New York: Holt, 1964.

Martínez, E. S. "Ideological Baggage in the Classroom: Resistance and Resilience Among Latino Bilingual Students and Teachers." In E. T. Trueba and L. I. Bartolomé (eds.), *Immigrant Voices in Search of Educational Equity*. Lanham, Md.: Rowman and Littlefield, 2000.

Martínez, T. A. "Toward a Chicana Feminist Epistemological Standpoint." *Race, Class, and Gender*, 1996, 3(3), 107–128.

Martínez, T., and Martínez, A. P. "Reality-Based College Loans: Present Programs Insure Lenders, Not Students." *Hispanic Outlook*, Jan. 2006, pp. 28–30.

Martínez Alemán, A. M. "Understanding and Investigating Female Friendship's Value." *Journal of Higher Education*, 1997, 68(2), 119–159.

Matute-Bianchi, M. E. "Ethnic Identities and Patterns of School Success and Failure Among Mexican-Descent and Japanese-American Students in a California High School: An Ethnographic Analysis." *American Journal of Education*, 1986, 95, 233–255.

Matute-Bianchi, M. E. "Situational Ethnicity and Patterns of School Performance Among Immigrant and Nonimmigrant Mexican-Descent Students." In M. A. Gibson and J. U. Ogbu (eds.), *Minority Status and Schooling: A Comparative Study of Immigrant and Involuntary Minorities*. New York: Garland, 1991.

McIntyre, A. *Making Meaning of Whiteness: Exploring Racial Identity with White Teachers*. Albany: State University of New York Press, 1997.

McSpadden McNeil, L. "Faking Equality: High-Stakes Testing and the Education of Latino Youth." In A. Valenzuela (ed.), *Leaving Children Behind: How "Texas-Style" Accountability Fails Latino Youth*. Albany: State University of New York Press, 2005.

Meier, D., and Wood, G. (eds.). *Many Children Left Behind*. Boston: Beacon Press, 2004.

Mendez v. *Westminster*, 64 F. Supp. 544 (S.D. Cal. 1946), 161 F. 2d 774 (9th Cir. 1947).

Michie, G. *Holler If You Hear Me: The Education of a Teacher and His Students*. New York: Teachers College Press, 1999.

Moll, L. C., Armanti, C., Neff, D., and González, N. "Funds of Knowledge for Teaching: Using a Qualitative Approach to Connect Homes and Classrooms." *Theory into Practice*, 1992, *31*(2), 132–141.

Monzó, L. D., and Rueda, R. "Shaping Education Through Diverse Funds of Knowledge: A Look at One Latina Paraeducator's Lived Experiences, Beliefs and Teaching Practice." *Anthropology and Education Quarterly*, 2003, *34*(1), 72–95.

Moraga, C. *Loving in the War Years*. Boston: South End Press, 1983.

Moreno, R. P. "Exploring Parental Involvement Among Mexican American and Latina Mothers." In R. M. De Anda (ed.), *Chicanas and Chicanos in Contemporary Society*. Lanham, Md.: Rowman & Littlefield, 2004.

Moreno, R. P., and Valencia, R. R. "Chicano Families and Schools: Myths, Knowledge, and Future Directions for Understanding." In R. R. Valencia (ed.), *Chicano School Failure and Success: Past, Present and Future*. (2nd ed.) New York: Routledge, 2002.

Naples, N. *Grassroots Warriors: Activist Mothering, Community Work, and the War on Poverty*. New York: Routledge, 1998.

National Collaborative on Diversity in the Teaching Force. *Assessment of Diversity in America's Teaching Force: A Call to Action*. Washington, D.C.: National Collaborative on Diversity in the Teaching Force, 2004.

National Commission on Excellence in Education. *A Nation at Risk: The Imperative for Educational Reform*. Washington, D.C.: U.S. Government Printing Office, 1983.

Nelson, G. "The Relationship Between the Use of Personal Cultural Examples in International Teaching Assistants' Lectures and Uncertainty Reduction, Student Attitude, Student Recall, and Ethnocentrism." *International Journal of Intercultural Relations*, 1992, *16*, 33–52.

Nieto, S. "A Gesture Toward Justice: Small Schools and the Promise of Equal Education." In W. Ayers, M. Klonsky, and G. H. Lyon (eds.), *A Simple Justice: The Challenge of Small Schools*. New York: Teachers College Press, 2000.

Nieto, S. (ed.). *Why We Teach*. New York: Teachers College Press, 2005.

Oakes, J. *Keeping Track: How Schools Structure Inequality*. New Haven, Conn.: Yale University Press, 1985.

Oakes, J., and Rogers, J., with Lipton, M. *Learning Power: Organizing for Education and Justice*. New York Teachers College Press, 2006.

Ochoa, E. C., and Ochoa, G. L. (eds.). *Latino Los Angeles: Transformations, Communities and Activism*. Tucson: University of Arizona Press, 2005.

Ochoa, G. L. "Everyday Ways of Resistance and Change: Mexican American Women Building Puentes with Immigrants." *Frontiers: A Journal of Women's Studies*, 2000, *20*, 1–20.

Ochoa, G. L. *Becoming Neighbors in a Mexican American Community: Power, Conflict and Solidarity*. Austin: University of Texas Press, 2004a.

Ochoa, G. L. "'Let's Unite So That Our Children Are Better Off Than Us': Mexican American/Mexican Immigrant Women." In R. M. De Anda (ed.), *Chicanas and Chicanos in Contemporary Society*. Lanham, Md.: Rowman & Littlefield, 2004b.

Ochoa, G. L., and Ochoa, E. C. "Education for Social Transformation: Chicana/o and Latin American Studies and Community Struggles." *Latin American Perspectives*, 2004, *31*(1), 59–80.

Odden, A. R., and Picus, L. O. *School Finance: A Policy Perspective*. New York: McGraw-Hill, 2004.

Ogbu, J. U. "Immigrant and Involuntary Minorities in Comparative Perspective. In M. A. Gibson and J. U. Ogbu (eds.), *Minority Status and Schooling: A Comparative Study of Immigrant and Involuntary Minorities*. New York: Garland, 1991.

Ogbu, J. U. "Variability in Minority School Performance: A Problem in Search of an Explanation." In E. Jacob and C. Jordan (eds.), Minority *Education: Anthropological Perspectives*. Norwood, N.J.: Ablex, 1993.

Olsen, L. *Made in America: Immigrant Students in Our Public Schools*. New York: New Press, 1997.

Omi, M., and Winant, H. *Racial Formation in the United States*. (2nd ed.) New York: Routledge, 1994.

Orellana, M. F., Ek, L., and Hernández, A. "Bilingual Education in an Immigrant Community: Proposition 227 in California." In E. T. Trueba and L. I. Bartolomé (eds.), *Immigrant Voices: In Search of Educational Equity*. Lanham, Md.: Rowman and Littlefield, 2000.

Orfield, G. "The Growth of Segregation." In G. Orfield, S. E. Easton, and the Harvard Project on School Desegregation (eds.), *Dismantling Desegregation: The Quiet Reversal of Brown v. Board of Education*. New York: New Press, 1996.

Orfield, G., and Yun, J. T. *Resegregation in American Schools*. Boston: Civil Rights Project, Harvard University, 1999.

Osler, A. *The Education and Careers of Black Teachers: Changing Identities, Changing Lives*. Bristol, Pa.: Open University Press, 1997.

Paley, V. G. *White Teacher*. Cambridge, Mass.: Harvard University Press, 1978.

Parenti, C. "Satellites of Sorrow: Los Angeles, Prison, and Circuits of Social Control." In D. Narang Sawhney (ed.), *Unmasking L.A.* New York: Palgrave, 2001.

Park, R. *Race and Culture*. New York: Free Press, 1950.

Parsons, T. *The Social System*. New York: Free Press, 1951.

Pearl, A. "The Big Picture: Systemic and Institutional Factors in Chicano School Failure and Success." In R. R. Valencia (ed.), *Chicano School Failure and Success: Past, Present and Future*. (2nd ed.) New York: Routledge, 2002.

Pérez, E. "Sexuality and Discourse: Notes from a Chicana Survivor." In N. Alarcón, R. Castro, E. Pérez, B. Pesquera, A. Sosa Riddell, and P. Zavella (eds.), *Chicana Critical Issues*. Berkeley, Calif.: Third Woman Press, 1993.

Pérez Huber, L., and others. *Falling Through the Cracks: Critical Transitions in the Latina/o Educational Pipeline*. Los Angeles: Chicano Studies Research Center, UCLA, 2006.

Pineda, D. "Analyzing the Formation of Social Support Networks and Intentional Communities Among Latina Undergraduates at Liberal Arts Colleges." Unpublished senior thesis, Department of Sociology, Pomona College, 2002.

Plessy v. Ferguson. 163 U.S. 537 (1896).

Portes, A., and Rumbaut, R. G. *Ethnicities: Children of Immigrants in America*. Berkeley: University of California Press, 2001.

Quijada, P., and Alvarez, L. "Cultivando Semillas Educacionales (Cultivating Educational Seeds): Understanding the Experiences of K-8 Latina/o Students." In J. Castellanos, A. M. Gloria, and M. Kamimura (eds.), *Abriendo Caminos: The Latina/o Pathway to the Ph.D.* Sterling, Va.: Stylus, 2006.

Ramirez, R. R. "We the People: Hispanics in the United States." Washington, D.C.: U.S. Census Bureau, 2004.

Robles, J. "It's Time." *California Educator*, Feb. 2002, pp. 27, 35.

Romo, H. D., and Falbo, T. *Latino High School Graduation: Defying the Odds*. Austin: University of Texas Press, 1996.

Rosenthal, R., and Jacobson, L. *Pygmalion in the Classroom*. New York: Holt, 1968.

Rueda, R., Monzó, L. D., and Higareda, I. "Appropriating the Sociocultural Resources of Latino Paraeducators for Effective Instruction with Latino Students." *Urban Education*, 2004, 39(1), 52–90.

Sadker, M. P., and Sadker, D. M. *Teachers, Schools and Society*. (7th ed.) New York: McGraw-Hill, 2005.

San Antonio Independent School District et al. v. Rodríguez at al., 337 F. Supp. 280 W. D. Tex. (1971), 37 L, Ed. 2d 16, 411 U.S. 1 (1973).

Schlesinger, A. *The Disuniting of America: Reflections on a Multicultural Society.* New York: Norton, 1991.

Segura, D. A. "Slipping Through the Cracks." In A. de la Torre and B. M. Pesquera (eds.), *Building with Our Hands.* Berkeley: University of California Press, 1993.

Serrano et al. v. *Ivy Baker Priest*, 487 P. 2d 1241 (Cal. 1971).

Shannon, S. M. "Minority Parental Involvement: A Mexican Mother's Experience and a Teacher's Interpretation." *Education and Urban Society*, 1996, *29*(1), 71–84.

Shannon, S. M., and Lojero Latimer, S. "Latino Parent Involvement in Schools: A Story of Struggle and Resistance." *Journal of Educational Issues of Language Minority Students*, 1996, *16*, 301–319.

Shor, I. *When Students Have Power: Negotiating Authority in a Critical Pedagogy.* Chicago: University of Chicago Press, 1996.

Sides, P. "Build Prisons or Build Schools?" In S. Karp, R. Lowe, B. Miner, and B. Peterson (eds.), *Funding for Justice: Money, Equity, and the Future of Public Education.* Milwaukee, Wis.: Rethinking Schools, 1997.

Sleeter, C. "How White Teachers Construct Race." In C. McCarthy and W. Crichlow (eds.), *Race, Identity and Representation in Education.* New York: Routledge, 1993.

Soto, L. D. *Language, Culture, and Power: Bilingual Families and the Struggle for Quality Education.* Albany: State University of New York Press, 1997.

Sowell, T. *Ethnic America.* New York: Basic Books, 1981.

Stanton-Salazar, R. D. *Manufacturing Hope and Despair: The School and Kin Support Networks of U.S.-Mexican Youth.* New York: Teachers College Press, 2001.

Suárez-Orozco, M. M., and Páez, M. M. "The Research Agenda." In
M. M. Suárez-Orozco and M. M. Páez (eds.), *Latinos: Remaking America*.
Berkeley: University of California Press and David Rockefeller Center for Latin
American Studies, 2002.

Tatum, B. D. *"Why Are All the Black Kids Sitting Together in the Cafeteria?" and
Other Conversations About Race*. New York: Basic Books, 1997.

Telles, E., and Murguia, E. "Phenotypic Discrimination and Income Differences
among Mexican Americans." *Social Science Quarterly*, 1990, 7(4), 682–696.

Torres, E. E. *Chicana Without Apology: The New Chicana Cultural Studies*.
New York: Routledge, 2003.

Valdés, G. *Con Respeto: Bridging the Distances Between Culturally Diverse Families
and Schools*. New York: Teachers College Press, 1996.

Valenzuela, A. *Subtractive Schooling: U.S.-Mexican Youth and the Politics of Caring*.
Albany: State University of New York Press, 1999.

Valenzuela, A. "The Accountability Debate in Texas: Continuing the Conversation." In A. Valenzuela (ed.), *Leaving Children Behind: How "Texas-Style"
Accountability Fails Latino Youth*. Albany: State University of New York Press,
2005.

Vasquez, M. "Confronting Barriers to Participation of Mexican American
Women in Higher Education." In A. Darder, R. D. Torres, and H. Gutierrez (eds.),
Latinos and Education: A Critical Reader. New York: Routledge, 1997.

Vasquez, M. "Journey to a PhD: The Latina/o Experience in Higher Education."
In J. Castellanos, A. M. Gloria, and M. Kamimura (eds.), The *Abriendo Caminos:
Latina/o Pathway to the Ph.D*. Sterling, Va.: Stylus, 2006.

Vigil, J. D. *Personas Mexicanas: Chicano High Schoolers in a Changing Los Angeles*.
Fort Worth, Tex.: Harcourt, 1997.

Villenas, S. "Latina Mothers and Small-Town Racisms: Creating Narratives of
Dignity and Moral Education in North Carolina." *Anthropology and Education
Quarterly*, 2001, 32(1), 3–28.

Viramontes, H. M. *Under the Feet of Jesus*. New York: Dutton, 1995.

Watford, T., Rivas, M. A., Burciaga, R., and Solorzano, D. G. "Latinas and the Doctorate: The 'Status' of Attainment and Experiences from the Margin." In J. Castellanos, A. M. Gloria, and M. Kamimura (eds.), *The Latina/o Pathway to the Ph.D.* Sterling, Va.: Stylus, 2006.

Watkins, W. H. "Our Country Is Rich, Our People Are Poor: Education, Justice, and the Politics of Structural Adjustment." In W. Ayers, M. Klonsky, and G. H. Lyon (eds.), *A Simple Justice: The Challenge of Small Schools*. New York: Teachers College Press, 2000.

Weber, D. J. *Foreigners in Their Native Land: Historical Roots of the Mexican Americans*. Albuquerque: University of New Mexico Press, 1973.

Wheelock, A. *Crossing the Tracks: How "Untracking" Can Save America's Schools*. New York: New Press, 1992.

"Where Schools Get Their Money." In S. Karp, R. Lowe, B. Miner, and B. Peterson (eds.), *Funding for Justice: Money, Equity, and the Future of Public Education*. Milwaukee, Wis.: Rethinking Schools, 1997.

Williams, J. "Per-Pupil Spending Varies Widely Between Districts." *San Francisco Gate*, Mar. 25, 2006. www.sfgate.com/cgi-bin/article.cgi?file=/n/a/2006/03/25/state/n095807S47.DTL.

Williams, D. L., and Stallworth, J. *Parent Involvement in Education Project, Executive Summary of the Final Report*. Austin: Southwest Educational Development Laboratory, 1983.

Wood, G. "Introduction." In D. Meier and G. Wood (eds.), *Many Children Left Behind*. Boston: Beacon Press, 2004.

Index

Rosenthal, R., 139–140
Rueda, R., 122, 124, 215
Rumbaut, R. G., 216
Rumberger, R., 26

S

Sadker, D. M., 228
Sadker, M. P., 288
Salazar, R., 64, 65
Saldana, E., 11; on allocation of
  resources in schools, 168–169; on
  impact of tracking, 157–158; on
  testing for tracking, 159
*San Antonio Independent School District
  v. Rodriguez,* 225
Schlesinger, A., 37
School counselors: allocation of, 167;
  positive impact of, 125–126, 127,
  155–156; reducing workload of,
  144–145; steering Latina/o students
  into easier courses, 23–24
School officials: importance of
  caring by, 108–109, 127; Spanish-
  speaking, 208–210
Schools: collaborative approach to
  improving, 220–221; creating
  inclusive atmosphere at, 208–216;
  diversifying, 214–216; funding,
  225–228; graduate, 18, 19, 108;
  multiple levels of change needed
  in, 144–146; reducing class size in,
  144–145, 171, 207–208; segregation in, 29–30, 33, 50. *See also*
  College; Education
Scientific management, 172
Scribner, J. D., 60
Segregation: California Supreme
  Court ruling against, 32–33; in
  public buildings, 33; school, 29–30,
  33, 50. *See also* Tracking
Segura, D. A., 35, 138, 150, 197, 205
Self-confidence, building students',
  193–196
Serrano v. Priest, 226, 227
Shannon, S. M., 61, 208
Shor, I., 82

Shyness, of Latina teachers as
  children, 109, 123–124, 129, 138,
  161, 198
Sides, P., 228
Skin color, 50–51
Social networks: as form of support,
  217–218; organizations as,
  117–118, 141–144, 145, 218;
  significance of, 109, 145. *See also*
  Peer networks
Socioeconomic class: of academic
  researchers, 39–40; and allocation of school resources, 169–170;
  diverse, of Latinas/os, 48–50; and
  financial aid for college, 221–224;
  and neoliberal economic policies,
  37; and parent participation, 58;
  and school funding, 225–228; and
  teacher placement, 137; and tracking, 151–152, 156–157
Sosa, V., 11; biography of, 15; on
  caring by parents, 219–220; family
  story of, 72–74; on impact of
  negative experience with teacher,
  137–138; on missing graduate
  school, 18; on mother's love of
  learning, 77–78; on not being
  taught Spanish at home, 90–91,
  93–94; on parents' educational
  expectations, 63; positive motivators for, 139; on students' self-
  perception with tracking, 160;
  teaching philosophy and techniques of, 74–77; on testing under
  NCLB, 177–178, 179, 187; on
  working while in college, 223–224
Soto, G., 199
Soto, L. D., 35, 93
South Americans, 41, 48
Sowell, T., 32
Spanish language: children rejecting,
  100–101, 131–132; discrimination
  for speaking, 90–92, 128–131; as
  foundation for teaching English,
  46, 47; high school classes teaching, 129–130; Latinas/os not being